Consenting to God and Nature

Princeton Theological Monograph Series

K. C. Hanson, Editor

Recent titles in the series

Richard Valantasis et al., editors
The Subjective Eye: Essays in Honor of Margaret R. Miles

Stephen Finlan and Vladimir Kharlamov, editors
Theōsis: Deification in Christian Theology

Sam Hamstra Jr.
The Reformed Pastor: Lectures on Pastoral Theology by John Williamson Nevin

David A. Ackerman
Lo, I Tell You a Mystery: Cross, Resurrection, and Paraenesis in the Rhetoric of 1 Corinthians

Paul O. Ingram, editor
Constructing a Relational Cosmology

Caryn Riswold
Coram Deo: Human Life in the Vision of God

John A. Vissers
The Neo-Orthodox Theology of W. W. Bryden

Michael G. Cartwright
Practices, Politics, and Performance: Toward a Communal Hermeneutic for Christian Ethics

Philip Harrold
A Place Somewhat Apart: The Private Worlds of a Late Nineteenth-Century University

Mark A. Ellis, translator
The Arminian Confession of 1621

Consenting to God and Nature

Toward a Theocentric, Naturalistic, Theological Ethics

BYRON C. BANGERT

Pickwick *Publications*
An imprint of *Wipf and Stock Publishers*
199 West 8th Avenue • Eugene OR 97401

CONSENTING TO GOD AND NATURE
Toward a Theocentric, Naturalistic, Theological Ethics

Princeton Theological Monograph Series 55

Copyright © 2006 Byron C. Bangert. All rights reserved. Except for brief quotations in critical publications or reviews, no part of this book may be reproduced in any manner without prior written permission from the publisher. Write: Permissions, Wipf & Stock, 199 W. 8th Ave., Eugene, OR 97401.

Pickwick Publications
A Division of Wipf & Stock Publishers
199 W. 8th Ave., Suite 3
Eugene, OR 97401

ISBN 10: 1-59752-524-3
ISBN 13: 978-1-59752-524-4

Cataloging-in-Publication Data

Bangert, Byron C.
    Consenting to God and nature : toward a theocentric, naturalistic, theological ethics / Byron C. Bangert.

    Princeton Theological Monograph Series 55
    xvi + 256 p.; 23 cm.
    ISBN 1-59752-524-3
1. Christian ethics. 2. Griffin, David Ray, 1939– . 3. Gustafson, James M. 4. McFague, Sallie. I. Title. II. Series.

BJ47 B36 2006

Scripture quotations from the New Revised Standard Version Bible are copyright © 1989 by the Division of Christian Education of the National Council of Churches in the USA and are used by permission.

Manufactured in the U.S.A.

In Memory of John Bunyan Spencer:

Scholar, Parishioner, Mentor, Teacher, Colleague, Friend

Contents

Preface / ix

1. Consenting to God and Nature / 1

2. James M. Gustafson's Theocentric Ethics: What More Can Be Said? / 45

3. Sallie McFague's Theology of Nature: Metaphor to the Rescue? / 92

4. David Ray Griffin's Case for Reenchantment: Apprehending God and Nature? / 145

5. A Synthesis for the Making / 207

Bibliography / 252

Preface

THIS book, an exploration in theological ethics, is motivated by two central questions. First: How can we think and speak with integrity about God as One who is active in human affairs *and* the world? How *can* God make a difference in our world and in our lives? Second, and no less important: What is the character of God's activity in the world, and how are we to relate and respond to this activity? How *does* God make a difference in our world and our lives, and what are some of the implications for our own actions?

These are not questions for which I believe there are definitive answers. All theological work is provisional. The same, of course, must be said about all other work, all other knowledge, all other conceptual schemes. Nonetheless, our lives do literally depend on the sorts of answers we find in our pursuit of those questions that touch on the ultimate realities of our existence. Throughout this book I seek to address questions about God, the world, and the relation of human beings to both God and world, in a way that takes seriously our current state of knowledge and understanding, and the limits of our human condition.

The method of the book is critical, comparative, and constructive. I examine, critique, and constructively appropriate the work of three major contemporary Protestant thinkers: James Gustafson, Sallie McFague, and David Ray Griffin. My claim is that each of these thinkers has a significant contribution to make to the conceptualization and articulation of an intellectually and religiously adequate theological ethics in our contemporary situation. The book is a sustained argument on behalf of that claim. The reader who is interested only in my conclusions may want to turn immediately to Chapter 5. The reader who wants to think along with me, sometimes forging through some very dense, murky, confused, or unfamiliar territory, is invited to proceed in the usual fashion, from beginning to end!

A prime motivation for writing this book is that I have found other approaches to theological ethics, and the theologies that fund them, to be either intellectually or religiously inadequate, or both. The various forms of theological fundamentalism obviously fail the test of *intellectual adequacy*, because they privilege authority and tradition over reason and experience. Theological liberalism is not always that much better. I have in mind those forms of theological liberalism that are basically moralistic in character. Lacking an apprehension of the deeply mysterious nature of all existence, employing God or religion primarily to warrant an essentially humanist perspective within an otherwise largely materialist worldview, they fail to evoke a sense of piety or awe toward anything worthy of our worship or ultimate devotion. Those sorts of theological liberalism fail the test of *religious adequacy*. But I really have not concerned myself here with either theological fundamentalism or moralistic theological liberalism as such. Rather, there are two other significant theological outlooks that I am subjecting to an implicit, and sometimes explicit, critique in this book.

The first theological outlook is one that might be called naive theological realism. Within Christianity, this is the general outlook of most believers, including fundamentalists, whose basic appeal is to traditional religious authority, and modernists, whose worldview is more consciously shaped by reason and experience. Naive theological realism is the view, or rather, it denotes the implicit assumption, that theological language is meaningful precisely because it refers to and describes *supernatural* realities. The referential or descriptive language may or may not be understood as literal, but it is understood as providing an account of a dimension of reality that is not subject to, but rather transcends, the presumed laws of nature and human events. For example, theological fundamentalists and theological modernists will differ greatly over the extent to which God may act in ways that disrupt or supervene the causal nexus of material events. Fundamentalists will affirm a literal virginal conception of Jesus, effected by the Holy Spirit, whereas modernists will more likely assume that God's special action, becoming incarnate in Jesus, takes place without violating the fundamental principles of human biology. Fundamentalists are likely to regard the resurrection of Jesus in terms hardly distinguishable from bodily resuscitation, while modernists may conceive of the event as reviving Jesus' spirit and restoring his subjectivity, with or without any supposition regarding the transmutation of Jesus' body. But both fundamentalists and modernists will agree that God has acted—and perhaps still acts—in ways that alter the course of events, and that these actions are not strictly conformed to the prevailing laws of cause and effect that are taken to govern material reality.

In my view, no theistic religion can dispense with the conviction that God acts in ways that shape the course of events. Intellectually speaking, this raises two unavoidable questions. One is whether there is any critically reasoned basis for thinking that the patterns and processes of events in the world exhibit some form of divine agency. The other is whether one can conceive of divine action in a way that is coherent with what we know and understand about the "real world" of events. I will argue for an affirmative answer to both of these questions.

The second theological outlook that I aim to critique in this book is commonly found only among academics and some church theologians. It goes by the name of postliberal theology. Postliberal theologians do not seem to be particularly concerned about the ontological status of the referents of their theological language. They appear to be non-realists, though their epistemological and ontological commitments are often unclear. In any event, their primary concern is with the "grammar" of theological language, or the "grammar" of faith. Postliberals share with most other Christians a more-or-less confessional stance toward the Christian faith and its tradition. They are not inclined to argue or test the truth of Christianity, but to accept and interpret its doctrines in relation to significant dimensions of human existence. To be a Christian is to speak the right language, with the proper grammar. It is to regard and interpret one's own life, and to regard and interpret the world, through the cultural-linguistic lens afforded by orthodox Christian tradition. Postliberals may engage in significant theological re-interpretation of the Christian faith, but not in its basic reformulation. The ancient creeds, for example, remain normative, and are neither dispensable nor susceptible of fundamental revision, precisely because they are regarded as definitive of the Christian faith.

In my view, postliberal theology represents an intellectual retreat from the quest for truth about the ultimate nature of reality. It is also misleading to the uninitiated. The typical Christian, for example, is a naive realist who takes it for granted that statements about God within the religious community are intended to be directly referential, and are intended to be true. Statements about God are taken to be warranted not solely because they conform to the "grammar" of the faith, but because they are thought to speak truthfully as well as faithfully of God and, in particular, God's relation with the world.

The non-realist approach of postliberal theology serves as a strategy for insulating traditional Christian doctrine from secular or scientific critique. To vouchsafe the truth of Christian doctrine, contingency upon empirically discernible realities is removed, reducing truth to conformity with received tradition. Ironically, whatever security may be purchased by this strategy comes at too great a cost to the integrity of religious language and the meanings ordinarily attributed to such language. Postliberal theology fails the test of religious adequacy, precisely due to its functionally non-realist response to the challenges of postmodernity.

Accepting the challenges posed by our contemporary, postmodern world, I seek to identify grounds that are valid and necessary for making any theological claims or affirmations. In doing so, I acknowledge that there is no way to think or speak meaningfully about God without the use of metaphors. Our language about God is not literal but metaphorical. Metaphor, as Sallie McFague has so effectively argued, has the character of "is–is not." We must never make a simple identification between the metaphor and its referent. This is not to say, however, that the metaphor is only a "mere" metaphor, as if it bears no reference to any actual reality. It is only to acknowledge that the reality is also other than, and probably more than, what is indicated by the metaphor.

When it comes to theological metaphors, the reality is doubtless far greater than any language can express. One of the greatest challenges facing theology is that of finding and employing language that is most congruent with, and faithful to, the reality to which it refers. Theological language is never simply the "grammar" of faith. It is also referential language, language that makes implicit truth claims, language that must be construed as a way of attempting to speak truthfully about ultimate realities. Metaphorical theological language possesses integrity when it speaks, not literally but faithfully and truthfully, of matters pertaining to God and God's relations with the world.

The title of this book is intended to be descriptive and informative. It is my conviction that a proper engagement in theological ethics requires both *consenting to God* and *consenting to nature*. By consenting to God I mean both the cognitive affirmation of assent to the reality of God, and consent to the reality that is God, the One with whom we ultimately have to do. Consenting to God requires an acceptance that is personal and engages the whole of one's being. By consenting to nature I mean both the cognitive affirmation of the existence of the natural or physical world as a reality quite apart from our own thought or actions, and acceptance of that reality as hugely determinative of the limits and possibilities of human life and all existence.

Both of these consentings have profound implications. Consenting to God means letting God alone be God. It means the refusal to domesticate God, or to instrumentalize God, for human ends. The Westminster Shorter Catechism has it right, at least on this score: The chief end of the human being is not self-fulfillment, certainly not self-aggrandizement, but rather the glorifying of God and the enjoyment of God.*

Consenting to nature means the full acceptance of the realities of embodied existence and the natural order. Human beings are creatures who are subject to the same temporal conditions and natural processes as the rest of existence. We do not exist above nature. We cannot rise above nature. We have no capacities or powers that free us from any of the constraints that govern the natural world. The salt of the seas courses through our veins, our bodies are composed of the dust of the stars.

Human beings may be a unique admixture of spirit and nature, as Reinhold Niebuhr claimed. That said, taking spirit to refer to a dimension of freedom and the possibility of self-transcendence, it will be one of the burdens of this book to argue that we are not utterly unique in being constituted of both spirit and nature. The claim will be that we do not inhabit a deterministic universe. The freedom or spirit that belongs to human existence may differ in degree but not in kind from that of all other forms of existence that we know.

While the *title* of this book may not raise any questions, the *subtitle* is bound to strike many prospective readers as oxymoronic. How can any perspective, theory, or approach be both "theocentric" and "naturalistic"? Does not the one rule out the other? It depends, however, on what one means by naturalistic. Some forms of naturalism are clearly deterministic, materialistic, and atheistic. They leave no room for any theological perspective, yet alone a theocentric one. I will argue not only that such forms of naturalism are not necessarily implied by our knowledge of the natural world but that, in fact, such forms of naturalism are far from being the most intellectually credible way in which to make sense of the complexities of human experience and scientific knowledge.

As will be evident from these brief remarks, this book reflects a strong commitment to a kind of realism. The primary criterion of my thinking, to the extent that I am making good on my intentions, is truthfulness, or adequacy to reality. I am not interested in defending any orthodoxy, ideology, theory, or theology that does not meet the test of adequacy to reality, as best reality can be known. There are major intellectual debates about the extent to which it is possible for human beings to know things "as they really are." I will touch on those at points in the book. It is certainly the case that all our knowledge is provisional. We can know nothing with absolute certainty. But we can know all kinds of things with a high degree of certitude. And so long as we recognize the inherent epistemological fallibility of the human condition,

---

* A paraphrase of the answer to the first question of the Catechism, "What is the chief end of man?"

our certitudes give us sufficient grounds for meaningful engagement with the world.

In the book I invoke the term "critical realism" to denote the epistemological fallibilism and ontological realism that define my basic worldview. It is also the implicit worldview of most scientists and, I would argue, the implicit view of most human beings when they are not behaving as naive realists. Naive realists fail to take adequately into account the deficiencies of language to reality and the fallibility of their knowing. Critical realists recognize the provisional nature of their language and knowledge, but are not thereby deterred from the quest for truth. Some philosophers, academicians, and other intellectuals claim to be non-realists, or anti-realists. Some even seem to want to deny that there is any world that exists independently of our knowing. In my view, their failure to consent to nature is egregious. It is hard to take seriously any non-realist perspective.

This does not mean that I reject wholesale the view that reality is a production of human thought and activity. Certainly our human *social* reality is a human product, a social construction. On the other hand, the non-human world is not socially constructed to any similar degree (even though it possesses some features of sociality). We may influence the existence of rocks, trees, and wild horses, and likewise be influenced by their existence. But rocks, trees, and wild horses do not need us to exist. On the other hand, economic markets, political systems, governments, art, music, and scientific theories are all human constructions, and would not exist without us. These are not, however, *mere* constructions. They are all rooted in the natural world, dependent on—though not exclusively determined by—what is given as possibility within the world of nature, including human nature as it exists in any particular place and time. Nonetheless, to the extent that we human beings can choose how our social world is constructed, we are responsible for those choices. We are also responsible for the choices we make in our relations with the non-human world. A critical realist perspective invites choices, within the limits of our knowledge and the powers of human agency, that are congruent with the way things really are and may yet become.

As a work in theological ethics, then, this book offers an overall perspective and identifies some major features of the landscape that provide the context for critical, faithful, theologically informed, ethical reflection. My hope is that it will also encourage thoughtful and engaged moral discernment and action.

Before proceeding with the argument, however, I must acknowledge my indebtedness to others and issue the usual disclaimer. There are at least a handful of people without whom this book could not have been written. These include my mentor and friend, John B. Spencer, who died long before

Preface

I began work on this project; my teacher and adviser, Richard B. Miller; and my life partner, Hayden M. Bangert. I am also profoundly indebted, of course, to James M. Gustafson, Sallie McFague, and David Ray Griffin, whose scholarly work has inspired, informed, provoked, and challenged me. Others who have read and commented helpfully on my work include David H. Smith, Ann Mongoven, and Noretta Koertge. I have also been grateful for the encouragement of many other teachers, colleagues, and friends, who will know who they are if they should ever have occasion to read these pages.

As for the disclaimer, none of these persons nor anyone else is at fault for any shortcomings in what I have written. If any mistakes find their way into the final text, they must either be mine or the mischief of some computer.

Byron C. Bangert
Bloomington, Indiana

1
Consenting to God and Nature

Introduction

JAMES M. Gustafson writes, "Ethics is shaped by the account one renders of God and God's relations to the world. How God is construed, and how the world is construed in the light of one's convictions about the ultimate power and powers that bring life into being, sustain it, and bear down upon it is the most critical choice made in theological ethics."[1] Gustafson speaks only of theological ethics, of course. There are non-theological varieties of ethics—including rationalistic and humanistic forms of philosophical ethics—in which it may be crucial how the world and the relations of human beings to that world are construed, but God is not in the picture. In this book, however, God, including the construal of God and God's relations to the world, is of central concern. Hence the placement of "theocentric" as well as "theological" in the subtitle.

The ethics to be explored here, nonetheless, is also "naturalistic." That is to say, it is not supernaturalistic. In most theological frameworks, God or the divine is associated with the supernatural, and the supernatural is understood in terms of intervention or disruption within the natural order of events.[2] The

---

[1] *Ethics from a Theocentric Perspective*, Vol. 2: *Ethics and Theology* (Chicago: University of Chicago Press, 1984) 27.
[2] Moreover, the association of God or the divine with the supernatural is hardly limited to those for whom it is a matter of conviction. J. Samuel Preus' book, *Explaining Religion: Criticism*

supernatural is taken to be precisely that which is capable of interrupting and superseding the causal nexus that otherwise characterizes and accounts for all that occurs in the natural world. There is no presumption here that such intervention actually occurs. To the contrary, the presumption is that such intervention does not occur.

However, this is to state the matter too simply. There is an ambiguity in what is to be meant by nature and the natural that will shortly have to be addressed. Certain kinds of naturalism are highly problematic from almost every theological perspective. A materialistic, deterministic view of nature and natural events, for example, is incompatible with nearly all theistic affirmations. The one possible exception is pantheism, the view that God is to be equated with all that exists. In order to articulate an ethics that is both theological and naturalistic, entailing a naturalistic construal of the world, Gustafson's question regarding how the world is construed must be treated in large part as a question of how nature is construed.

As a first step, I will endorse the understandings of the natural world that come to us from contemporary science, in particular, the view that there are no exceptions to the universality and inviolability of the causal nexus that is constitutive of all events. I will not, however, endorse certain metaphysical assumptions that are also commonly associated with the scientific worldview. Drawing upon insights from process philosophy and theology, I will ultimately argue the need for a non-deterministic, non-materialistic conception of nature—that is, of the real world—one that does not preclude and in fact may indicate the need for certain kinds of theistic affirmations.

For the most part, then, the naturalistic approach pursued here attempts to take quite seriously those interpretations of our world and its events that derive from human reason and experience, and are thus consistent with current scientific understandings. This approach rejects uncritical appeals to authority and tradition, in particular religious authority and tradition, for an understanding of what is really going on in our world. Religious authority

---

and Theory from Bodin to Freud, is taken by David Griffin as illustrative of the widespread mistake of identifying the theological, religious, and transcendent with the supernatural; Griffin, *Religion and Scientific Naturalism: Overcoming the Conflicts*, (Albany: SUNY Press, 2000) 36. Sociologist of religion Rodney Stark provides another example when he begins his book, *One True God*, with the assertion, "All religions involve conceptions of the supernatural" (Princeton: Princeton University Press, 2001) 9. Stark's observation may be generally true of modern forms of religion, but one must recognize the historical and cultural contingency of this way of conceptualizing the divine. It is clearly anachronistic, for example, to use the term "supernatural" to describe the content of religious beliefs pre-dating the emergence of the idea of nature in Western culture. A main concern here is that the uncritical (and, in my view, mistaken) identification of the divine with the supernatural tends to make religious belief contingent upon continuing belief in the supernatural.

and tradition may have much to contribute to our understanding of the nature of our existence, including its moral and ethical dimensions, but such authority and tradition lack any *a priori* claim upon our interpretation of the events that constitute the world of our experience. On the other hand, this approach also rejects implicitly metaphysical claims that are often made in the name of science, namely claims to the effect that all events are fully explicable in terms of their material causes, and that science thus provides the singular methodology for acquiring the knowledge necessary exhaustively to explain all events.[3]

As these introductory remarks suggest, there are formidable challenges to the formulation of an adequate theological ethics in the current intellectual environment. These challenges go beyond a careful definition of terms and the achievement of intellectual coherence. An adequate theological ethics must be situated in and responsive to some religious tradition if it is to gain acceptance among religious adherents. It must take God seriously, not simply as an idea but as divine reality. To be intellectually defensible, however, theological ethics must not invoke any religious tradition's authority *a priori*. It must share what Franklin Gamwell has called "the modern commitment," namely the affirmation that our understandings must finally be validated "by appeal in some sense to human experience and reason as such."[4]

An adequate theological ethics must also be consonant with prevailing critical assumptions regarding the nature of reality, including in particular all that is usually identified as the world of nature in contradistinction to those features of reality that are contingent upon human perception, thought, language, and action. In other words, the construal of the world must be critically realistic. Furthermore that construal must be such that the construal of God's relation to the world is not dependent on the existence of features of the world that have only become present with the emergence of human beings. Human subjectivity, for example, must not be a feature of the world on

---

[3] Ian Barbour characterizes the form of epistemology rejected here as scientific materialism; see, e.g., *When Science Meets Religion: Enemies, Strangers, or Partners?* (New York: HarperCollins, 2002) 12–14. It is also commonly denoted as scientism, or scientific reductionism. In his book, *Religious Experience* (Berkeley: University of California Press, 1985), Wayne Proudfoot argues that the distinguishing mark of the distinctively religious experience is that it is believed by the subject to be incapable of exhaustive explanation in naturalistic terms (217 and passim). Proudfoot clearly implies, however, that the subject may be mistaken in this belief. Given that his understanding of naturalism is essentially materialistic and deterministic, and contrary to his extensive denial, his position represents a form of scientific reductionism. The contrasting view taken here is that no experience whatsoever is susceptible to exhaustive explanation in materialistic terms.

[4] *The Divine Good: Modern Moral Theory and the Necessity of God* (New York: HarperCollins, 1990) 3, 4.

which God's relation to the world necessarily depends. This is necessary in order to speak meaningfully of God as creator of the world. A robust conception of divine agency that is not contingent on the existence of human agency must be possible. For religious reasons, God's relation to the world must be construed as primordial.[5]

Moreover, there being no clear evidence or reason to the contrary, continuity is to be assumed in the constitutive character of God's relation to the world throughout the entire natural history of the world. This rules out, for example, claims to an age of miracles and similar ideas that are sometimes proposed to account for purported past modes of divine agency for which no current instances are to be found. God should not be assumed to relate to the world any differently now than in the past. The converse, however, should not be taken as true. The emergence of human beings, for example, introduced into the world new ways in which to be related to God.

An adequate theological ethics must also be consonant with current (i.e., natural and social scientific) understandings of how reality is to be known. It is not uncommon for theologies to be constructed so as to be insulated from any conflicts with scientific claims. A typical strategy is to argue that there is no overlap between the referents of theological language and those of scientific language. Religion and science are understood to be entirely separate and distinct domains or universes of discourse. Even when they appear to be talking about the same thing, for example a human being, they really are not. Religion may be talking about the human being in terms of what it means to be a volitional person or experiencing subject, whereas science may be talking about the human being in terms of how to explain the behaviors of a bio-chemical organism or psycho-social entity. The perspective taken here, on the other hand, is that both religion and science make claims about the way things really are, and that those claims often mutually bear on one another. Thus, neither religion nor science can be indifferent to the epistemologically substantive claims of the other. In particular, if the way in which the world is construed is crucial to theological ethics, then scientific understandings of the world are also crucial. It is precisely for this reason that the approach taken here is naturalistic.

In this context, it bears repeating that an adequate theological ethics must also be theological. God-talk may come cheap in public and religious life, but it is often at a premium in academic circles, even among philosophers and theologians. One must take care not to say more than human knowledge and experience can warrant about God. Nonetheless, theological ethics must articulate some understanding of (1) the nature or being of that

---

[5] As we shall see later, there are also theological, philosophical, and specifically metaphysical reasons for this assumption.

ultimate reality traditionally referred to as God; (2) how God is to be known; and (3) how the relation between God and the world—both human and non-human—is to be understood.

Finally, an adequate theological ethics must be sufficiently indicative of what is to be valued in human experience and in the knowable world to inform, judge, and guide human action in the world. In some approaches to ethics, the question of what is to be valued lies at the center. In ethics with a theocentric focus, there is an important sense in which God is what is ultimately to be valued. But then the question becomes one of how the finite human being is to embody and express this valuation within the temporal world. As we will see, following Gustafson, the answer has something to do with relating "ourselves and all things in a manner appropriate to our and their relations to God."[6]

Thesis

James Gustafson is one of several contemporary Protestant Christian thinkers who have developed distinctive theological perspectives, approaches, or world-views that address the critical intellectual, scientific, and conceptual challenges confronting religious belief today. My aim is to examine, critique, and appropriate his work and that of two others, Sallie McFague and David Griffin, each of whom has made significant contributions to the articulation of a naturalistic theological ethics that is responsive to the Christian tradition while also sharing the modern commitment's appeal to human experience and reason. Each of these three thinkers eschews *a priori* appeal to the authority of religious tradition, and each rejects supernaturalism. Each is a critical realist who takes seriously scientific knowledge of our world. As religious thinkers who find parallels, intersections, and/or convergences between science and religion, each accents ways in which current scientific understandings inform, and in some cases are informed by, contemporary appropriations of the language and thought of Christian tradition. Each is also concerned to relate his or her approach to human valuing, life, and action. A critical appraisal of the work of these three thinkers will show that none provides a sufficient basis for an intellectually *and* religiously adequate theological ethics, but that each contributes elements necessary to the articulation of such an ethics within the Protestant Christian tradition as it confronts the religious and intellectual challenges of today's world.

---

[6]Op. cit., 146. In one of his best-known essays, "The Center of Value," H. Richard Niebuhr made a philosophical argument from a theocentric perspective for a relational value theory in which God is identified as the center, source, and end of value; *Radical Monotheism and Western Culture* (New York: Harper and Row, 1970) 100–113.

Setting the Context

To provide a context for the discussion of the work of each of the three thinkers that is to follow, it will be helpful to set forth the perspectives that inform my argument on a number of critical matters. There are four preliminary issues I wish to address. First, there are different ways in which the relationship between science and religion has been understood. Some further specification of those ways that are appropriate to a theocentric, naturalistic, theological ethics is called for. Moreover, it is also important to expand and clarify the meanings of the two terms, naturalistic and theocentric. Naturalism can be variously defined. A second issue, then, is to identify how naturalism will be understood. Theocentricism carries implications that would not be fully connoted by the term, theism. A third issue is to discuss some of these implications. I have also indicated that my epistemological perspective, like that of Gustafson, McFague, and Griffin, may be characterized as critical realism. As a fourth issue, critical realism needs to be further explained.

There are also recurring themes that will appear in my critiques in Chapters 2, 3, and 4. These deserve to be articulated and elaborated at some length. These may be briefly identified as divine agency; divine purpose and a personal God; construal vs. construction in the interpretation of experience and the formulation of theology; the indicative and the imperative (or the "is" and the "ought"); and the relation of theology and ethics to each other.

Finally, the title of this book, "Consenting to God and Nature," should be explained and justified. Therefore, the remainder of this chapter will be devoted to an explication of preliminary issues, a discussion of recurring themes, and a concluding word on why the theocentric, naturalistic perspective claimed for this project suggests the book's title.

Preliminary Issues

1. The Relationship between Science and Religion

As already indicated, how the relationship between religion and science is to be understood is very critical to a naturalistic theological ethics. Various proposals have been developed to summarize the ways in which this relationship is actually conceived. Physicist and theologian Ian Barbour has identified four views of this relationship that are widely held today. He calls these conflict, independence, dialogue, and integration.[7]

---

[7] *Religion in an Age of Science* (New York: HarperCollins, 1990) 4–30; *Nature, Human Nature, and God* (Minneapolis: Fortress, 2002) 1ff.; *When Science Meets Religion*, 10–38. John F. Haught proposes a very similar typology in his book, *Science and Religion: From Conflict to*

In the conflict view, religion and science are clearly at odds. Biblical literalists, for example, reject any scientific claims that conflict with their interpretation of events recounted in the scriptures, from the creation of the world to the possibility of miracles. Scientific materialists, on the other hand, dismiss all claims of divine agency or involvement affecting the outcome of actual events, insisting that God is superfluous to a full account of the origins of the universe and its evolution to the present. On moral questions such as those that are posed by homosexual behavior, the biblical literalist will find grounds for condemning all such behavior, whereas the scientific materialist may regard such behavior to be nothing more than the inevitable outcome of genetic and/or environmental factors. In the conflict view, either the religious or the science perspective is taken to be right, and is so construed that when the two perspectives differ the other must necessarily be wrong.

The independence view, already previously alluded to, holds that "[s]cience and religion deal with differing domains and contrasting aspects of reality."[8] A particularly clear instance of this from the side of science was articulated by evolutionary biologist Stephen Jay Gould. Gould wrote,

> each subject has a legitimate magisterium, or domain of teaching authority—and these magisteria do not overlap (the principle that I would like to designate as NOMA, or "nonoverlapping magisteria"). The net of science covers the empirical universe: what is it made of (fact) and why does it work this way (theory). The net of religion extends over questions of moral meaning and value. These two magisteria do not overlap, nor do they encompass all inquiry (consider, for starters, the magisterium of art and the meaning of beauty). To cite the arch clichés, we get the age of rocks, and religion retains the rock of ages; we study how the heavens go, and they determine how to go to heaven.[9]

Conversation. His categories are conflict, contrast, contact, and confirmation; (New York: Paulist, 1995) 3–26. Arthur Peacocke develops a different and more complex typology, but the substantive features of his own position are close to those of Barbour; *Theology for a Scientific Age: Being and Becoming—Natural, Divine, and Human*, enlarged ed. (Minneapolis: Fortress, 1993) 20ff. In a pedagogical vein, Gustafson describes and illustrates what he calls "eight different themes about how other disciplines have been and are related to theological ethics"; *Intersections: Science, Theology, and Ethics* (Cleveland: Pilgrim, 1996) 136–43. Though he indicates his own preferences, his purpose is not to advance a normative position. In his most recent book, Gustafson works with a simplified three-fold typology of the relation of scientific and religious accounts, *rejection*, *absorption*, and the broad spectrum of possible forms of *accommodation* between these two extremes; *An Examined Faith: The Grace of Self-Doubt* (Minneapolis: Fortress, 2003) 6–7 and passim.

[8] Barbour, *Nature, Human Nature, and God*, 1.
[9] "Nonoverlapping Magisteria," *Natural History* 106 (1997) 19–20. Gould purports to find common ground on the science and religion question with recent Roman Catholic teaching about evolution and human ensoulment.

The same sort of argument can be made from the side of religion, to wit, science studies the "what" and "how" of things, religion is concerned with the "why." Other independence approaches are variations on the claim that science and religion have different languages and meaning structures. In effect, they are two distinctly different universes of discourse; they do not speak to or about each other. In the view taken here, the independence view of the relation of science and religion fails to acknowledge that the epistemological claims of science and religion are by no means always mutually exclusive.

What Barbour calls the dialogue view tends to assume that science and religion are relatively independent, but is also oriented toward comparison of methods as well as exploration of similarities, analogies, and complementarities. Barbour notes that in both religion and science "conceptual models and analogies are used to imagine what cannot be directly observed (God or a quark, for example)."[10] Dialogue may also be prompted by limit-questions, e.g., "when science raises questions at its boundaries that it cannot answer, such as: why is there a universe at all, and why is it orderly and intelligible?"[11] In the dialogue view, religion and science each have something to contribute to the other, and something to learn from the other, especially with respect to methodology. Neither, however, is likely to be significantly challenged or transformed by the other.

The fourth view, which Barbour calls integration, is the one he considers "the most promising option."[12] He identifies three primary ways in which such integration has been sought. One is *natural theology*, the view that evidence for and knowledge of God can be gained through the exercise of reason in light of our knowledge of the natural world. Another is *theology of nature*, which "starts from a religious tradition based on religious experience and historical revelation"[13] and argues "that many of its beliefs are compatible with modern science but some beliefs should be reformulated in light of particular scientific theories."[14] A third variation on the integration view is systematic synthesis, the most prominent example of which is *process philosophy*, "which systematically elaborates a set of concepts relevant to both science and religion."[15]

Barbour finds value within the dialogue perspective, especially with respect to methodological and conceptual parallels between scientific and theological inquiry. For the most part, however, he favors integrationist approach-

---

[10] *Nature, Human Nature, and God*, 1.
[11] Ibid.
[12] Ibid., 2.
[13] *When Science Meets Religion*, 31.
[14] *Nature, Human Nature, and God*, 2; cf. *Religion in an Age of Science*, 26.
[15] Ibid. The term "systematic synthesis" comes from Barbour's other two cited books.

es, specifically a theology of nature and critical appropriation of process philosophy. For my purposes, what is most significant are the ways in which the integrationist approaches are reflected in the work of James Gustafson, Sallie McFague, and David Griffin. The primary approach of both Gustafson and McFague, I will note, is that of a theology of nature. In Gustafson's case there are also elements of a natural theology, as well as some understated affinities with process philosophy or theology. In McFague's case, process theology plays a secondary but significant role, but there is little opening to natural theology. She is also attentive to the methodological parallels between religion and science that Barbour attributes to the dialogue view. For Griffin, on the other hand, the dominant approach is that of process philosophy and theology. However, there are also overtures to natural theology, especially in his most recent work, and there are certain significant claims he wants to make as a Christian that are clearly more congruent with a theology of nature approach than anything else.

2. Refining the Definition of Naturalism

Thus far I have defined naturalism primarily in terms of what it is not, namely, supernaturalism. But I have also identified three ways in which naturalism is often construed that are to be rejected, namely, materialism, determinism, and reductionism. And I have at least intimated that naturalism can be consistently defined in terms of an epistemological commitment to human experience and reason. The reasons for rejecting supernaturalism are essentially empirical and scientific. But, as noted, there are compelling theological reasons for rejecting the materialism and determinism that constitute scientific reductionism. In a wholly materialistic and deterministic world there would be no meaningful role for God.

There are also compelling reasons from the perspective of ethics, however, for rejecting materialistic and deterministic conceptions of the world. Ethics only makes sense in a world where there are beings who are capable of reflection, deliberation, choice, and freedom of action. In whatever way naturalism is to be understood, therefore, it must allow for human freedom. Now, if human freedom is taken to be an empirical reality, and not mere illusion, then a further challenge is presented to reductionist assumptions. Moreover, it can and will be argued (primarily in Chapter 4) that the knowledge of science itself leads to an apprehension of the natural world, including human beings, that no materialism can explain.

The task remains, then, to clarify how naturalism may be positively understood, yet clearly distinguished from those forms of naturalism that must be rejected. Of our three thinkers, David Griffin provides by far the most thorough and satisfactory treatment of the subject, specifically in his book, *Religion and Scientific Naturalism*, and most succinctly in his contemporaneous article, "Religious Experience, Naturalism, and the Social Scientific Study of Religion."[16]

Griffin identifies eight kinds of naturalism, based on the contextual meaning of the term as used by authors who claim a naturalistic perspective.[17] He further distinguishes among these four forms of epistemic naturalism and four forms of ontological naturalism. He accepts all but one form of epistemic naturalism, and he rejects all but one form of ontological naturalism. Those forms of naturalism that are rejected include:

1. a form of epistemic naturalism called sensationism, the view that "we can have no experience of anything beyond ourselves except through our physical sensory organs";[18]
2. a form of ontological naturalism that Griffin calls finite causation, or atheism, the view that there are no causal powers beyond the totality of finite causes;
3. a form of ontological naturalism denoted as materialism, the view that denies the existence of any other than physical or material entities; and
4. a form of ontological naturalism, denoted as natural law, that rejects personal causation "because it holds that everything, from the behavior of subatomic particles to the operation of the human mind and the course of history, is governed by natural laws."[19]

Those forms of naturalism that Griffin accepts, on the other hand, include:

1. the form of epistemic naturalism that rejects epistemic supernaturalism, or the view that some ideas are to be accepted because they originate from an authoritative revelation;
2. the form of epistemic naturalism denoted as domain uniformitarianism, which insists that "religion is to be explained in terms of the same causal categories that are used in other cultural domains";[20]

---

[16]*Religion and Scientific Naturalism: Overcoming the Conflicts* (Albany: SUNY Press, 2001); *Journal of the American Academy of Religion* 68 (2000) 99–125. See also Griffin's recent and more popular treatment of scientific naturalism in *Two Great Truths: Christian Faith and Scientific Naturalism* (Louisville: Westminster John Knox, 2004).
[17]"Religious Experience"; the particular authors whose work he critiques are J. Samuel Preus, *Explaining Religion: Criticism and Theory from Bodin to Freud* (New Haven: Yale University Press, 1987), and Robert A. Segal, *Religion and the Social Sciences: Essays on the Confrontation* (Atlanta: Scholars, 1989) and *Explaining and Interpreting Religion: Essays on the Issue* (New York: Lang, 1992).
[18]"Religious Experience," 107.
[19]Ibid., 110.
[20]Ibid., 105.

3. the form of epistemic naturalism that Griffin calls "empirical groundedness," which—inasmuch as religious claims are rooted in experience—does not radically differentiate religious from scientific claims in terms of susceptibility to empirical testing; and
4. the ontological naturalism that rejects supernaturalism, understood as the capacity of a supernatural being to intervene in the causal nexus of events and interrupt the world's normal causal processes. This latter naturalism may also be more broadly understood as ontological uniformitarianism, "the insistence that no causes operated in the past other than the kinds of causes operating today."[21]

It is beyond the scope of this chapter to attempt a thorough account and analysis of Griffin's taxonomy of naturalisms. Suffice it to say that he has gone a long way toward rescuing and untangling the possible meanings of the term. In so doing he has helped to subvert the modern consensus that theistic belief is incurably authoritarian in character.[22] The rejection of authoritarian religious tradition and the epistemic supernaturalism by which it is generally accounted for is widely thought to entail an anti-theistic metaphysics, or simply a materialistic world-view. Griffin shows a way to cut the knot that is assumed to bind theism to epistemic and ontological supernaturalism. His exposition suggests that there are implicit metaphysical commitments in each of the forms of naturalism. Some of these metaphysical commitments are neutral with respect to theistic belief, others are clearly hostile. Of course, our judgment of the truth or validity of any of these forms of naturalism must not be contingent solely upon their compatibility with theistic affirmations. In the chapter on David Griffin's work I will explore further the warrants for accepting certain of these forms of naturalism while rejecting others. For the time being, however, I indicate my provisional agreement with Griffin in his rejection only of those forms of naturalism that he denotes as sensationist, atheist, and materialist—as well as the final form, which he sees as an aspect of materialism, but may also be characterized as determinist. The other forms of naturalism accepted by Griffin are hereby accepted.

3. Theocentrism—Critique and Alternative to Anthropocentrism

Within a Christian context, a theocentric focus or emphasis bears double significance. In the first place, such a focus stands in contrast to the greater particularity of Christocentrism. Christocentric theologies typically empha-

---

[21] Ibid., 108.
[22] Cf. Franklin Gamwell's discussion of "The Dominant Consensus," in *The Divine Good*, 9–14.

size the unique if not exclusive role of Jesus Christ as bearer of divine revelation, redemption, and salvation. The Christian community, the Church, and its scriptures, the Bible, are understood to have secondary but necessary roles as means by which Jesus Christ is mediated to the believer. This means, among other things, that special epistemological significance is attached to Jesus Christ, as revealed in the scriptures, church sacraments, preaching, and teaching, through the mediating work of the third "Person" of the Christian Trinity, the Holy Spirit. Jesus Christ becomes definitive for the fullest possible knowledge of God and of human being, as the lens through which God and world are most perfectly to be seen and/or as the singularly perfect incarnation of God and true humanity.

A theocentric focus in Christian theology may acknowledge the uniqueness of the revelation of God in Jesus Christ. However, it does seek to articulate a less particularistic and decidedly less exclusive understanding of God and God's relations to the world. Theocentrism provides a broader view of how God comes to be known. If the idea of revelation is retained, it is not limited to God's special revelation in Jesus Christ but is conceived to be more generally manifest. The locus of such revelation may include nature, history, and other religious communities and traditions, in other words, not just the Bible and the Church. Supernaturalistic conceptions of revelation tend to be qualified if not relinquished.[23]

Most importantly, with respect to Christocentrism, a theocentric theology shifts the focus away from God's work of redemption in Jesus Christ to God's work in creation. In Christian theology the first "Person" of the Trinity, God the Father, is typically though not exclusively associated with the work of creation. The second "Person" of the Trinity, God the Son (Jesus Christ), is typically though not exclusively associated with the work of redemption. Redemption is understood to encompass both "fallen" humanity and the whole creation, which has been implicated in humanity's fallen-ness. In actual practice, the emphasis on redemption in Christocentric theology tends to result in a focus on the salvation of human beings. After all, it is human sin that is believed by most Christians to lie at the root of the human and worldly conditions that occasion the need for redemption in the first place. Thus the primary work of God from a Christocentric perspective is God's work in Christ, which is likely to be seen as the salvation of human beings from sin and all its consequences, in persons and in the world. In a theocentric theology, on the other hand, God's primary work is much more likely

---

[23]A well-known example of a distinctively Christian yet clearly theocentric interpretation of revelation that, in my judgment, does not imply any epistemic supernaturalism, is to be found in H. Richard Niebuhr's book, *The Meaning of Revelation* (New York: Macmillan, 1960).

to be understood in terms of creation, and God's redemptive work is viewed in light of God's primary creative activity of bringing the whole world as we know it—including humanity—into being.

The three Protestant theologians whose work is to be examined here understand themselves and their work to stand in a distinctively Christian tradition. In contrast to Christocentric approaches, however, the work of each of the three must be characterized as decidedly theocentric in character. Yet, to my knowledge, none of the three explicitly defines his or her position in contrast to Christocentrism.[24] Neither does my position here call for an emphasis on the various ways in which a theocentric focus is likely to provide a contrast to Christocentric approaches. My purpose here is simply to note that such a contrast exists, because this will help to provide a context in which to interpret and understand some of the features of the theological perspectives of Gustafson, McFague, and Griffin to be considered later.

There is a second way in which a theocentric focus is to be understood that is more fundamental to the perspective I share with the three thinkers to be examined in the following chapters. Theocentrism represents an alternative to, and critique of, anthropocentrism, the view that places human beings at the center of attention and value. Gustafson, McFague, and Griffin all reject anthropocentrism. Admittedly, there is something anthropocentric about all human thought. We human beings can scarcely transcend our human's-eye view of the world, in order to attain a God's-eye view. Yet it is possible to attain a perspective on God and all that pertains to God, rather than the human being, that provides a sense of the whole in our theological and ethical reflections. It is also important, in this connection, to note our common tendency as human beings to dissociate ourselves from nature, and thus to speak of the natural world as if we were not an integral part of it. A critique of anthropocentrism must lead to a greater identification of human beings with nature and the human world with the natural world.[25]

As we will see later, Gustafson is most emphatic in his rejection of anthropocentrism in the name of theocentrism. McFague's theocentric critique of anthropocentrism, while explicit, is much less rigorous and emphatic than Gustafson's. Griffin, with his process theology approach, addresses key theological issues from within a distinctive philosophical framework with a vo-

---

[24]In a recent article, however, Gustafson clearly contrasts his view with what he terms the "orthodox" view that "God chose to reveal Godself in a unique and exclusive way in a single historical event, Jesus Christ"; "Just What Is 'Postliberal' Theology?," *The Christian Century* 116 (1999) 354.

[25]As Gustafson says, "human life is to be construed in continuity with 'nature' as much as in distinction from it"; *Ethics from a Theocentric Perspective*, Vol. 1: *Theology and Ethics* (Chicago: University of Chicago Press, 1981) 282.

cabulary that does not employ the terms anthropocentrism and theocentrism. Yet it is clear that his perspective entails the simultaneous though partially qualified rejection of anthropocentrism and acceptance of theocentrism.

The chief axiom in a theocentric critique of anthropocentrism is that God, not humankind, is the measure of all things. Humankind may be the *measurer* of all things, certainly of all things that belong to human experience, but humankind is not the be-all and end-all of existence. The cosmos was not created for humankind. The rest of the creation must not be regarded as merely instrumental to the service of human ends. It is not all about us. Only God can be God.[26]

Much of the language I am using here reflects James Gustafson's way of putting the matter. Though it seems clear to Gustafson that the cosmos is not all about us, it is not clear what the cosmos is all about.[27] Gustafson balks at traditional treatments of what he calls "the basic issue of theological ethics in the West: Are God's commands right because he commands them or does he command them because they are right? Are God's ends good because he chooses them or does he choose them because they are good?" The dichotomy in this way of posing the question has forced an unnecessary choice that has always been made in favor of what is perceived to be right and good from a human perspective, says Gustafson.[28] What is required is at least a much more expansive perspective on what constitutes the right and the good. Moreover, there are neglected strands in the biblical and Christian tradition to corroborate the sense that God's purposes may not be consistent with human perceptions of what is in our own interests.[29] Gustafson also demurs on the question of whether God actually possesses an ultimate aim or purpose for the universe.[30]

Gustafson, we will see, is very reticent in speaking of God. It is simply beyond our human ken to claim much knowledge of God. Consequently, Gustafson's theocentrism serves a negative function first of all, precisely as a critique of anthropocentrism.[31] In this respect, his work belongs to the *via negativa* in theology. But there are also clearly identifiable positive implications of theocentrism, which I will attempt to specify more fully in the respective chapters on Gustafson, McFague, and Griffin. Here I will note two

---

[26]Cf. Gustafson, ibid., 15, 82; also, "A Theocentric Interpretation of Life," *Christian Century* 97 (1980) 754–60.
[27]Ibid., 90ff.
[28]Ibid., 95.
[29]Ibid., 96.
[30]*A Sense of the Divine: The Natural Environment from a Theocentric Perspective* (Cleveland: Pilgrim, 1994) 72.
[31]Gustafson understands himself to be engaged in a critique that challenges the dominant anthropocentric tendency in Christian thought. Indeed, it is the dominant tendency in Western philosophy as well. In his lectures on moral philosophy, the noted moral and political

important features of the theocentric perspective that I wish to emphasize and advocate for an adequate theological ethics.

The first feature is a commitment to a large perspective or view of things. This is a key commitment that McFague and Griffin share with Gustafson. If human beings are not the end and goal of the cosmos, then the concern of an adequate theological ethics must not be merely with human beings and their welfare. Our concern must encompass as much as possible of the whole creation. I do not mean to suggest that a moral obligation exists to agonize over the fate of galaxies millions of light years away. We are not ethically obligated beyond the reach of our own influence. But we are in some measure obligated to act and respond with interest and concern so far as our knowledge and influence do extend.

Second, in this proposal for a theocentric ethics God may be best understood as the center, source, and end of all value. I do not claim that there is only one locus of value in the cosmos. Indeed, every entity in the universe may be said to have value, as I will explain in the chapter on David Griffin's work. Even so, all value is to be understood as such in ultimate relation to God. It will later be necessary to give further specification to the meaning of value. At this point I simply highlight the fact that the theocentric commitment requires a great expansion of our perspective on where value is to be found, one that qualifies all our human valuations and thoroughly relativizes our own sense of importance, by locating ultimate and absolute value only in God.

4. Critical Realism

Another distinguishing feature of the three thinkers whose works are being considered here is that each may be characterized as a critical realist. There are various forms of critical realism in science and philosophy, but no attempt will be made to distinguish among them. A general, nontechnical understanding of critical realism should suffice to illuminate what is distinctive and important to this study. In brief, and first of all, critical *realism* assumes a realist ontology. That is to say, there is a real world that exists independently of

---

philosopher, John Rawls, observed: "[W]hat gives Kant's view a religious aspect is the dominant place he gives to the moral law in conceiving of the world itself. For it is in following the moral law as it applies to us, and in striving to fashion in ourselves a firm good will, and in shaping our social world accordingly that alone qualifies us to be the final purpose of creation. Without this, our life in the world, and the world itself, lose their meaning and point." *Lectures on the History of Moral Philosophy* (Cambridge: Harvard University Press, 2000) 160–61. Needless to say, Gustafson would vigorously disagree that we are "the final purpose of creation" and that without "the moral law as it applies to us" the world would lose its meaning and point. In Gustafson's view, Kant's ethics are decidedly untheocentric; cf. *Ethics II*, 135–36.

our perception of it. If a tree falls in the forest it effects a disturbance. If there is no one there to hear it, any debate over whether or not it makes a sound is only a matter of semantics. There can be no doubt but that the disturbance it effects would be both seen and heard if anyone were present to perceive it.

Critical realism also acknowledges, however, that human perception and knowledge of reality is fallible and incomplete. For one thing, all sensory experience is selective, if due only to the limited receptivity of the human sense organs. It is possible for there to be too much light, or not enough, for the eye to see. Moreover, only certain electromagnetic frequencies register in the eye as light, just as only certain frequencies of vibration register in the ear as sound. The range of smells detectable by a dog clearly exceeds the range of humanly perceptible smells, leaving curious dog-owners wondering what they are missing. With advances in technology, of course, it has become possible for human beings to detect, measure, and sometimes observe the presence of many real-world phenomena that escape normal sensory perception.

Even so—and this is what most proponents of critical realism emphasize—our knowledge of the world can never be said to correspond precisely and completely to things as they are. All experiences are necessarily interpretations. Our apprehension of the world is limited not only by our perceptual abilities but also by the conceptual frameworks we bring to all events. All our feelings, all our encounters, all our observations of events, result in interpreted experiences that are shaped by our conceptual frameworks. Thus, in a scientific context, it can be said that all data are theory-laden. In a religious context, it can be said that implicit cosmological or theological assumptions lie behind all substantive claims. In general, it can be said that there are no uninterpreted "facts."

This does not mean, however, that we do not have knowledge of the real world after all. As John Haught helpfully summarizes,

> though scientific "facts" are always in some sense our own constructs, and are inevitably theory-laden, they are not simply wild guesses that have no reference to a real world existing independently of our preferences. In some way, though chastened by our new understanding of the social nature of knowing, we may still trust that both scientific and religious ideas refer to a real world, one that transcends mere wishing. This appreciation of the mind's capacity to put us in touch—in an always provisional way—with the real world is known as "critical realism." Critical realism, as distinct from naive realism, maintains that our understanding, both scientific and religious, may be oriented toward a real world, whether the universe or God, but that precisely because the universe and God are always too colossal for the human mind to encompass, our thoughts in both science and religion are

also always open to correction. . . . Scientific theories and religious metaphors, in this epistemological contract, are not just imaginative concoctions, as much modern and postmodern thought asserts. Rather, they bear an always tentative relationship to a real world and its ultimate ground. This world beyond our representations is always only incompletely grasped, and its presence constantly "judges" our hypotheses, inviting us continually to deepen our understanding both in science and religion.[32]

As implied by this statement, critical realists tend to regard their formulations as revisable, and thus, improvable. In science, critical realism entails a critical stance with regard to current knowledge and theory. As Arthur Peacocke puts it, "Critical realism recognizes that it is still only the *aim* of science to depict reality and that this allows gradations in acceptance of the 'truth' of scientific theories . . . It must never be forgotten that the realism is always qualified as 'critical' since the language of science is . . . fundamentally metaphorical and revisable, while nevertheless referring."[33] It should also not be forgotten, of course, that this stance assumes that growth in scientific knowledge is possible, that development and revision in theory are on the whole progressive. In other words, whatever the deficiencies of scientific theories to reality, they are presumably always partially correctable, but therefore never perfect and complete.

Although critical realism denotes an epistemological stance within both science and religion, these observations accent features that tend to make this stance more welcome in science than in religion. Peacocke regards critical realism as "the implicit, though often not articulated, working philosophy of practising scientists who aim to depict reality but know only too well their fallibility in doing so."[34] Whether or not most scientists are as aware of their own fallibility as claimed by Peacocke, certainly members of the scientific community are not given to public declarations of infallibility. The same cannot be said of all members of the various religious communities. Nor are religious beliefs so widely regarded as revisable and improvable among religious thinkers as are beliefs about reality among scientists. The critical realist stance taken here, and by the three thinkers to be considered, will meet significant resistance in religious communities precisely because it is critical. On the other hand, the realism of this stance is the implicit if not always articulated conviction of most religious believers. That is to say, most religious believers use religious language as referential language, language that says something

---

[32] *Science and Religion*, 20–21.
[33] *Theology*, 12–13.
[34] Ibid., 11.

to them about the way things really are. This seems true whether religious people understand their language to be literal, analogical, or metaphorical. In any case it is language about things that are taken to be real. It is language about which it makes sense to say that it may be true, or false, or partially true and partially false.

This observation bears significantly on the case I will be making regarding the elements necessary to an adequate theological ethics. Such an ethics must have a theology that is adequate from a religious perspective. Contemporary theological perspectives that are non-referential, or non-realistic, do not do justice to the sensibilities of most religious believers. A critically realistic theological perspective certainly presents a major challenge to the naive realism of many religious believers. But it is clearly more adequate than any non-realistic alternative, for it does not do violence to the typical religious person's understanding of his or her religious experience.[35] Rather, it is more or less consonant with the religious person's implicit and often deeply held assumptions regarding the truth of religious language in reference to divine realities.[36]

This discussion about critical realism has touched briefly on the question, what kind of language is religious language? I have indicated that it is to be regarded as referential language, language that is taken to refer to things, actualities, or entities that are real. I have also indicated that within certain non-realist theological frameworks religious language is understood to be non-referential. Religious language may be viewed as a special kind of language, with its own particular set or system of symbols and structures of meaning. Such language "functions in a special way as an expression of the

---

[35] Wayne Proudfoot rightly observes that it is erroneous to attribute to the subject of a religious experience or belief "an indifference with regard to the existence of the object of that experience of belief." He goes on to note, "The force of religious experience is best accounted for by the fact that the criteria for identifying an experience as religious include reference to an explanatory claim. The experience is perceived by the subject as eluding explanation solely in terms of his own mental states but as having been produced in such a way that it supports his beliefs about the world, beliefs that are distinctive of the tradition within which it is being characterized as religious. The experience provides support for and confirmation of those beliefs"; op. cit., 208, 216. Though I find other features of Proudfoot's argument problematic (cf. n.3 above), I believe he is quite correct in regarding the view that ordinary religious believers hold with respect to religious beliefs and truth claims as realistic and referential. As I note in the following paragraph, religious experience thus calls for explanation as well as interpretation.

[36] As Gordon Kaufman notes, "religious rituals and symbol systems . . . can function effectively . . . only if they are believed 'true,' that is, only if they are taken to represent more or less adequately . . . 'how things really are' with humanity, the world roundabout, and God (or the gods or other resources of life and meaning)"; *In Face of Mystery: A Constructive Theology* (Cambridge: Harvard University Press, 1993) 432.

various forms of the religious consciousness."[37] The appropriate way to understand such language is by means of interpretation, conceived specifically as "the method required for grasping the rules that govern a certain system of symbols or conventional practices" of the sort that one finds in religious texts, myths, and actions.[38] The view taken here is not that religious language is never expressive. It may very well be expressive, for example, of religious feelings, dispositions, and meanings. But it is not merely so. It is also referential. In particular, it is referential with respect to the assumed source or sources of religious experiences. Thus religious experiences, beliefs, and practices implicitly assume, and call for, explanation.

However, it must also be added that religious language is largely analogical and metaphorical, not literal. In fact, as Barbour and Peacocke have emphasized, scientific language is also analogical or metaphorical.[39] All religious as well as all scientific understandings of reality are based on interpretations of experience. That is, they are construals or constructions intended to depict as fully and precisely as possible the way things really are. I have argued that, in contradistinction to a naive realism, a critical realism explicitly takes this circumstance into account. Much more needs to be said, however, especially from a theological perspective, regarding the criteria by which to judge the adequacy of metaphorical religious language. The critical and empirical methods of science continually serve as a check on all scientific models and theories. Is there anything comparable from the side of religion to assess the truthfulness of theological doctrines, systems, and beliefs?

In Chapter 3 we will see that an emphasis on the metaphorical character of religious language—indeed, of all language—is central to the work of Sallie McFague. McFague has characterized much of her work as "metaphorical theology." In one sense, the modifier is redundant—all theology is metaphorical. However, McFague uses the term to denote something quite specific and distinctive about her method. She raises the metaphorical character of religious language to self-consciousness in order to critique tendencies to literalism, which she regards as an idolatrous confusion of the metaphorical with the literal. She thus hopes to create space for the introduction of new metaphors that will make religious language more relevant, especially to

---

[37]Proudfoot, op. cit., 45.
[38]Ibid., 43. Proudfoot helpfully observes that there are two traditions of thought regarding the meaning of interpretation. The more specific and distinctive meaning referred to here belongs to the hermeneutic tradition. The more general meaning, which he identifies with the pragmatic tradition, uses the term "to refer to the active moment in perception, or to the mind's construction of reality"; 45. To say that all experiences are interpretations, or that there are no uninterpreted facts, is to conceive of interpretation in this latter sense.
[39]For example, Barbour, *When Religion Meets Science*, 24ff.; Peacocke, *Theology*, 11ff.

those who find themselves excluded by traditional, patriarchal language for God. But her metaphorical theology is also a strategy for claiming a vigorous first-order language for religion in the face of what she regards as severe epistemological limits on what can actually be known about God as ultimate reality. In Chapter 3 I will focus in particular on an explication and critique of her metaphorical approach in order to assess its potential as an method for articulating a religiously adequate–and thus also truthful—theological ethics.[40]

Recurring Themes

The foregoing discussion of preliminary issues is intended to set forth four of the most significant base points that shape the argument of this book. These base points are 1) a largely integrative view of science and religion; 2) a particular form of naturalism that is neither materialistic nor deterministic; 3) theocentrism as a fundamental theological orientation that also functions as a critique of anthropocentrism; and 4) critical realism in epistemology. In addition to these base points, there are some recurring themes that will characterize my examination and inform my critique of the work of Gustafson, McFague, and Griffin. I do not intend to take up these themes in any deliberately systematic manner in the following chapters. Nonetheless, each of these themes will play a significant role in my treatment and evaluation of the works under consideration. Consequently, I wish to devote some space here to a more focused exploration and elaboration of these themes, their significance, and their possible implications for the remainder of this work.

1. Divine Agency

One of the most difficult problems for any contemporary theology that seeks to be consonant with contemporary scientific understandings of the world is the matter of divine agency. When God is understood in supernatural terms, divine action is understood in terms of disruption of the normal causal nexus

---

[40]Lisa H. Sideris devotes the latter half of the second chapter of her book, *Environmental Ethics, Ecological Theology, and Natural Selection*, to an extensive critique of the scientific adequacy of McFague's ecological ethics. In brief, she contends that "McFague's environmental ethic lacks a solid scientific grounding" (60), in that her ecological ethic appears to trump all other considerations. Thus she does not seriously attend to key features of evolutionary thought that are not congenial to her ethic (New York: Columbia University Press, 2003). I will focus most of my examination and argument in Chapter 3 on McFague's theological method and the ways in which it is implicated in her ecological ethic. Though I find Sideris' argument persuasive and telling, it remains to be seen what ramifications the scientific inadequacy of McFague's work may have for the religious adequacy of her approach.

of events in the world. But there is no empirical evidence or scientific warrant for such disruption. Consequently, in some theologies it is assumed that God no longer acts or intervenes in the world of events in the manner that God must have so acted in order to effect those events that are recorded in scripture and tradition as manifestations of miraculous, or supernatural, power. Needless to say, from a critical perspective such a view is regarded as a form of special pleading. Only if scriptural or traditional attestations of miraculous events are accepted *a priori* as authoritative evidence does the argument carry any weight. And even if one accepts claims regarding miracles in the past as authoritative, one is faced with devising an explanation to account for the fact that no comparable miracles are currently in evidence. Why, in other words, does God no longer perform such feats of power today?

A more sophisticated argument on behalf of divine agency distinguishes between primary and secondary causes. God is said to be the primary cause of all that happens in the world, while empirical investigation has only to do with secondary causes. That is to say, God—being omnipotent—has brought the world into being, created order, established all the laws that govern the interactions of all existing entities, and set everything in motion. God may even be said to continue to engage in the activity of sustaining the world. But all that is accessible to human knowledge are those actions and relations that manifest the secondary causes and the laws by which they are governed. God's sustaining activity is usually assumed to take place on a wholly different plane, and is undifferentiable with respect to all particular events. Except for such sustaining activity, divine agency in this view is not ordinarily constitutive of natural events. Most theologians who have held to this distinction between primary and secondary causation in order to account for the perceived orderliness and explicability of natural events, however, have also postulated that there are special exceptional occasions when God intervened in miraculous or supernatural ways.[41] Nonetheless, assuming some alternative way of dealing with the claims of supernaturalism, one might conceive of God's agency solely in terms of primary causation. The chief problem with such a conception of God is that it hardly does justice to most religious sensibilities. A God who acts only as primary cause is not a God who can be petitioned in prayer, or experienced and related to in any meaningful way.

Apart from the claim that such a God continues to act to sustain the world, albeit on another non-intersecting level or plane, there is no practical difference between the conception of God as primary cause and traditional deism. Deism, of course, has been another way of conceiving God to avoid

---

[41]Cf. Griffin, *Reenchantment without Supernaturalism*, 144ff.; *Religion*, 38–40; also Barbour, *Nature*, 25–27.

the complications of supernaturalism. But a deistic God has long been regarded as too remote, inaccessible, and inactive to bear resemblance to the God of religious faith, a God "who continues to be intimately involved with the world and human life."[42] And, to the immediate point at hand, contemporary divine agency is lost altogether in a deistic conception of God.

Ian Barbour identifies and outlines four additional ways in which efforts have been made to interpret God's relationship to the world while preserving a meaningful notion of divine agency. According to one of these views, God is the determiner of indeterminacies:

> Quantum events have necessary but not sufficient physical causes. If they are not completely determined by the relationships described by the laws of physics, their final determination might be made directly by God. What appears to be chance, which atheists take as an argument against theism, may be the very point at which God acts. Divine sovereignty would be maintained if God providentially controls the events that appear to us as chance.[43]

Religious thinkers who hold this view acknowledge that such divine action would not be scientifically detectable, but claim that under some conditions very small differences could result in significant large-scale effects. They may also argue that God only influences some quantum events, not all. And they tend to supplement their views of divine agency at the quantum level with other views of divine agency, for example, top-down causality.[44]

God as top-down cause and God as communicator of information are two additional views of divine agency described by Barbour. In one version of top-down causality, God's relation to the world is viewed as analogous to the relation of the mind to the body in human beings. To characterize God's role as communicator of information, different analogies are invoked, for example, that of a choreographer of a dance. Certain of the insights of each of these views, Barbour notes, have their counterparts in the fourth view he presents, that of process theology.[45] Since we will be examining process theology's approach to divine agency in Chapter 4 on the work of David Griffin, it is not important to say more at this point about these other alternative views. The fact that such views have been developed, however, attests to the need felt

---

[42]Barbour, *Nature*, 26. The statement applies at least to religious faith within the Jewish, Christian, and Islamic traditions. Barbour notes that one now finds the deistic view in scientifically more sophisticated garb: God as designer of a self-organizing process (25–26). As a religious conception, however, this reformulation is hardly more adequate that previous deistic conceptions.
[43]Ibid., 27.
[44]Ibid., 27–28.
[45]Ibid., 28–38.

by many theologians, especially those with scientific training, to articulate a conception of divine agency that cannot easily be refuted by science. In the absence of such a conception, theological claims that God acts in the world, exercises influence upon temporal events, and contributes to human experience appear to be entirely unwarranted to anyone who is not predisposed to believe such claims. At the same time, the absence of a credible conception of divine agency leaves people of religious faith exceptionally vulnerable to the suspicion, by themselves as well as others, that their faith in a God who makes a difference in their lives and in the world is but wishful thinking.

2. Divine Purpose and a Personal God

In philosophy, the concept of agency usually implies subjectivity. An agent is "a person (or other being) who is the subject when there is action." An agent is thought to possess the capacity to choose among options, and to act on that choice.[46] However, in scientific contexts it is common to think of an agent in impersonal terms. In chemistry, for example, a particular substance may be denoted as a cleansing agent, another as a bonding agent; light may be an agent of photosynthesis; heat may be an agent of oxidation, or combustion—and so on. In these instances, the primary connotation of agency is causation. In light of the scientific world-view, the primary issue at stake in discussions about divine agency is divine causation. How is it possible to think of God as a cause, or the cause, of events in the natural world? The preceding review of approaches to the question of divine agency has focused on agency with respect to this question of causation. Although most conceptions of divine agency assume divine subjectivity, I think it will be helpful to regard the question of whether God can be understood as personal and purposeful as separate and distinct from the question of whether God can be conceived as causal agent.

It is possible to conceive of an agent in impersonal and non-purposeful terms. Even God may conceived as a capricious and arbitrary force. However, it is highly problematic if not impossible to have an impersonal, non-purposeful view of God within the Christian tradition. Within that tradition, human beings are understood to be made in the "image and likeness" of the Creator God. Metaphors for God are inescapably rooted in human experience, and draw heavily upon human activity and relationships. In short, Christianity seems to require a purposeful as well as an agential view of a personal God.

Sallie McFague notes that the root metaphor or original theological model in the Judeo-Christian tradition "is characteristically expressed in terms of per-

---

[46]Jennifer Hornsby, "Agent," in *The Oxford Companion to Philosophy*, edited by Ted Honderich (Oxford: Oxford University Press, 1995) 18.

sonal relations. The biblical root-metaphor is that of a personal deity relating to the human and natural world as its source and its transformer—traditionally articulated in the models of 'creation' and 'redemption'."[47] In the biblical tradition, various personal qualities, dispositions, and features are attributed to God. God is loving and kind, forgiving and long-suffering, gracious and merciful, just and righteous, all-seeing and all-knowing. God becomes angry, God grieves, God expresses jealousy and compassion, God rejoices and laments, God even repents. To God is ascribed a heart and mind, hands and ears and eyes, a backside and a face. God walks in the primeval garden, and speaks to the prophets, chastises the erring and succors the weak. God is not only active and personal, God has a will. God has plans and purposes to fulfill. God instructs, leads, guides, legislates, judges, executes decisions, rescues, restores, delivers, and saves. The language is metaphorical, but it is richly suggestive of an active, personal, and purposeful Being who enters into active, personal relationship with the creation, and most especially, with us human beings.

Although it seems necessary from a religious and theological perspective to have a personal, purposeful conception of God, such a notion can be highly problematic from a theocentric perspective, precisely with respect to theocentrism's critique of anthropocentrism. If God is conceived as a Person writ large, a critical question arises: Is it we human beings who have been created in God's image, or have we human beings created—or constructed—God in our own image? If we understand God in terms of human qualities of being, have we not continued to make human beings the measure of all things? Yet how are we to conceive of the nature of any being except in terms of the being we know through our own self-knowledge? In fact, most theologians insist that what we know of God is only that of which we are capable, given the epistemological limits to our knowing and the rational and experiential limits to our understanding. No presumption should be made that what we know of God is by any means complete with respect to the totality of God's being.

There remains this inescapable dilemma in our thinking about God. Our highest conceptions of God seem to depend on our highest conceptions of what it means to be human.[48] Yet the highest form of human existence is said to be the *imitatio Dei*, the imitation of God. Thinking about God in personal terms involves us in circular thinking. But a critical theocentric

---

[47] *Metaphorical Theology: Models of God in Religious Language* (Minneapolis: Fortress, 1982) 104.
[48] This is made quite explicit in orthodox Christian thought regarding the figure of Jesus Christ, where his complete identification with, and full embodiment of, humanity is at one and the same time grounds for affirming his true divinity. Cf. Hebrews 1:1-3c: "Long ago God spoke to our ancestors in many and various ways by the prophets, but in these last days he has spoken to us by a Son. . . . He is the reflection of God's glory and the exact imprint of God's very being, and he sustains all things by his powerful word."

perspective can keep it from becoming a vicious circularity. For one thing, as just noted, it should never be presumed that what we can know of God is by any means complete. For another, a theocentric perspective seeks to inform our thinking about God and God's relations to the world in ways that do not center on human experience, interests, and concerns. In this respect it is an expansive conception of God, a conception that transcends familiar categories of the personal. Nonetheless, an inherent tension does seem to exist between a theocentric perspective that critiques anthropocentrism on the one hand, and a personal conception of a purposeful and agential God on the other. A more adequately textured account of this tension and its possible implications will be taken up in the following chapter on Gustafson's work, and will provide the context for examining how successfully McFague and Griffin provide alternative proposals for conceiving God in personal terms without losing the theocentric commitment.

In traditional Christian thought, God is understood not only in personal and agential terms, but also as one who has purposes with respect to humankind and the whole creation. Ordinarily we associate purposes with intentions, and one term is often used to define the other.[49] To have purposes is to have ends or aims that one establishes, envisions, or sets forth for oneself to effect. One may have wishes or desires, but these are different from purposes or intentions in that they do not presume one's own effective agency in prospective action. Purposes assume effective agency.

It is not so clear that purposes make sense only if attributed to a personal being or power. Certainly we tend to associate the personal and the purposeful in our thinking, however. And certainly within Christian thought the purposes of God have been viewed in light of God's personal being. God is thought to have purposes that are characteristic of a personal being. Consequently, just as God's person has been expressed in terms similar to those used to describe the human person, so also God's purposes have generally been understood in light of the purposes of human beings.[50] Thus, a conception of God as purposeful, like a conception of God as personal, is problematic for a theocentric critique of anthropocentrism. Just as a theo-

---

[49]Gustafson makes a distinction between purposes and intentions in a discussion of his conception of God. Pointing to the functional interdependence of things, he attributes purposes to God. He does not believe God to be "an intentional agent, active like human agents are," however ("Liberal Questions: A Response to William Placher," *Christian Century* 116 (1999) 425). I find his distinction unpersuasive. See also Harlan Beckley and Charles Swezey, editors, *James M. Gustafson's Theological Ethics: Interpretations and Assessments* (Macon, Ga.: Mercer University Press, 1988) 215.

[50]It is a crucial prophetic insight that "my thoughts are not your thoughts, nor are your ways my ways, says the LORD" (Isaiah 55:8). Such theological insight, while not rare, is seldom taken to heart.

centric ethics requires a de-centering of human beings in our thinking about God and God's relations to the world, it also requires a de-centering of human beings in our thinking about the divine purposes.

In a theocentric ethics, the divine purposes will not be seen as focused exclusively or even primarily on human beings. Those purposes must be thought of as much larger, spatially and temporally, than the realization of any conceivable human ends. However, it remains essential that human ends are comprehended by divine purposes. If the divine purposes have no bearing on human purposes, that is, if there is no way in which human beings can share in the divine purposes, then human existence would seem to be lacking any ultimate meaning.

To be sure, some people who profess no religious faith seem to manage without any convictions regarding the ultimate purpose of their lives, but no one seems to manage without purposes that extend beyond themselves. In moments of extremity, if not often in the course of daily life, virtually everyone recognizes the need for some reasons or purposes larger than self to go on living. Most people of religious faith consciously recognize and articulate the need for those reasons or purposes to be directed toward some ultimate and consummate end. That end must not be simply a terminus or conclusion. It requires the character of realization or fulfillment. It must give meaning to the life of which it is the culmination and outcome, so it must be somehow fitting and right. It must also endure, for if it comes to nothing, then it can be no more than a penultimate end, in which case it raises the question of ultimate meaning all over again. In cultures where Christianity has been the dominant religion, and in terms of its implication for human existence, that end has typically been understood in terms of heaven or an afterlife, a kind or quality of existence that is assumed to be enjoyed without end in the presence and favor of God.

Traditional notions of heaven or an afterlife, inasmuch as they are anthropocentric, are—again—problematic for a theocentric ethics. I will argue that such notions, and the subjective immortality they imply, are not essential for a religiously adequate theological ethics. On the other hand, what is essential is some way to conceive of the meaningfulness of human activity in terms of its participation in, or contribution to, that which is ultimate and enduring. In other words, for human purposes to be adequately meaningful, at least from a religious standpoint, the effort and activity that are expended toward their attainment must be regarded as enduring contributions to the life of God. In more conventional religious language, a life lived in accord with the divine will and purpose must be regarded as an imperishable service to God.

As we will see in Chapter 4 when we examine the work of David Griffin, process theology provides a concept of objective immortality that addresses the need for a sense of ultimate and enduring meaning and purpose. The idea of objective immortality is responsive to the widespread sensibility that the assurance of meaning in existence, with respect to both human beings and the rest of the creation, is contingent upon a conception of the God–world relationship such that God comprehends and preserves all that contributes to the divine purpose. Griffin also argues that process theology allows for the possibility of continued subjectivity or life after death, and we will see why this is a significant moral and religious consideration for him.[51] The prospect of life after death is certainly congenial to most religious believers. However it tends to reflect an inordinately anthropocentric preoccupation with human destiny. From a theocentric perspective one must insist that the affirmation of this prospect is not critical to a religiously adequate conception of God in relation to the human questions of ultimate meaning and purpose.

3. Construal vs. Construction in the Interpretation of Experience and the Formulation of Theology

From a critical realist perspective, all scientific theories and all theologies are necessarily interpretations. That does not mean that they lack truth, in the sense of being adequate to the realities to which they refer. As we have seen, however, the truth of scientific theories, and theologies as well, must be understood in relative terms, inasmuch as some theories and theologies may finally be judged to be more adequately representative of reality than others.[52] The question then arises, how is the truth or adequacy to reality of scientific theories and theological statements to be judged? Our three thinkers provide somewhat different answers to that question, and it will be important to note, compare, and contrast those answers in the chapters to come.

One significant clue to the differences is reflected in the language that each employs to denote the interpretive task. As noted at the very outset of this chapter, in James Gustafson's view it is critical to theological ethics how God is construed, but also how the world is construed. Gustafson is very much aware of the fact that both of these construals figure prominently in the formulation of his ethics. He consistently uses the term "construal" to acknowledge that his work involves a critical interpretive dimension. I believe he also uses the term construal, rather than construction, precisely to avoid

---

[51] *Reenchantment without Supernaturalism*, 234–46; *God and Religion in the Postmodern World: Essays in Postmodern Theology* (Albany: SUNY Press, 1989) 91–108.
[52] Cf. p. 17 and n. 33 above.

identification with certain forms of theological constructivism on the one hand, and critical theory on the other.

On the theological side, Gustafson clearly distinguishes himself from the sort of "postliberal" theology best exemplified in the work of George Lindbeck.[53] Lindbeck argues that theology is a cultural-linguistic system that operates according to its own distinctive, internally derived, set of rules. Questions regarding the truth of theology are to be settled in terms of these rules, not by reference to external criteria or realities. Gustafson rejects such an approach as a form of epistemological relativism that provides "justification for affirming the truth of beliefs without worrying about whether they are true for more than those who affirm them."[54]

On the scientific side, Gustafson clearly wants to distinguish himself from those critical theorists whose general theoretical outlook obliges them to take a jaundiced view of scientific (as well as other) claims to knowledge. Surely he is alluding to the influence of major deconstructionist thinkers when he comments, "Perhaps some who have imbibed certain forms of critical theory would call science the myth of the twentieth century in that it provides the symbols for understanding reality."[55] In context the comment is even more pejorative than it appears here. Gustafson does not deny the constructive character of all knowledge claims, nor does he entirely reject the cultural and linguistic critiques of the critical theorists. Rather, he simply sees such critiques being carried too far, resulting in an undue epistemological skepticism and relativism with respect to both theological and scientific truth claims.

In attempting to distinguish between construal and construction I have found it helpful to invoke Wayne Proudfoot's distinction between two different meanings of interpretation, which he associates with two traditions of thought, the pragmatic and the hermeneutic.[56] The general meaning of interpretation, which belongs to the pragmatic tradition, understands that all data are theory-laden. There are no uninterpreted facts. As previously noted, the more specialized meaning of interpretation, belonging to the hermeneutic tradition, conceives of interpretation as "a method for grasping the rules that govern

---

[53]George A. Lindbeck, *The Nature of Doctrine: Religion and Theology in a Postliberal Age* (Louisville: Westminster John Knox, 1984). See Gustafson, "Tracing a Trajectory," *Zygon* 30 (1995) 187.
[54]"Liberal Questions," 422. See the two preceding articles in this series, James M. Gustafson, "Just What Is 'Postliberal' Theology?"; and William C. Placher, "Being Postliberal: A Response to James Gustafson," *Christian Century* 116 (1999) 353–55, 390–92, as well as the full article cited, 422–25. See also Gustafson, *An Examined Life*, 9, 16.
[55]*Intersections*, 32.
[56]Op. cit., 43–45; cf. n. 38 above, p. 19.

a certain system of symbols or conventional practices."[57] Within that non-realist tradition, language has a primarily expressive rather than referential function. For Gustafson, there is no question that language, whether theological or scientific, has a primarily referential function. The language of construal retains this referential connotation. The language of construction, on the other hand, lends itself more readily to the hermeneutical meaning of interpretation.

In any event, Gustafson eschews both abstract philosophizing and epistemological constructivism. For all practical purposes, he believes that it is possible to acquire a knowledge of "how things really are," and that such knowledge is to be gained through historical and scientific study.[58] "I am so incorrigibly empirical," he asserts in response to others' misgivings regarding the modesty of his theological affirmations.[59]

So far as empirical or scientific knowledge is concerned, then, "construal" signals Gustafson's recognition of the interpretive element in such knowledge while seeming simultaneously to imply that such knowledge does have to do quite directly with reality.[60] The imprecision in this way of stating the matter reflects my perception that Gustafson himself is either intentionally vague, or unwilling or unable to provide a more definitive statement of his epistemology. In any case, as we will see, Gustafson remains vulnerable to the charge of naive realism, just because he typically fails to distinguish between scientific interpretations of reality and reality as such. When it comes to Gustafson's *theological* construals, however, we will see that there are additional qualifications and ambiguities to be noted regarding the realism of his perspective. The main point here is that Gustafson looks to scientific accounts to provide as reliable a description and explanation as possible of how things really are. He judges the adequacy of theological accounts precisely in terms of their congruence with scientific accounts of the world, but also—as we will see—from the perspective of his theocentric piety.

Sallie McFague is much more interested than Gustafson in methodological issues pertaining to the epistemological status of our language about God

---

[57] Ibid.
[58] *Intersections*, xvi.
[59] *James M. Gustafson's Theocentric Ethics*, 229.
[60] I use the term "directly" for lack of a better word to indicate the conviction that I attribute to Gustafson, and also share, that we do experience and thus have knowledge of the real world. I cannot provide adequate argument for this assertion here. Suffice it to say that, for my part, this assertion entails rejection of epistemologies that claim not to be able to know things in themselves in favor of an ontology that eschews the very notion of a *thing-in-itself*, because it regards the basic entities of existence as events, not discrete substances or things. Along these lines, as we will see in Chapter 4, David Griffin sets forth a conception of human perception that "provides direct knowledge of other actualities"; *Reenchantment without Supernaturalism*, 340.

and the world. McFague also seems more interested than Gustafson in the derivation of theological language, and less attentive to the actual knowledge of science. For McFague, scientific and religious thought are both interpretive enterprises that rely on metaphors and models to construct the theories and theologies by which they comprehend their respective spheres. "Thinking by metaphor and hence by models is not optional but necessary. And this is true in the sciences as well as in the humanities."[61] Thus, scientific theories and theological systems are among the many constructions that constitute our socially constructed world.[62] McFague realizes that this raises questions regarding the reference and truth of metaphor. "The centrality of metaphor in all constructive fields—our world as modeled and we as the modelers—means that the question of the truth of metaphor cannot be dealt with in a direct, literalistic, positivistic way." Rather, the truth of a metaphor—for example, a scientific hypothesis—is a matter of fit, an assessment of the extent to which it is an "apt, fitting way of interpreting reality."[63]

In Chapter 3 I will explore much more fully how metaphors and models function as constructions in McFague's metaphorical theology, and reflect on the implications of her approach for establishing criteria for making assessments of truth. The point here is to note that McFague's language of construction, in contrast to Gustafson's language of construal, seems to put us somewhat further removed from the sense of knowing how things really are. Interpretation, understood as construction, seems to be much more dependent on the interpreter, much less constrained by and conformed to what is being interpreted. At the same time, McFague insists that her epistemology is a form of critical realism.[64] The case is easier to make with respect to her views regarding scientific metaphors, models, and theories than it is with respect to her theological method.

There is in fact an evolution in McFague's thought on these matters from her earlier books, *Speaking in Parables* and *Metaphorical Theology*, to her more mature and better known *Models of God* and *The Body of God*, that makes any brief statement about her epistemology inadequate.[65] Nonetheless, the following excerpt from *Metaphorical Theology*, where she deals most extensively

---

[61] *Metaphorical Theology*, 24. I will deal more specifically with how McFague defines metaphors, models, and theories in Chapter 3.
[62] Ibid., 33.
[63] Ibid., 40–41.
[64] Ibid., 101.
[65] *Speaking in Parables: A Study in Metaphor and Theology* (Philadelphia: Fortress, 1975); *Models of God: Theology for an Ecological, Nuclear Age* (Philadelphia: Fortress, 1987); *The Body of God: An Ecological Theology* (Minneapolis: Fortress, 1993).

with methodological issues, highlights major contours of a constructivist view of interpretation within a critical realist perspective:

> [W]e have said from the beginning that the outstanding characteristic of metaphor is its tensive "is and is not." Metaphor has a positive as well as a negative pole and the positive pole is an assertion, albeit an indirect one, of reference to reality. That reference is, however, not only indirect but redescriptive; that is, metaphorical construction refers to reality both in the sense of creation as well as discovery. The epistemology that lies behind this statement is, of course, "critical realism . . . ."[66]

We will subsequently need to attend at greater length to McFague's critical realist claims.

Like McFague and Gustafson, David Griffin understands himself to be a critical realist who acknowledges that all our knowledge and theories about God and the world are matters of interpretation. Unlike the other two, however, Griffin says relatively little to call attention to this interpretive dimension in our apprehension of reality. For one thing, he devotes little space to descriptive accounts of the world as known to science. For another, he is not preoccupied with the metaphorical character of our scientific and theological language. He is first of all a philosopher and a metaphysician who is seeking to present a coherent general account not simply of the way things appear to be, but of the way things really are at a fundamental level. In doing so, he recognizes the provisional character of his and all philosophical work. It is clearly a constructive enterprise, but it is by no means pure speculation. Commenting on the fact that his (postmodern) approach to theology does not claim certain ideas to be true because they happen to come from divine revelation, he writes:

> This sets it apart from premodern forms of theology. Insofar as postmodern theology does think of some ideas as resulting from divine revelation to a greater degree than others, it seeks to establish their truth first. The reason for this epistemic approach is also rooted in the understanding of the God–world relation. Because all creatures have their own creativity *vis-à-vis* divine creativity, and because human beings have a very high degree of this power to be self-determining in relation to the divine influence upon them, no human ideas can be thought to have been directly implanted by God. All human ideas,

---

[66]*Metaphorical Theology*, 132. This is certainly not McFague's definitive last word on constructivisim in theology. In *Models of God* she actually advocates a heuristic approach, and seems to pull back to a weaker constructivist view of scientific knowledge. The citation serves primarily to set the stage for subsequent discussion.

whether about God or the world, are largely free interpretations. Although there is a prelinguistic, preinterpretive, "given" element in experience, including a direct experience of God, all conscious ideas are constructed by the creative power of human experience. The premodern idea of "revealed theology" must therefore be totally abolished. *All* theological ideas are human constructions. Accepting this idea fully, postmodern theology must rest its claim to truth wholly upon the intrinsic convincingness of its ideas, and this means upon their self-consistency, adequacy to all the facts of experience, and illuminating power.[67]

Griffin's reference here to his theology as postmodern should not be misunderstood. He defines postmodern largely in terms of the epistemological and metaphysical departures from Cartesian dualism and scientific positivism that contemporary science and the philosophy of Alfred North Whitehead require. He is obviously not referencing the poststructuralist and deconstructionist movements in literature and some streams of continental philosophy that take their bearings from the work of Jacques Derrida. As we will see in Chapter 3, Sallie McFague also makes frequent recourse to the term postmodern, most often as a modifier of science. In this respect, she uses the term much as Griffin does. However, because she has also been influenced by the deconstructionist movement in literary criticism, her use of the term tends at times to have constructivist and anti-realist connotations, so that when she writes of "the picture of reality" provided us by postmodern science, it is difficult to say just how, or to what extent, she regards the picture to be true to the reality. In any event, both Griffin and McFague call for a thorough revision of the modern worldview and its replacement with a postmodern worldview or cosmology. McFague writes of this as a constructive task. For Griffin it is a work of critique and reconstruction.[68]

---

[67] *Primordial Truth and Postmodern Theology* (Albany: SUNY Press, 1989) 203.
[68] In a new "Introduction to SUNY Series in Constructive Postmodern Thought," of which Griffin is the general editor, he writes: "The postmodernism of this series can . . . be called *revisionary, constructive,* or—perhaps best—*reconstructive*. It seeks to overcome the modern worldview not by eliminating the possibility of worldviews (or "metanarratives") as such, but by constructing a postmodern worldview through a revision of modern premises and traditional concepts in the light of inescapable presuppositions of our various modes of practice. That is, it agrees with deconstructive postmodernists that a massive deconstruction of many received concepts is needed. But its deconstructive moment, carried out for the sake of the presuppositions of practice, does not result in self-referential inconsistency. It also is not so totalizing as to prevent reconstruction. The reconstruction carried out by this type of postmodernism involves a new unity of scientific, ethical, aesthetic, and religious intuitions . . . While critical of many ideas often associated with the modern science, it rejects not science as such but only that scientism in which only the data of the modern natural sciences

In a general sense, all three thinkers, Gustafson, McFague, and Griffin, regard interpretation as a matter of construction. However, as will be noted more fully in the chapters to come, Gustafson does not employ the term and appears to want to differentiate his theology as construal or perspective from most constructivist approaches, particular those that are indebted to non-realist epistemologies.[69] McFague readily uses the term in her major works, but with varying nuances that may be at least partially explained in terms of the evolution in her thought as well as significant ambiguities in the way she implicitly and explicitly differentiates between construction in science and in theology. Griffin seldom has recourse to the term, though his entire process philosophy may be viewed as a constructive alternative to the dominant scientific and theological constructions of the modern period. One of my primary concerns in this book will be to assess the adequacy of the interpretations of God and the world provided by these three thinkers. The terminologies they employ to describe the general epistemological standpoints of their presumably critical-realist approaches should aid in this task.

4. The Indicative and the Imperative, or Getting from the "Is" to the "Ought"

A naturalistic ethics, as construed here, rejects any *a priori* appeal to non-naturalistic or supernaturalistic sources of knowledge. Whatever ethical rules, principles, or other prescriptive formulations such an ethics may propose cannot be warranted by divine laws or commands, or any other form of supernaturally revealed truth. Nor can appeal be made to transcendental norms or values that presumably can be grasped only by means of intuition, insofar as such norms or values are conceived to exist, not only in distinction from, but independently of, the world of nature. In short, there are no norms or "oughts" that a naturalistic ethics can import from beyond or outside the world as it is to construct or justify its ethical claims.

The question arises, how does one get from the descriptive to the prescriptive, from facts to values, from the indicative to the imperative, from the "is" to the "ought"? There are two major facets to the so-called "is-ought"

---

are allowed to contribute to the construction of our public worldview." See Catherine Keller and Anne Daniell, editors, *Process and Difference: Between Cosmological and Poststructuralist Postmodernisms* (Albany: SUNY Press, 2002) ix.

[69]At the same time, Gustafson can seem to reject metaphysical realism; cf. *Ethics I*, 258. In my view, Gustafson is sufficiently averse to abstract philosophy and metaphysics that he wishes to avoid identifying himself with any philosophical label, even if it happens to fit. Philosopher Robert Audi also notes with respect to the same passage referenced here that Gustafson need not give up ontological realism "if it is conjoined with an *epistemological* fallibilism"; "Theology, Science, and Ethics in Gustafson's Theocentric Vision," in Beckley and Swezey, 179.

problem. The first is simply a logical problem. As Hume objected, one must have an "ought" in the premises in order to derive an "ought" in conclusion. A purely descriptive account of an event or situation carries no moral implications, according to this objection. I believe that is correct, although one might demur that no purely descriptive account of anything is possible. Nonetheless, the logic of the objection is sustained: Were a purely descriptive account of an event or situation possible, it would carry no moral implications.

The second facet of the problem pertains to the identification and specification of the good, or that which is to be valued. Any attempt to define the good in natural terms seems to beg the question. If the good is defined as the pleasurable, for example, then it may be asked, "But what is the good of that which is pleasurable?" If one says simply that what is pleasurable is good, and what is not pleasurable is not good, it seems that one has succeeded in defining the good only by replacing it with the pleasurable. But what warrants are there for this substitution? Is the pleasurable really unexceptionally good? The substance of the objection here is, in effect, the identification of some "is" (e.g., the pleasurable) with the "ought" (i.e., the good). But grounds are lacking to justify this identification. The meaning of the good can hardly be exhausted by identification with any specified "is". Because it appears from this perspective that the good cannot be adequately defined by any natural terms, G. E. Moore called the attempt to do so the naturalistic fallacy. A naturalistic ethics, therefore, seems vulnerable to both logical and morally substantive criticisms.

Both Gustafson and Griffin take note of the "is-ought" problem. McFague, to my knowledge, does not. Gustafson's treatment is very brief, while Griffin goes to some length to answer both the logical and the moral criticisms raised against naturalistic ethics.[70] Gustafson to a large extent, and McFague to a more limited extent, have an *implicit* answer to the "is-ought" problem, while Griffin offers a very *explicit* response.

As I see it, the critical realism of these three writers goes hand in hand with a kind of moral realism. All three may be said to address the logical facet of the "is-ought" problem by a kind of general imperative that is constitutive of their moral realism. None of these three thinkers, in fact, brings a merely descriptive approach to the world. Insofar as they are critical realists they seek to know things, so far as possible, "as they really are." But as ethical think-

---

[70]Gustafson, *Ethics II*, 111, 295; Griffin, "The Holy, Necessary Goodness, and Morality," *Journal of Religious Ethics* 8 (1980) 330–49; *Reenchantment without Supernaturalism*, 313–19; *Primordial Truth*, 40; cf. 52, 127; Griffin, *Spirituality and Society: Postmodern Visions* (Albany: SUNY Press, 1988) 153, n. 1; Griffin, William A. Beardslee, and Joe Holland, *Varieties of Postmodern Theology* (Albany: SUNY Press, 1989) 47–48.

ers there is a reason why they are critical realists. They all regard morality as having something rather directly to do with living and acting in accordance with the way the world is actually constituted. This is why science, with the knowledge it provides us of our world, is so important to their thinking. Yet, as McFague explicitly notes, their work is not merely about shaping theology, or theological ethics, to science.[71] They are also theologians for whom the "ought" is not simply derivative of the "is."[72]

As we will see, Gustafson does not think the "oughts" can be deduced simply from an "isness." The patterns and processes of the natural world provide a basis or foundation for moral discernment, but they are not definitively prescriptive.[73] McFague attributes moral significance to the "picture of reality" that is provided us by contemporary science, precisely because it is indicative of certain imperatives regarding how we ought to live on this planet, but it is also clear that some of her imperatives derive more from religious tradition and imagination than from a merely descriptive account of the way things are.[74] Griffin explicitly formulates the general moral principle according to which human beings should act: "*in any concrete situation we should seek to maximize importance insofar as it is attainable by us in that situation.*"[75] Since it is always God's aim to maximize importance, however, this is tantamount to adopting the divine aim as one's own.[76]

Thus, it is never entirely true that "how things really are" yields the "ought" in the work of these three thinkers. In general terms, the primary reason for this is that each has a processive rather than a static view of reality. In this regard, each clearly sees human beings as active participants in the world process, although God's role is variously understood. Human actions help give shape to what "is"; divine influence may also be significant. Regardless of whether and to what extent each reckons God to be directive of the world process, however, each implicitly distinguishes between a conformist view of ethics and some kind of transformative perspective. The sense of the possibilities for transformation is quite strong with McFague, and also with Griffin,

---

[71] *The Body of God*, ix.
[72] Griffin comes closest to assuming this derivation when he footnotes: "The widespread acceptance among ethicists that it is logically fallacious to derive human morality from the nature of things . . . has done nothing to change the fact that human beings do so. Rather than attacking the connection between is and ought, reality and morality, postmodern thought seeks to spread a new understanding of reality, from which will follow a better morality"; *Spirituality and Society*, 153, n. 1. Griffin's philosophical conception of reality adds a good deal of complexity to any account of the "is," however.
[73] *Ethics I*, 111, 295–96
[74] *Models*, 111; *Body*, ix; cf. Sideris, op. cit., 60–90.
[75] *Reenchantment without Supernaturalism*, 305; emphasis preserved.
[76] Ibid., 310.

while much less so with Gustafson, who has often been criticized for his apparent stoicism.[77] But, as just pointed out, even Gustafson hardly believes that a naturalistic ethics calls for simple conformation of our lives to the way things currently are.[78]

In broadest terms we may say that undergirding the work of each of these three thinkers is a kind of moral imperative that, given his or her distinctive sense of the possibilities within existence, can be roughly formulated as follows: *we ought to live and act, so far as possible, in accordance with the way things really are; the way things really are, being neither static nor entirely predetermined, is dependent in part on our contributions to the evolving realization of inherent possibilities in the way things really are.* That there are "inherent possibilities in the way things really are" implies that there are also inherent limitations. All things are by no means possible. The "ought" must lie within the realm of possibility, or else it is meaningless. The realm of possibility is largely determined by, but not limited to or circumscribed by, what is. Thus, knowledge of the "is" is basic but not entirely decisive for discerning the "ought".

It may still be objected, following Hume, that a naturalistic ethics has no place for any imperatives, on the assumption that naturalism provides a basis for indicatives, for whatever "is," but not for any imperatives, or "oughts." Thus, not even the imperative to live and act in accordance with reality, however construed, has a place in naturalistic ethics. If we grant the objection we must concede that there appears to be no solution to the logical facet of the "is-ought" problem within a naturalistic perspective. Ethics either becomes impossible, because there can be no "ought," or there must be resort to some form of supernaturalism or ethical transcendentalism. But the objection need not be granted. A ready solution to the logical facet of the "is-ought" problem can be found in the processive view of reality itself. As we will see more fully in Chapter 4, reality itself exercises a claim upon us precisely because there is intrinsic value or goodness in all that is.[79]

---

[77] Gustafson has apparently accepted the appellation, as he identifies himself as a "Christian stoic" or "stoical Christian" in his latest book, *An Examined Faith*, 106.
[78] Cf. *Ethics I*, 327–28.
[79] Suffice it to say here that the "is" is not simply to be equated with the "ought," if only because what is given includes both actuality and possibility. Only some small portion of what is given as possibility can ever be realized at any moment. Choices must be made regarding alternative possibilities and their respective values. However, in my view the claim that intrinsic value or goodness resides in all that is does not by itself render human action truly *meaningful.* Meaningfulness, as I will argue, also requires that intrinsic value or goodness be constitutive of, or contributive to, an enduring entity who we call God.

All that naturalistic ethics need claim is that, *in varying degrees*, value or goodness resides intrinsically in what is given in existence, both what is given in actuality and what is given as possibility. The primary concern of ethics is to orient human thought and action toward the realization of greater rather than lesser degrees of value or goodness. If it is credible to speak of the inherent value or goodness of that which is, then the "ought" may be understood to refer either to some possibility in which the greatest attainable value or goodness would be realized, or to that human action whereby such a possibility would become actuality. In other words, we can speak of how things *ought* to be within some horizon of possibility, or of what *ought* to be done in order to actualize the envisioned possibility. In either case, we are speaking of the "oughtness" that attaches to the realization of intrinsic value or goodness.

A naturalistic ethics may thus claim that the "ought" is given in the "is" precisely in the sense that the "ought" refers to the moral imperative that attaches to the realization of the greatest potential intrinsic value or goodness residing within some particular set of actualities. Right action, then, is action in accordance with the way things really are, where "the way things really are" includes the possibilities that are given in the actualities at hand, toward the realization of the greatest of those possibilities, where "the greatest of those possibilities" denotes those potential actualities that would be of greatest intrinsic value or goodness.[80]

---

[80]It may be helpful to contrast more traditional theistic forms of ethics, in which it is virtually taken for granted that goodness is to be identified with God. It follows from such identification that God's actions, including God's laws or commands, must be good. The attempt to derive the "ought" from divine laws or commands may appear to avoid the logical objection to naturalistic ethics, namely that the "is" cannot yield the "ought." In traditional theism the ought is derived from God's good will.

However, it can be argued that the presumed logical difficulty of naturalistic ethics, deriving the "ought" from the "is," is not avoided in traditional theism but simply displaced from the realm of the natural to the supernatural. The "re-location" of the good in a God who is understood in supernatural terms still leaves us in a situation where it is clear that our thinking about the "ought" has necessarily required us to postulate a locus of goodness or value. Whether the locus of goodness or value is understood in naturalistic or supernaturalistic terms, whether it is spoken of as God or not, the logic is the same. Goodness or value must be taken to be in some sense intrinsic to, and definitive and constitutive of, that locus. The "ought" must be assumed to be implicated in some fashion in the "is."

Another way to frame the argument here is to point out that metaphysical dualism offers no more logical resolution of the "is–ought" problem than does ethical naturalism. It only seems to do so by treating the non-natural, whether it be identified with God or some other source of transcendental norms, as uniquely productive of value or goodness.

Moreover, the logic of divine goodness invariably raises the theodicy question: If God is supremely powerful, and God is good, how can there be evil in the world? Traditional theism argues, on behalf of God's goodness, either that the evil is illusory, or that God's exercise of power is not such as to prevent the evil, or both. (The Augustinian tradition regards evil, in

The logical facet of the "is–ought" problem need not detain us further, but there is still the question of the substantive identification and specification of the good. To the extent that the "ought" can be understood in terms of living and acting in accordance with how things really are, both in actuality and in possibility and prospect, the primary task in addressing the substantive moral problem in a naturalistic ethics becomes one of discerning the most important features of world processes and events. Certain sorts of questions need to be asked and at least provisionally answered. For example: What features of reality hold greatest significance for comprehending the nature of things? How are we best to understand what is going on? In what ways can we relate to what is going on so that our lives and actions contribute to the whole of existence? And, assuming that God is integral to the natural process, how can the theological character of naturalistic ethics be most adequately acknowledged, articulated, and conveyed? The following chapters may be understood in large part as explorations toward answering such questions from within the Christian Protestant tradition.

What we will discover is that Gustafson, McFague, and Griffin exhibit a remarkable congruence with respect to the broad outlines and substance of their ethical concerns. The work of each of them is marked by opposition to all metaphysical and ethical dualisms; a processive view of, and deep appreciation for, the natural world; emphasis on relationships and interdependence; focus on wholes, not just parts; a de-centering of the human being as the touchstone of all values; an ecological ethic; and a personal commitment to the religious life in some form as integral to the shaping of our moral sensibilities and/or the sustaining of our moral energies. But the paths by which they come to their common concerns and perspectives are decidedly different. As part of the expository section in each of the next three chapters I will trace and assess these different paths.

---

essence, as a privation of being, in effect, a non-reality. It and other theodicies also see evil to be occasioned by human freedom, and thus subservient to and ultimately transmuted by God's highest purposes in the creation.)

But evil hardly seems illusory. In fact, there seems to be more evil than can be rationally accounted for in any traditional theistic scheme. Therefore, God's exercise of power is not such as to prevent evil. Thus, the attempt to ground the "ought" by resort to a supernaturally divine source of moral knowledge, such as divinely revealed commandments, introduces its own logical dilemma regarding the divine power and goodness. How can we be confident of the goodness of God, and hence of God's commands, in a world permeated with evil that appears irrational and wholly undeserved?

5. The Relation of Theology and Ethics to Each Other

I began this chapter by quoting James Gustafson: "Ethics is shaped by the account one renders of God and God's relations to the world."[81] The statement appears in the second volume of *Ethics from a Theocentric Perspective*. At an earlier point in the same volume he notes, "the entire volume seeks to fulfill a general purpose by answering a single general question: How does the theocentric perspective qualify ethics?"[82] Clearly, Gustafson believes that theology has ethical implications. That is to say, what and how we think about God, and God's relations to the world, informs and shapes our valuations of things, including our perceptions of what is morally relevant, what relationships are most significant, and what place we human beings have in the totality of all that is going on.

So central is Gustafson's conviction of the crucial role of theological construal for ethics that he regards his distinctively theocentric project as a call to conversion—a conversion of perspective, but also I think a conversion to a theocentric piety that would help re-shape the moral life. In other words, an altered theological perspective has significance not only for ethical reflection but also for the religious life and the morality of the actions that flow from such a life. From Gustafson's perspective, theology clearly has priority over ethics. On the other hand, theology does not arise in a vacuum. That one can say anything about God in the first place is largely a matter of piety, in Gustafson's view. "Theology is an enterprise that extrapolates from piety, and other affective responses to the world, to say some things about God," he writes.[83] Yet what can be said about God is profoundly constrained by our understanding of the world and the patterns and processes according to which it appears to be governed. In the following chapter we will want to examine whether the way Gustafson construes the world is as determinative of his construal of God as his construal of God is determinative of his construal of the world.

Sallie McFague seems equally committed to the view that theology makes a difference in how we see things and, ultimately, how we live and act. In *The Body of God* she writes, "the principle task of an ecological theology . . . is to change consciousness, to develop a new sensibility about who we are in the scheme of things so that when we deal with concrete issues we can do so differently than in the past. The focus of this essay is on *thinking differently* so that we might behave differently."[84] This is a theme that appears throughout her writings.[85]

---

[81] *Ethics II*, 27.
[82] Ibid., 3.
[83] *Ethics I*, 235; cf. 164, 251, 257.
[84] *The Body of God*, 202; emphasis preserved.
[85] Compare, for example, *Metaphorical Theology*, xi; *Life Abundant: Rethinking Theology and Economy for a Planet in Peril* (Minneapolis: Fortress, 2001) xi.

Like Gustafson, McFague is also hoping to effect a conversion, not just in consciousness or perception but in ethical reflection and moral action. Her appeal to metaphorical theology is not simply an acknowledgment of the inescapably metaphorical nature of language, especially theological language. It is also a move that allows her to employ new images and metaphors to think and speak about God. Since none of our metaphors are literally descriptive of God, we are free to experiment with new metaphors, to construct new models that speak of God in ways deemed more appropriate to an ecological, nuclear age.[86]

Theology serves a functional or instrumental role in McFague's work that contrasts rather sharply with Gustafson's approach, in which all human considerations are judged to be subordinate to divine aims. As she says, "The goal of theology, as I see it, is to be *functional*, that is, to actually work in someone's life."[87] Another way to state the difference is to note that, for McFague, ethics often seems to take priority over theology. Her existential moral concerns, arising from gender discrimination, nuclear and ecological perils, and economic exploitation, greatly influence her selection of potentially suggestive and fruitful metaphors and models of God. She also emphasizes the need to overcome a complex of dualisms in Western culture that she believes lie at the root of many of our most intractable human problems. These dualisms include spirit/flesh, human/nonhuman, male/female, objective/subjective, reason/nature, and supernatural/natural.

The Christian tradition is doubtless an important source of McFague's moral concerns, and in that respect, her ethics is indebted to theological sources. More so than either Gustafson or Griffin, she draws on biblical imagery and traditional theological themes, e.g., crucifixion, the Trinity, and eschatology, in the construction of her theology. At the same time, she intends for her primary theological model, the world as God's body, to be "in keeping with the view of reality coming to us from contemporary science."[88] In Chapter 3 we will further explore ways in which her theological heritage, her attention to scientific knowledge, and her motivation to address the moral and ethical issues she has identified by re-mythologizing the Christian faith appear to be interrelated.

The central focus of David Griffin's work is the articulation of a philosophical world view that integrates scientific and religious understandings. In agreement with anthropologist Clifford Geertz, Griffin claims that "a religion always consists of a 'world view' and an 'ethos,' with the latter understood as

---

[86]*Models*, 40.
[87]*Life Abundant*, 15; emphasis preserved.
[88]*Body*, ix.

values, attitudes, emotions, motivations, and conduct—both moral and ritualistic conduct."[89] His focus is on the world view, but it is very much for the sake of the ethos.[90] As a general statement of the rationale for his major work in philosophy of religion, Griffin notes, "The provision of cosmological support for the ideals needed by contemporary civilization is one of the chief purposes of philosophy in our time."[91] A disciple of the process philosopher, Alfred North Whitehead, Griffin observes that Whitehead's "entire philosophy is intended to provide support for the moral life."[92]

In light of these remarks, it is clear that Griffin shares the conviction of Gustafson and McFague that our conceptions about God and God's relation to the world are of critical significance to our moral valuations and ethical reflections. Griffin differs most from Gustafson and McFague with respect to the need for a philosophical as well as theological understanding of how it is that God is related to the world. Theology risks incredibility if it cannot articulate an understanding of this relationship in which it makes sense to speak of God as personal and purposive, possessing powers of causal efficacy, and thus as exercising divine agency in the world.

Griffin notes that there is widespread agreement among most process thinkers on certain ideals. These include "the need for a politics and economics for the common good, for an ecological ethic, and for a post-patriarchal culture." He is also committed to another ideal that he takes "to be implied by and inclusive of those three: the movement to a democratic world order."[93] Each of these ideals is viewed as concomitant with that enlargement of our interests and sympathies in keeping with his one general moral imperative, to maximize importance.[94] Griffin also explicitly seeks a way beyond the sorts of dualisms highlighted by McFague and also largely rejected by Gustafson. Yet it must be acknowledged that to date Griffin has not produced any major work that could be characterized as theological ethics. He has identified only one general moral principle that follows from his philosophical and theological construal of the world. Consequently, it will require a certain amount of extrapolation to comment further on the significance of his theology for his ethics.

---

[89] *Reenchantment without Supernaturalism*, 13.
[90] One of Griffin's current works in progress is in fact an extensive argument for global democracy, as will be discussed briefly in Chapter 4.
[91] Ibid., 7.
[92] Ibid., 285.
[93] Ibid., 311. Griffin says nothing more here about his views on global democracy. However, he does so in at least one of his forthcoming books, available to me in lecture form with the title, *Thy Kingdom Come*. Cf. n. 90 above.
[94] 35, n. 75 above.

On the other hand, there are clearly moral and ethical concerns that help motivate Griffin's philosophical and theological work. Moreover, his conception of God must meet the test of intelligibility, judged in light of scientific knowledge and critical-realistic, naturalistic philosophy. He also takes seriously major traditional religious conceptions about God that, if not exclusively Christian, probably continue to have more currency among Christians than any other religious group. These include such qualities as personal agency, purposiveness, supremacy in power, and perfection in goodness.[95] And, in some of his most recent work, he identifies what he calls "hard-core commonsense notions" about the way things are that we invariably presuppose in practice, and assigns to philosophy the task of showing how these can be true–a task that has clear implications for an understanding of God.[96] One of our tasks in Chapter 4 will be to explore more fully and critically the various sorts of arguments Griffin makes on behalf of his conception of God.

As this initial review of the relation of theology and ethics to each other in the work of Gustafson, McFague, and Griffin makes clear, no single formula can capture this relation. At this point I want to emphasize that the articulation of a theological ethics is not a linear process, beginning with theology and ending with ethics, but a much more complex holistic undertaking. As I hope the remainder of this book will illustrate, if such an undertaking sometimes begins with empirical observations or ethical concerns, with feelings of piety, apprehensions of mystery, or convictions of meaning, that does not speak against the integrity of the theological enterprise, nor does it bespeak the adequacy of the concomitant moral judgments. When making moral judgments, one must seek a coherence that encompasses what is known and what is believed, what is experienced and what is taken on authority, what is felt and what is reasoned, what is discerned to be and what is discerned to be required—or at least a gestalt of patterns and relationships that is sufficiently evident to warrant one's interpretation of the situation and sufficiently indicative to authorize one's discernment of what that situation calls oneself and others to be and do.

Consenting to God and Nature

I have claimed throughout this chapter that the writings of Gustafson, McFague, and Griffin may each be interpreted as both theocentric and naturalistic. This claim cannot be made without some qualifications, and I have

---

[95] Cf. *Religion and Scientific Naturalism: Overcoming the Conflicts* (Albany: SUNY Press, 2001) 90.
[96] Cf. ibid., 101.

tried to indicate in a preliminary way what some of those qualifications must be. But I have also set out to define my own perspective in theological ethics as one that is both theocentric and naturalistic. My purpose in this book is not simply to examine and critique the work of others, but to do so in order to identify key ideas, perspectives, and approaches in their work that can be appropriated for a theocentric, naturalistic ethics that holds promise of being more intellectually compelling and religiously adequate than the ethics they have thus far produced. As previously stated, I believe that Gustafson, McFague, and Griffin each contributes elements necessary to the articulation of a more adequate theological ethics within the Protestant Christian tradition as it confronts the contemporary world.

Every endeavor must begin somewhere, and every intellectual endeavor must begin with certain assumptions. Two key assumptions that undergird this study are implicit in the title. Both assumptions are metaphysical; one is theological, the other ontological. First, I believe it makes sense to speak of God, and to do so largely within the framework of Christian theism. Second, I believe it makes sense to speak of the real world, and to do so largely in terms of the world of nature. Moreover, I find that there are good reasons within the Christian tradition, especially in its Reformed expressions, for adopting a *theocentric* theological perspective. And I find that there are good reasons from the perspective of natural science for adopting a *naturalistic* world view. There is of course a long history of conflict within Western culture between religion and science, exacerbated since the seventeenth century, reflecting the judgment that any kind of theistic affirmation, with the exception of pantheism, is incompatible with a naturalistic worldview. I have indicated that I believe this perceived conflict can be resolved, and I will continue throughout this book to explore and elaborate how it can be resolved.

However, I will not attempt to make a case for Christian theism as such, and will only make the case for theocentrism within a context in which Christian theism is assumed. Nor will I attempt to make a case for ontological realism, the conviction that a world exists independently of human experience or knowledge. I will assume the critical-realist claim that this world is at least partially accessible to human experience and knowledge, including by means of scientific investigation. In fact, scientific study of the world has yielded such knowledge of regularities in structures, patterns, processes, and relationships in the world that we speak of it as the world of nature. And even though the world of nature as a whole is not contingent on the existence of human beings, we humans being are an integral part of the natural world. Whatever else we are, we are creatures of nature.

Thus I begin with the assumption of two realities, God and the world of nature. But a bit more than assumption is implied in the title, "Consenting to God and Nature." We typically assume that which appears to be obvious, or that which is convenient. We acknowledge the evidence, for example, that the interactions of all kinds of physical phenomena can be described by laws or calculated by equations, and so we may *assume* that there is a "nature" to things. We have fears, anxieties, aspirations, yearnings for meaning, and experiences of wholeness, otherness, and awe, and so we may *assume* that there is a "God" who is present in temporal events and who mysteriously oversees the course of human destiny. But what does it mean to consent?

To consent requires more than intellectual acknowledgment. It connotes acceptance. Consent is closer to personal affirmation than it is to resignation. I have borrowed the term from Gustafson, who speaks of consenting to divine governance, in order to indicate certain matters of consequence regarding where this study begins. As we will see more fully in the next chapter, to consent to God, and to undertake a *theocentric* theological ethics, is not simply to assume a theistic belief. It is to take seriously God as God. It is to regard God as the primary and ultimate reality with whom we have to do, and to do so in affirmation that our highest calling is the service of God.

Similarly, to consent to nature, and to engage in a *naturalistic* theological ethics, is not simply to dismiss or discount the supernatural. It is to take seriously the reality and integrity of the world as it exists, mostly not of our own making. It is also to take seriously that we human beings are creatures of nature whose experiences of the world are necessarily mediated by our bodies. We are creatures whose possibilities and limits reside in our bodies and in the natural environments that surround, sustain, and impinge upon our human existence. On the one hand, to consent to nature is to accept our finitude as creatures, while on the other hand it is to recognize and affirm our participation in and communion with all that exists. Thus, this undertaking toward a theocentric, naturalistic, theological ethics is not a casual matter of intellectual preference or convenience, though one of its aims is intellectual coherence. It is more a matter of seeking to be responsive and faithful within a context of fundamental apprehensions about the way things really are.

2

James M. Gustafson's Theocentric Ethics: What More Can Be Said?

Introduction

As both a teacher and a scholar, James Gustafson has been a dominant—if not *the* dominant—figure in the field of Protestant theological ethics for most of his professional life. Indeed, Roman Catholic theologian Richard McCormick has called him "the most distinguished theological ethicist of our time."[1] Protestant ethicist Stanley Hauerwas has called him "the master teacher of our craft."[2] Theological ethicist Harlan Beckley has characterized Gustafson's major systematic work, *Ethics from a Theocentric Perspective*, as "the first proposal in theological ethics since Paul Ramsey's *Basic Christian Ethics* (1950) with a potential to reorient the field and the first proposal with such breadth of Christian and non-Christian sources since Reinhold Niebuhr's *The Nature and Destiny of Man* (1941–43)."[3]

No work in theological ethics, at least in America, has received more focused attention than Gustafson's *Ethics*. But neither has any such work been subjected to more thorough critique. In its Spring 1985 issue, *The Journal of*

---

[1] Review of *Intersections: Science, Theology, and Ethics*, in *America* 177 (1997) 2.
[2] "Time and History in Theological Ethics: The Work of James Gustafson," *Journal of Religious Ethics* 13 (1985) 4.
[3] "The Raft That Floats: Experience, Tradition, and Sciences in Gustafson's Theocentric Ethics," *Zygon* 30 (1995) 201.

Religious Ethics devoted half its space to a focus on Gustafson's ethics, with essays by major scholars in the field, including McCormick and Hauerwas. Most of these essays were sharply critical of Gustafson's work.[4] Later that year a symposium was held in Lexington, Virginia, on the *Ethics*, with eight scholars invited to make formal presentations. The papers and edited discussions issuing from that event were later published in a volume edited by Beckley and Charles M. Swezey titled *James M. Gustafson's Theocentric Ethics: Interpretations and Assessments*.[5] On the whole, these papers are more appreciative and less harsh in their critique than those that appeared in *The Journal of Religious Ethics*. Nonetheless, participant Edward Farley could still characterize the reception given Gustafson's *Ethics* with the memorable line, "his critics do not damn him with faint praise, but praise him with shouted damns."[6] Yet a third, briefer, collection of papers focusing on Gustafson's work appeared in the June 1995 issue of *Zygon*.[7] Of course, Gustafson's *Ethics*, and his other writings as well, have also occasioned many other articles, reviews, and comments in academic literature and religious journals.[8]

Clearly, James Gustafson is a theological ethicist to be taken seriously. As must already be evident, his work is very important to the structure and content of this book. The widespread attention given his work, and the extensive published responses to that work, raise a practical question: What more can be said? Certainly much has already been said by others, both to highlight the assumed strengths and expose the perceived weaknesses of Gustafson's theological ethics. I will not attempt to summarize even a significant portion of the scholarship that his work has generated. I will of course draw on some of that scholarship in my own examination and critique of certain features of his ethics, as well as in my own constructive appropriation of his work. But I will also attempt to draw attention to issues raised by Gustafson's work that merit further attention or can be more adequately framed. The way in which an issue becomes framed depends largely on the assumptions and questions that the student, the critic, or the inquirer brings to the matter under study. Very few of Gustafson's critics seem to share both his naturalistic and theocentric commitments. As someone who does share those commitments, at least to greater extent than most students of Gustafson's work, I hope to provide a fresh perspective on the issues raised by his theological ethics, in

---

[4] "Focus on the Ethics of James M. Gustafson," op. cit., 1–112.
[5] Macon, Ga.: Mercer University Press, 1988.
[6] "Theocentric Ethics as a Genetic Argument," ibid., 40.
[7] "Profile: James M. Gustafson," *Zygon* 30 (1995) 159–226.
[8] These include an additional series of four largely appreciative articles published in the *Annual of the Society of Christian Ethics* 17 (1997) 13–43.

large part because I bring a distinctive set of assumptions and questions to the task. From my self-consciously theocentric, naturalistic perspective, there is certainly more to be said about Gustafson's theological ethics

There is yet another sense or meaning to be noted in the question, What more can be said? Gustafson leaves a lot of questions unanswered. Sometimes he is admittedly ambiguous.[9] Often he writes with such care and understatement that he sounds vague and equivocal.[10] Consistently he demurs from what he regards as the abstractions and generalities of philosophy and metaphysics.[11] Above all, as we will see, Gustafson refuses to make some of the traditional affirmations about God and God's intentions for humanity that other Christian theologians take to lie at the heart of the Christian faith.[12] An important part of the task of this chapter, and this book, is to indicate what more, if anything, can be said about God and human destiny within the context of a theocentric, naturalistic perspective that seeks to honor if not always concede the intellectual scruples that inform and constrain Gustafson's theological work.

Establishing the Perspective

Gustafson begins his *Ethics* with a lengthy chapter entitled, "An Interpretation of Our Circumstances."[13] The chapter opens with the statement, "Every effort to develop a coherent theology is shaped to some extent by the author's perceptions of the circumstances in his or her culture and in the churches."[14] Gustafson's first step is to set forth his view of theology "as a way of construing the world."[15] He then sets out his account of the circumstances that are constitutive of his construal.

Gustafson moves subtly from description and interpretation to increasingly explicit critique as he calls into question the preeminent role that human beings have assigned to themselves in the scheme of all things.[16] He then

---

[9]"Response to Rottschaefer, Beckley, and Konner," *Zygon* 30 (1995) 222.
[10]See Jeffrey Stout's incisive observations to this point in *Ethics after Babel: The Languages of Morals and Their Discontents* (Boston: Beacon, 1988) 173ff.
[11]Gustafson's naturalism, along with his historicism and relativism, clearly put him at odds with various forms of philosophical idealism. However, even where he recognizes an affinity with process philosophy and theology he eschews the metaphysics. Cf. *Ethics I*, 56–61; "Tracing a Trajectory," *Zygon* 30 (1995) 183. In *An Examined Life*, Gustafson's brief but perjorative references to process theology suggest that he wants to distance himself further from this metaphysical option; cf. 41, n.6, 111; 51.
[12] "Tracing a Trajectory," 188.
[13]*Ethics I*, 1–85.
[14]Ibid., 1.
[15]Ibid; in n. 5, p. 3, Gustafson acknowledges indebtedness to Julian Hartt for conceiving theology in this way.

notes how religion itself functions instrumentally in the service of subjective temporal human ends. Gustafson does not claim that religion should have no value to its adherents. Rather he questions whether religion ought to be justified on utilitarian grounds. He observes that religion typically is promoted and defended precisely for its human benefits.[17] A section on "Religious Studies" recounts how such studies have made us much more knowledgeable about the instrumental character of religious beliefs and practices.[18] Gustafson argues, on behalf of religious studies, that "religion has no privileged position among human phenomena that isolates it from being interpreted and explained by principles that are not its own historically privileged ones."[19] At the same time, he questions whether it is sufficient for the defense of religion to regard it only in terms of its instrumental, utilitarian value. He questions whether the descriptive and explanatory accounts of religious studies are "the adequate (and only defensible) normative basis for religious beliefs and practices."[20]

This brief sketch of the opening pages of the *Ethics* is intended only to suggest how Gustafson begins to make what becomes a very explicit case for theocentrism. When human beings see themselves as ends in themselves, and religion is regarded as merely subservient to human ends, "God (or the gods) is put in the service of human beings."[21] The implication, of course, is that this is all wrong: human beings are to be in the service of God. At the same time, we see Gustafson making a less explicit case for naturalism. He couches this case in terms of the validity of religious studies, where religious phenomena are studied by the same methods of investigation that are employed in the study of all other human phenomena.

A certain irony attends the claims that Gustafson makes about religious studies, however. On the one hand, such studies rightly deny religion a privileged position with respect to the methods of investigation employed to study human phenomena. On the other hand, such studies have more fully exposed the functional, utilitarian role of religion. But if the naturalistic study of religion only confirms the instrumental value of religion, what basis is there for asserting any distinctively theological claims on behalf of religion? In particular, what grounds are there for asserting a theocentric interpretation of life and the world? There is an inherent tension between Gustafson's naturalism and his theocentrism that is never quite resolved. This will be evident in much that follows.

---

[16]Ibid., 15.
[17]Ibid., 16.
[18]Ibid., 26.
[19]Ibid., 30.
[20]Ibid., 31.
[21]Ibid.

It bears noting that Gustafson's critique of anthropocentrism, including religious anthropocentrism, is not wholly dependent on his theocentric commitments. As he interprets the circumstances of our existence, he notes that "there is no overcoming the fundamental human conditions of finitude: biological conditions and historical and cultural conditions."[22] As someone whose outlook is highly informed by the sciences, Gustafson knows that life on planet Earth will not go on forever.[23] Even on this planet other life will probably outlast us. Nor have we reason to assume we are the pinnacle of cosmic existence. In short, there are also empirical grounds for calling into question the prevailing human tendency to place ourselves at the center of value and to regard ourselves as the measure of all things. As Gustafson puts it, "We may not be sure what the ultimate purpose of life is, but we can be certain that we are finite, limited. We may not be sure that there is an ultimately sovereign and purposive power governing all things, but we can be sure that we are creatures, and that we are not God."[24] Human finitude is a theme that runs deep throughout Gustafson's work, and is integral to both his naturalistic and theocentric perspectives. The anthropocentric critique is warranted by both perspectives.

The Development of a Comprehensive Theological Ethics

In his *Ethics* Gustafson identifies four distinguishable base points in relation to which a comprehensive theological ethics must be developed. These are:

> (a) the interpretation of God and God's relations to the world and particularly to human beings, and the interpretation of God's purposes; (b) the interpretation of the meaning or significance of human experience—of historical life of the human community, of events and circumstances in which persons and collectivities act, and of nature and man's participation in it; (c) the interpretation of persons and collectivities as moral agents, and of their acts; and (d) the interpretation of how persons and collectivities ought to make moral choices and ought to judge their own acts, those of others, and the states of affairs in the world.[25]

I cannot begin to undertake a thorough examination of how Gustafson deals with each of these base points. In what follows I will attempt to review only a few selected features of Gustafson's *Ethics* that correspond to each of

[22]Ibid., 14.
[23]In *An Examined Life* he writes of the "plausible cosmological accounts of the future demise of our species and the planet on which it developed," 11.
[24]*Ethics I*, 8–9.
[25]*Ethics II*, 143. The same base points are first set down in his *Protestant and Roman Catholic Ethics: Prospects for Rapprochement* (Chicago: University of Chicago Press, 1978) 139–40.

these four facets of his approach. However, primary attention must be given to Gustafson's understanding of God, and to his theological perspective in general, inasmuch as he claims that his theology provides the primary basis for his theological ethics. This will necessitate a more extensive and careful look at how Gustafson's naturalistic perspective significantly qualifies his theological outlook. It will also lead us to consider the sources and dimensions of the religious piety that infuse Gustafson's religious perspective. Then it will be helpful to identify other significant features of Gustafson's theological construal and method that define the general theological perspective and approach of his ethics, some of which touch on his interpretations of human experience, moral agency, and moral decision-making. The chapter will conclude with a review and assessment of what I take to be the most problematic issues to be addressed, if not resolved, in order to appropriate Gustafson's work for a more adequate theological ethics.

Theology, Theocentrism, and the Role of Scientific Knowledge

In both volumes of his *Ethics* Gustafson reiterates his conviction that theology, in particular the theological construal of God and the world in relation to God, provides the most decisive basis for theological ethics.[26] Near the end of volume 1 he summarizes the case he has been making for theocentric ethics:

> Theology, to repeat Julian Hartt once more, is a way of construing the world. Construing involves a perception of the world. The theocentrism I have developed provides a perspective from which the human species is perceived and interpreted in relation to the rest of the universe. The primary turn is one that has been reiterated several places in this book; it is from self to other, from anthropocentrism to God as the primary object of attention. I have properly denied that this enables human beings to see things from "God's point of view." But it does force persons to perceive and interpret man in relation to the ultimate power and orderer of all of the creation. Man is perceived and interpreted in relation to the purposes of the divine governance that can be grasped by humans, and the divine governance is of the whole of the creation.[27]

Gustafson claims that God is "the primary object of attention." But who, or what, is God? And how is God perceived? And what are the purposes of the divine governance?

In one of his most succinct and complete statements about God, Gustafson states:

[26] Cf. *Ethics II*, 144, for example.
[27] *Ethics I*, 308.

God is the ultimate power that brings all things into being; sustaining, ordering, and bearing down upon them; and creating the conditions for possibility of change and development in them. God is the determiner of the ultimate destiny of all things. In piety the patterns and processes of interdependence that we perceive and conceptualize are indicators, signals, or signs of the divine governing and ordering of life. Through these patterns and processes man can know some things about the ultimate ordering power that determines the destiny of all things. But these patterns and processes are indicators or signs only; they are not evidences or proofs of an immutable divine order to which all relationships of persons and things must necessarily be conformed. They inform and give direction to what persons, institutions, and communities are to do to relate things in a manner appropriate to their relations to God. They are not, however, a clear and infallible guide in and of themselves of God's moral will.[28]

These are the terms in which Gustafson characteristically speaks of God: creator, governor, ultimate power that orders, sustains, and bears down on all things. God is the "powerful Other"[29] who "provides conditions of possibilities for human activity and even a sense of direction."[30] As previously noted, God may be said to have purposes, but not intentions.[31] Gustafson thinks of purposes in terms of "the functional interdependence of things."[32] He thinks of intentions as "the fruits of our rational activity relative to ends."[33] He rejects any notion of divine intention or agency that suggests human-like intelligence and a will or capacity to control events in a manner analogous to human control.[34]

What, then, may be said of the divine purposes? "The purposes of the ultimate power can be deemed generally good without necessarily claiming that they have to be good for human beings."[35] The attribution of such purposes, however, does not necessarily entail the assumption of any final or ultimate *telos* or cosmic purpose.[36] So far as general attributes of God are concerned, this is about as specific as Gustafson ever gets. One must look to the particularities of the patterns and processes of actual natural and historical events to discern anything more specific about God's governing purposes, understood in terms of God's ordering, sustaining, and bearing down upon us.

---

[28]*Ethics II*, 293.
[29]*Ethics I*, 167.
[30]Ibid., 264.
[31]Chapter 1, 25, n. 49.
[32]Beckley and Swezey, 215.
[33]Ibid., 215.
[34]*Ethics I*, 270.
[35]Ibid., 271; cf. 202; also 110: "The salvation of man is not the chief end of God; certainly it is not the exclusive end of God."

Gustafson's theocentric perspective provides a powerful critique of anthropocentrism. He insists that human beings must always be viewed as a part of the whole, and in relation to the whole, of creation. Moreover, human beings are to be viewed, along with all the rest of the universe, in relation to the ultimate power that creates, orders, and governs all things. Furthermore, the purposes of this power, while deemed to be good, are not to be regarded as in the service of specifically human ends. Finally, God's powers and governing are not to be comprehended by analogy to such human powers as will, intelligence, agency, and intention. God is not to be cast in the image of humankind. Human beings are not the measure of all things.

But while Gustafson provides a compelling critique of anthropocentrism, many critics argue that he does not provide an adequate or compelling view of God.[37] By his own admission, Gustafson has nothing to say about God as God might be *in se*, in God's own being. In his view, it is not even possible to think about God in such terms.[38] More problematic, however, is the fact that Gustafson has so little to say about God as known to human beings. For some critics it is damning enough that Gustafson has abandoned certain traditional Christian convictions in failing to share a number of classic Christological, soteriological, and eschatological views.[39] At a more fundamental level, however, the question is whether any notion of God is even necessary to Gustafson's "theocentric" construal of the world. Alternatively framed, the question is whether the distinction Gustafson makes between God and nature makes any difference.

David Griffin simply identifies Gustafson as a pantheist for whom there is no real distinction between God and the totality of all finite things, processes, and relationships.[40] Lisa Cahill observes that there are "many striking parallels in Gustafson's uses of the terms "God" and "nature."[41] Jeffrey Stout, noting that "[w]e are simultaneously told that God's purposes should be the focal point of all ethical reflection and that we lack the means for bringing either God or his purposes into clear focus," wonders why Gustafson "insists on speaking of God or divine purposes at all."[42] Gordon Kaufman maintains that Gustafson has conceived of God in a "completely dehumanized

---

[36] Beckley and Swezey, 215; also *A Sense of the Divine*, 72; *Ethics I*, 262. Gustafson offers a minimalist summary of this and the preceding point in *Intersections*, 125: "I offer an aphorism of my own: God (through nature) is the source of human good, but does not guarantee it."
[37] Cf. especially, the essays by Lisa Sowell Cahill, Stephen Toulmin, and Richard A. McCormick in the Spring 1985 issue of *Journal of Religious Ethics*; also those by Gordon Kaufman, Edward Farley, and Robert Audi in Beckley and Swezey, op. cit.; also Stout, op. cit., 178ff.
[38] *Ethics I*, 270.
[39] "Tracing a Trajectory," 188.
[40] *Reenchantment*, 136.

and depersonalized way"[43] that Kaufman "would be inclined to call simply 'nature'"[44]— "little more than a kind of reification, into a unified structure, of natural powers and orders."[45] Edward Farley does not think Gustafson identifies God with nature, but he sees Gustafson's "functional definition of God" to be undifferentiated in content from "the perceivable orderings of world process."[46]

Even Gustafson himself can hardly say what difference his theology and his theocentric perspective make for his construal of the world and the place of human beings in that world. In the earlier-cited passage from the *Ethics* where Gustafson provides a summary review of his theocentric perspective he goes on to say,

> This is not to claim that . . . many others cannot adequately perceive the place of man in nature without a theology or an avowed theocentric interpretation of life. The enlargement of vision that a theocentric perspective enables certainly can be achieved, at least in considerable measure, from nontheological perspectives. But the theocentric view does enlarge the context within which humanity is perceived and interpreted.[47]

It is easy to miss what Gustafson is not saying in these carefully measured words. First, he is not saying that many others actually do succeed in adequately perceiving the place of humankind in nature without a theocentric perspective. Second, he is not definitively saying that the enlarged context within which humanity is perceived and interpreted by a theocentric view exceeds what can be attained by other approaches. In other words, while clearly claiming benefits for his theocentric perspective in terms of an enlargement of vision, he remains non-committal regarding whether these benefits can be, or have been, equally fully attained by other perspectives that are nontheological. It is not at all clear, therefore, that Gustafson's construal of God is essential to what Gustafson himself would judge to be an adequate construal of the world and humanity's place in the world.

The way in which Gustafson has subsequently described the theological task may be significant in this connection. Commenting in 1995 on his *Ethics*, he says, "The general conviction of those volumes . . . is that theology

---

[41]"Consent in Times of Affliction: The Ethics of a Circumspect Theist," *Journal of Religious Ethics* 13 (1985) 132.
[42]*Ethics after Babel*, 178.
[43]"How Is *God* to be Understood in a Theocentric Ethics?" Beckley and Swezey, 27.
[44]Ibid., 28.
[45]Ibid., 33.
[46]"Theocentric Ethics as a Genetic Argument," Beckley and Swezey, 51.
[47]*Ethics I*, 308.

deals with the meaning and significance of life, both human and nonhuman. It is a way of construing the world which provides a framework for the ordering of life in the world."[48] It seems strange that someone for whom the construal of God had earlier been of first and most critical importance speaks here only of construing the world.[49]

In his book, *Intersections: Science, Theology, and Ethics*, Gustafson has this to say about the theological task:

> For theology, I believe, the critical issues are the importance of "creation" and how it is explicated and becomes a basis for ethical norms and human values. A theology in which the second article of the Apostle's Creed is the most important approaches nature differently from one that accents the first article, belief in God as the "creator of heaven and earth." How God, the creator, is interpreted with reference to nature is the second important choice.[50]

God is now mentioned, but the prior issue is the interpretation or construal of creation, or nature. And here God is to be interpreted with reference to nature, whereas in the *Ethics* nature is to be interpreted, or the world is to be construed, in light of one's convictions about God. It is hard not to see in these more recent statements an implicit concession from Gustafson that his theology is hardly determinative of his construal of the world. Rather, his theology—his construal of God and God's relations to all things—now appears to be contingent on his interpretation of nature and his construal of the world.

I have no doubt that Gustafson's own personal religious convictions have continued to shape his perceptions and thus inform his construal of the world, even though he acknowledges that others may come to a similar construal of the world without sharing his religious convictions. The issue, however, is whether Gustafson's religious convictions figure in any significant way in his conceptualization of the relation between God and the world. The question is, does the way in which Gustafson conceives God's relation to the world require, assume, or even allow for the possibility that God makes a difference in the world? If God does not make a difference in the world then, presumably, one can give an adequate description and explanation of how things really are—or at least of how some things that we are sufficiently

---

[48]"Tracing a Trajectory," 187.
[49]Yet even in the *Ethics* Gustafson can define theology in terms that sound less theocentric than instrumentally anthropocentric: "Theology is an effort to make sense out of a very broad range of human experiences, to find some meaning in them and for them that enables persons to live and to act in coherent ways"; *Ethics I*, 158.
[50]109.

informed about are—in terms of the materialistic assumptions still common to the physical and social sciences.[51]

It may be impossible to pin Gustafson down on this issue. In a comment in the *Ethics* regarding one of his earliest books, *Treasure in Earthen Vessels*, a sociological study of the Christian Church, he speaks of aspects of the life of the Church "that could be explained in great part by social theories."[52] He claims neither that *all* aspects of the life of the Church can be explained, nor that any aspect can be *completely* or *fully adequately* explained, by such theories, however.[53] A couple of pages later he seems to say quite clearly that social scientific studies are not fully adequate when it comes to explaining religious phenomena.[54] On the other hand, in one of his *Zygon* essays of 1995, Gustafson seems to suggest that a cultural or psychological explanation may adequately account for certain "senses" that he identifies as aspects of piety or the religious affections.[55] At the same time he claims that a religious or theological interpretation of these senses "can cohere in significance with other explanations of the same experiences."[56] What we seem to have here is a conviction that a religious interpretation of at least certain kinds of phenomena or events can add dimensions of meaning or significance to our understanding, even if the religious interpretation adds nothing by way of explanation. This is consistent with Gustafson's statement, cited above, that "theology deals with the meaning and significance of life."[57] On Gustafson's terms, however, it does not seem possible to claim anything more than human origins for this meaning and significance, since God is never credited with the capacity to effect a religious sensibility or perception in human beings.[58]

If Gustafson's intention were simply to say that we can never be certain when and where God is active in the world, shaping events, influencing outcomes, effecting certain kinds of sensibilities and perceptions, one would have to applaud his humility and intellectual integrity. The problem is that Gustafson presents us with a God who is powerful Other, creator and gov-

---

[51]As the discussion in Chapter 1 indicates, I do not mean to suggest that the physical and social sciences are necessarily wedded to materialistic assumptions, only that they are still typically thought to be.
[52]*Ethics I*, 26.
[53]In the conclusion to *Treasure in Earthen Vessels*, Gustafson states, "Both doctrinal and social reductionism must be avoided in an understanding of the Church," 105. He basically finesses the question of divine causation, however: "The issue of causal relation is taken care of in the highly ambiguous language of God *acting in* history," 108.
[54]*Ethics I*, 28. Nowhere, to my knowledge, does Gustafson comment on the possible adequacy of social scientific, or natural scientific, accounts of *nonreligious* phenomena.
[55]Cf. *Ethics I*, 130ff., for a description of these senses.
[56]"Response to Rottschaefer, Beckley, and Konner," 223.
[57]See p. 54, n. 48; cf. *An Examined Faith*, 9.

ernor, who bears down, orders and sustains, possesses purposes, and is the source of human good, and yet he provides no way to conceive how God exercises any influence within or upon the world, including the minds of human beings. If anything, he denies that God is necessary to interpret and explain all that transpires in the world. God seems to be entirely superfluous to an adequate intellectual apprehension of the universe.

The Role of Piety in Gustafson's Perspective

And yet there is every indication that Gustafson is a deeply religious man.[59] It is critical for understanding the form and content of his *Ethics* to appreciate the role that religious piety plays in his life and thought. "Theology," he says, "is an enterprise that extrapolates from piety, and other affective responses to the world, to say some things about God."[60] Gustafson consistently claims, in the *Ethics* and in subsequent statements and writings, that "in piety" he can affirm that "the patterns and processes of interdependence that we perceive and conceptualize [through our empirical observations of the world] are indicators, signals, or signs of the divine governing and ordering of life."[61] In an extended response that he gave at the 1985 symposium on his *Ethics* in Lexington, Virginia, Gustafson elaborates:

> I have a naturalistic basis for theology and a naturalistic basis for ethics—though a box called naturalism is not quite right. But Midgley[62] asks, does the ordering need an Orderer? Is God identified with the patterns and processes of interdependence or is there more to God? . . . I do not argue that the ordering logically necessitates an Orderer, but that *given a set of observations about life in the world and given piety, the outcome, both affectively and reflectively, is construed from the tradition in a way that I, at least, can affirm an Orderer.* Does the piety need a Deity? Not necessarily, but again *construing things out of my Reformed theological and religious roots, I assent to saying there is one.* Does the Deity act as the ultimate relativizer? Yes, in the sense that all that is is related to God. So what else does God mean for moral life?
> *If* God is the Ultimate Orderer and Power, the determiner of the

---

[58] Cf. "Response to Rottschaefer, Beckley, and Konner," 223.
[59] This is evident, e.g., in some of the personal reflections one finds in *The Sense of the Divine*. It can also be inferred from his report that, in retirement, he not only continues to read in his field, e.g., Ernst Troeltsch, but also that he engages in daily biblical readings; see "Just what is 'postliberal' theology?" 353, and "Liberal questions: A response to William Placher," 424. See also *An Examined Faith*, 21.
[60] *Ethics I*, 235.
[61] *Ethics II*, 293; the words are from a passage previously cited on p. 51 above, n. 28.
[62] Mary Midgley, one of the presenters and respondents at the symposium.

ultimate destiny of all things, natural piety is both focused and intensified. *If* God, then the language of stewardship and service appropriately point to the awesomeness of human responsibility.... To use metaphors used in Edwards and Puritanism, and in Calvin and others, there is a difference in taste and sight, a difference (to use less "spooky" terms) in perception and valuation, because it is finally God with (if I may resort to a personal term) whom human beings and the world have to deal. There is a difference in human disposition and affectivity. In these respects, at least, I perceive myself to be very much in a biblical tradition.[63]

We can see here, perhaps as clearly as in anything Gustafson has written, that his religious sensibilities are not grounded in an intellectual apprehension of the world; they are not the logical outcome of rational thought processes; they are not a matter of being convinced by empirical evidence of one sort or another. They are a matter of piety, or religious affectivity, the shape of which reflects strong influences from the Reformed theological tradition with its central emphasis on the sovereignty of God and its high regard for the authority of scripture. "In piety," and only "in piety," Gustafson "can affirm" that there is a Deity, an Orderer, a Creator—belief in the existence of which (or, whom) is not in any way compelled by empirical evidence in the natural, social, or historical world. As Gustafson acknowledges in the *Ethics*, citing and then amending Ernst Troeltsch, "The idea of God is admittedly not directly accessible in any other way than by religious [piety]. Yet it asserts a substantial content which [cannot be incongruous] with the other forms of scientific knowledge and also [must] be in some way indicated by these."[64]

In light of my aims in this book, this statement is highly important. It appears in a section titled *The Use of Scientific Explanations in the Retrieval and Reconstruction of Theology*.[65] Gustafson's modifications of Troeltsch's statement merit our first attention. Gustafson substitutes "piety" for Troeltsch's "belief," explaining that piety "is a necessary condition for ideas of God to be subjectively meaningful and intellectually persuasive." He then adds that "the worthwhileness of the theological enterprise is apparent within the context

---

[63]"Response," in Beckley and Swezey, 217; I have italicized the two passages (but not the two "Ifs") for emphasis.
[64]*Ethics I*, 251, 257; the bracketed portions are Gustafson's amendments, substituting "piety" for "belief" and "cannot be incongruous" for "must stand in harmony." In his latest book, *An Examined Faith*, he offers without comment a slightly different revision, in which he amends only "harmony with" to "critically self-conscious relationship to," 94. He does not substitute "piety" for "belief" in this latest amendment. Is this an oversight, or does it signal that Gustafson has come to regard "belief" as the more fitting term for denoting the means by which one comes to the "idea of God"? I am inclined to think the latter, and that the

of personal and communal piety."[66] Piety, in contradistinction to belief, is more affective than cognitive.[67] It is a kind of religious virtue for Gustafson. It evokes and sustains attitudes and dispositions that are "important features of morality in a theocentric perspective."[68] It is "a settled disposition, a persistent attitude toward the world and ultimately toward God. . . . [A]we and respect are the fundamental and persisting characteristics of piety."[69] In a very real sense, piety is the word Gustafson finds most adequate to express a manner of relating to the universe. No one, to my knowledge, has found reason to gainsay this claim of the centrality of such piety to Christian life and thought.

The main reservations and objections regarding Gustafson's work focus on the theological *content* of his theocentric ethics. This content, he tells us, "cannot be incongruous (rather than must be 'in harmony') with well-established data and explanatory principles established by relevant sciences."[70] Gustafson actually lessens Troeltsch's requirement of "harmony" with the knowledge of the sciences. The change appears to reflect his desire to guard against views of the relation of science and religion that mix and confuse scientific and theological language and explanation.[71] On the other hand, Gustafson retains Troeltsch's requirement that ideas of God "must . . . be in some way indicated" by forms of scientific knowledge. Gustafson claims to stop short of a natural theology. One cannot read God directly from nature, or natural processes. Nor can one claim sufficient evidence for God's existence in the ordering of nature. "At most one might say that a 'governance' is occurring."[72] Nonetheless, the patterns and processes of interdependence in the natural world provide indicators of an ordering, of "the presence of pow-

---

single change, which calls for a "critically self-conscious relationship" between the idea of God and scientific knowledge, indicates that Gustafson now sees either more room for cognitive tension, or less possibility for complete cognitive congruence, between the idea of God and scientific knowledge than when he wrote the *Ethics*. Possible corroboration of this judgment may be seen in his statement in *An Examined Faith*, "Current efforts to *integrate* science and theology are ultimately futile," 83.

[65]*Ethics I*, 251–79.
[66]Ibid., 251.
[67]The affective and the cognitive are not to be understood as mutually exclusive or even distinctly separate, however. Gustafson does not "draw overly sharp distinctions among the affective, cognitive, and volitional aspects of experience"; Stout, 180. "[I]n theology as well as ethics I insist on holding the affective and cognitive together"; Gustafson, in Beckley and Swezey, 212. Cf. *Ethics I*, 191.
[68]*Ethics II*, 10.
[69]*Ethics I*, 203.
[70]Ibid., 257.
[71]Cf. ibid., 257–58.
[72]Ibid., 262.

ers bearing down on us and sustaining us."[73] It is not merely possible, but "necessary" both "to test what is said theologically in the light of relevant sciences, and to use indicators from the sciences in what one says substantively about God."[74]

Scientific knowledge thus plays both a negative or constraining role, and a positive or constructive role, in Gustafson's theology. In terms of Ian Barbour's outline of different views of the relation of science and religion, discussed in Chapter 1, the negative role corresponds most closely to a theology of nature.[75] Grounded in religious piety and the theology of the Reformed tradition, Gustafson explicitly modifies or rejects elements of the Christian tradition only insofar as he finds them to be incongruous or incompatible with the well-established knowledge of the sciences. This means, in particular, the rejection of theological doctrines or formulations that necessarily suppose some form of supernaturalism.[76] Although it may appear to some critics that the approach is simply one of trying to reduce Christianity, or Christian theology, to the barest possible minimum, this is clearly not the case. It does seem true, however, that where Gustafson finds incongruities between the theological content of the Christian tradition and scientific knowledge, the latter trumps the former.[77]

Gustafson adds complexity to this conception of the relation between theological ideas and scientific knowledge, however, when he asserts that the sciences also provide "indicators" of what one may say substantively about God. This raises major questions, as he notes:

> What indications from the various sciences are relevant to what is said about the characteristics of the powers that bear down upon us and sustain us? What data and theories from the sciences are appropriate tests of the intelligibility and plausibility of theological affirmations? Which are proper tests of a theological construing of the world? With which theories must theological statements be congruous? Answers to

---

[73] Ibid., 260.
[74] Ibid., 258.
[75] 6–9 above.
[76] Edward Farley might take exception to this claim, based on a definition of supernaturalism as "any theological or philosophical-theological tradition that makes a distinction between God and the world order"; Beckley and Swezey, 61. In his view, Gustafson remains a supernaturalist. But his definition is not what is generally meant by the term, and is not accepted here. Cf. Gustafson, *Ethics I*, 226.
[77] In the *Zygon* 30 (1995) article, "Tracing a Trajectory," Gustafson claims that in his *Ethics* "neither the Christian tradition nor modern sciences nor experience finally trumps the other two" (188). Perhaps in his ethical reflections upon, and judgments about, particular matters this statement holds true, but it does not seem true with respect to his general conception of the relation between the content of theological ideas and scientific knowledge.

these questions cannot be fully developed here, but a general response to them and some illustrations of particular answers are necessary to further the argument of this book.[78]

The complexity of Gustafson's theological perspective reflects more than the complexity of the task he outlines for himself here. There is the additional complexity resulting from the positive influence that Gustafson gives to the "relevant" indications that he derives from scientific knowledge in the reformulation of theological ideas. The negative and positive roles that scientific knowledge plays in Gustafson's theology are really complementary, and not clearly distinguishable. The sciences provide Gustafson with the requisite knowledge for the construal of various features of the world. These construals function negatively and positively, removing obvious incongruities and introducing necessary modifications to bring theology into closer congruity with these construals. The result is a theological perspective that departs significantly from traditional Christian thought.

I have already noted Gustafson's rejection of the notion of divine agency. There are no indicators of such agency in his construal of the natural world. Gustafson rejects traditional Christian eschatological views for similar reasons. The evidence is lacking to support a teleological construal of nature. Likewise, the realization of human good hardly seems to be the central focus of the world process, and thus must qualify any claim Christians might make regarding God's goodness in relation to humankind.[79] On the other hand, Gustafson does find evidence for ordering in the patterns and processes of interdependence in the natural world. While the "indicators" of ordering do not compel the conclusion that there is an Orderer, as we have seen, "in piety" Gustafson can affirm that there is an Orderer.

Despite Gustafson's disclaimers, there does seem to be a kind of natural theology at work here. That is to say, Gustafson's theological affirmations regarding a divine Orderer that (or, who) bears down upon us and sustains us seem to depend on "evidence . . . gained through the exercise of reason in light of our knowledge of the natural world."[80] In the absence of similar evidence, Gustafson declines to make affirmations regarding divine agency, intention, and ultimate telos.[81] Does Gustafson believe there is simply an absence of evidence, or "indicators," for these things? Or does the evidence actually speak against divine agency, intelligence, and telos? It seems to be the former, not the latter. Then why not affirm these things "in piety," inasmuch as they are not clearly contraindicated by the evidence?

---

[78]*Ethics I*, 258.
[79]Ibid., 271.

The answer, I think, is two-fold. One is that the construal of nature does function, positively, to add warrant to some of Gustafson's theological affirmations. The other is that Gustafson's theocentrism mitigates against any conception of God that can too readily be enlisted in the service of anthropocentric perspectives and concerns. Gustafson scrupulously avoids any conception of God that may be construed to claim that human beings are the ultimate beneficiaries of God's goodness.

This much is clear: Gustafson's theocentric critique of anthropocentrism is not simply a consequence of his naturalistic perspective. It surely derives much of its intensity and force from Gustafson's appropriation of the Reformed tradition's central emphasis on the sovereignty, majesty, and holiness of God.[82] Gordon Kaufman sees this in Gustafson's reference to God as the "powerful Other," which evokes our reverence and awe.[83] Gustafson explicitly acknowledges the affinity between his theocentric perspective and Calvin's theology, at least on this point, though he departs from Calvin at various other points.[84]

It also seems clear that Gustafson's view of divine sovereignty has been refracted through the lens of his mentor, H. Richard Niebuhr's, radical monotheism. For Gustafson, as for Niebuhr, God is the center of value. All things receive their value ultimately in relation to God. But, as Jeffrey Stout observes, the austerity of Gustafson's conception of God makes his monotheism even more radical than Niebuhr's radically theocentric orientation. "We are simultaneously told that God's purposes should be the focal point of all ethical reflection and that we lack the means for bringing either God or [God's] purposes into clear focus."[85] Niebuhr could speak of what God is doing in the world, but Gustafson explicitly eschews such language.[86] Gustafson's strictures against anthropomorphic theological language, in particular, greatly complicate any attempt to conceive of the Divine being, nature, and activity.

It seems possible that the sense of awe and reverence so integral to Gustafson's piety derives from his apprehension of nature's beauty, magnitude, and powers as much as, or more than, it does from specifically religious sources. But however Gustafson has come by this piety—his sense of awe

---

[80]Chapter 1, 8.
[81]Cf. *Ethics I*, 271.
[82]Edward Farley notes, "It is important not to permit Gustafson's critical and selective use of Christian doctrines to obscure the important, even central, place tradition has for him"; Beckley and Swezey, 56. The observation is germane here and at many other points in Gustafson's theology.
[83]Kaufman, 22ff.
[84]*Ethics I*, 167.
[85]Stout, 178; cf. Farley, op. cit., 49.

and reverence and humility[87] before that which he calls God—it is a matter of piety, *not a lack of piety*, that accounts for the severity of his critique of anthropocentrism. And it is this same piety that seems most responsible for the austerity of his radical monotheism. "In piety" Gustafson affirms that there is an Orderer, not just an ordering, of the natural world. "In piety" Gustafson also declines to affirm that this Orderer possesses agency, will, intelligence, intention, or ultimate purpose. God must not be so construed to be confused with humankind.[88]

In this interpretation of Gustafson's theocentric perspective, the sorts of questions philosophers of religion might raise about the relation between God and the world figure minimally, if at all. Recall that Gustafson eschews abstract philosophizing and metaphysics. His reasons for rejecting divine agency, for example, have little or nothing to do with the difficulty of trying to provide an intellectually coherent account of how God might exercise influence in the world. Of course, Gustafson may be fully aware of this difficulty, yet see no need to bring it up. Indeed, if Gustafson is actually a pantheist, then questions about divine agency, will, and intention would seem to be moot. The idea that there is a God, distinct from nature, who acts within and upon nature, is at odds with pantheism. On the other hand, it is not inconsistent with a pantheistic perspective to claim that nature has an order, and that natural patterns and processes manifest an ordering. These claims simply make more explicit what is already implicit in the idea of nature. Nonetheless, if Gustafson may correctly be called a pantheist, I doubt that he is self-consciously so, if only because he resists such labels.[89]

The pantheistic label is also problematic precisely because Gustafson affirms that the ordering of nature has an Orderer. Why this personification, not of nature itself, but of a power manifest in nature—unless Gustafson conceives of God as somehow distinct from nature? Indeed, this Orderer "creates," "governs," "bears down," "sustains," and "determines." Moreover, Gustafson typically speaks of *an* Orderer, *an* ultimate power, or *a* powerful Other, and on occasion even of God as Creator, Sustainer, Governor,

---

[86]Cf. Beckley and Swezey, 226.
[87]Cf., e.g., *Ethics II*, 11.
[88]Cf. Stout: "Many of the doctrines for which Gustafson finds insufficient evidential warrant 'even in piety' (271) are also, in his judgment, incompatible with full affirmation of the sovereignty and majesty of God. They conflict, directly or indirectly, with a central theme of the tradition, a theme that is warranted by a sense of dependence upon and grateful obligation to God. Fully to affirm God's sovereignty and majesty, in Gustafson's eyes, entails refusing to limit our conception of the Deity by ascribing anthropomorphic attributes, especially those that are really designed to flatter us and not God at all. Gustafson's book attempts to turn an austere doctrine of divine sovereignty derived from the Reformed tradition against everything in the tradition that in fact glorifies humanity rather than God," 172.

Judge, and Redeemer.⁹⁰ Such singular, personal language hardly connotes a pantheistic conception of God. On the other hand, Gustafson does not seem to regard the affirmation of "a single powerful Other" to be decisively incompatible with his naturalistic perspective, which assumes "something like [William] James's 'pluralistic universe.'"⁹¹ Of course, Gustafson's resort to anthropomorphic language about God would also seem to qualify his anthropocentric critique. In any event, there seems to be no way to speak of God in terms that bear significance for human existence without resort to some language, however metaphorical, that receives its meaning by analogy to human activity and nature.

In the final analysis, it becomes impossible to give precise philosophical definition to Gustafson's conception of God. One strongly suspects that he wants it that way. The one thing that really seems to be decisive for his theocentric affirmation is the piety, the sense of awe and reverence and all the other "senses" that he claims for religious affectivity.⁹² *What* may be said of God is certainly shaped, both positively and negatively, by our scientific knowledge of the world. But *that* one affirms a God about which (or, whom) anything can be said, as well as much of *what* can and cannot be said about that God, remains a matter of piety.

Gustafson's Construal of the World

Thus far I have concentrated on interpreting key features of Gustafson's construal of God and God's relation to the world. Consequently, little has been

---

⁸⁹In his "Response" in Beckley and Swezey, Gustafson acknowledges but does not specify affinities with Spinoza, whose theology was pantheistic (209). In the same "Response," however, he states that he does not think he has claimed simple identity between "divine activity" and "perceived world processes," or "whatever happens" (216).

⁹⁰*Ethics I*, 236.

⁹¹Ibid., 226. Stout expresses puzzlement over Gustafson's theistic, and in particular monotheistic, construal when he notes that Gustafson "never explains clearly why one ought to speak of 'the powers that bear down upon us' as divine or what this addition in fact adds. Nor does he explain why the powers, which he nearly always refers to as plural, should be construed monotheistically" (182). Farley also wonders how, given Gustafson's grounding of his theology in objective reality, he can "take the step to monotheistic conviction"; Beckley and Swezey, 49–50. William A. Rottschaefer observes, "I am in complete agreement with Gustafson in his rejection of anthropocentrism. However, I do not believe there is sufficient scientific evidence at present to center objective values in one purposive though nonintentional source, let alone to characterize that source as divine"; "Gustafson's Theocentrism and Scientific Naturalistic Philosophy: A Marriage Made in Heaven?", *Zygon* 30 (1995) 218–19.

⁹²Commenting on the sense of awe, as an example of a religious affectivity, Gustafson says, "It is not necessary to be able to give a theological explanation of the natural occurrences to which one responds in order to have a religious response. One does not need to have an Aristotelian-Thomistic philosophical theology of a prime mover, or a process theology. . . . [T]he perception is prior to explanations"; *Ethics I*, 228.

said about Gustafson's construal of the world. His basic position is that our understanding of the world is empirically and experientially based, and highly reliant on the knowledge of the sciences. But, we may observe, there is no single science that offers a comprehensive view of all things. Moreover, not all scientific theories and perspectives are equally well confirmed, or equally validated, and they are certainly not all mutually compatible. Discerning what is relevant for a construal of the world is a highly complex task, no less so than discerning what indications from the various sciences are relevant for the task of theological construal.[93] In fact, Gustafson never proposes to provide a construal of the world as a whole.[94] The knowledge of the sciences may tell us "how things really are," but always with respect to particular circumstances, or particular kinds of phenomena, or in relation to a certain set of issues or concerns that define a certain context.

Edward Farley characterizes Gustafson's general framework for interpreting events in terms of a *commonsense* ontology, "because of its relatively nontechnical language and its presumed self-evidence."[95] Gustafson seems to have given at least a qualified acceptance to the designation at the time,[96] though he subsequently writes of his "commonsense empiricism," a designation I suspect he finds more apt.[97] On the whole, Gustafson's commonsense empiricism serves him well, precisely because he is a careful observer and critical thinker who discriminately appropriates the knowledge of the sciences in his ethical reflections and practical moral reasoning. I find little reason to fault Gustafson for the particular ways he uses scientific sources of knowledge. There is reason to question how he conceptualizes the status of scientific knowledge in terms of its comprehensiveness, coherence, and adequacy to reality, however.

I wish to make two general observations regarding how Gustafson goes about construing the world. One of these pertains to Gustafson's naturalistic perspective. At times, when Gustafson claims this perspective he puts it in quotation marks.[98] On at least one occasion, cited above, he says that "a box called naturalism is not quite right."[99] Here again I think we see Gustafson's

---

[93] The complexity of the latter task is noted above, 59–60. To my knowledge, however, Gustafson does not explicitly discuss the inherent difficulties for construing the world that arise from the nature of the scientific enterprise itself.

[94] "I take it as axiomatic," says Gustafson, "that no human being can perceive, conceive, and respond to "*the* whole," that is, to the totality of all things and the interrelationships of each of the differentiable parts"; *Ethics II*, 15.

[95] Op. cit., 41.

[96] Beckley and Swezey, 219; Gustafson marks the designation with quotation marks, as if to indicate equivocation about its meaning.

[97] "Tracing a Trajectory," 181.

reluctance to be pinned down to any abstract conceptualization of how things transpire in the world. For David Griffin, as a philosopher of religion, it is very important to distinguish among various forms of epistemological and ontological naturalism.[100] Gustafson never seeks such clarification. When he equivocates in denoting his own naturalistic perspective, perhaps he is signaling that there are certain forms or definitions of naturalism that appropriately characterize his thought while there are others that do not. The problem is that we cannot be sure.

We have already seen that there are ambiguities in how Gustafson understands the relationship between God and the world. We have also seen that Gustafson is unclear regarding whether the natural or social sciences can provide fully adequate explanations of events on their own terms, though he seems to suggest so in his more recent writings. Lacking any notion of divine agency, and rejecting the idea that God "causes" things to happen—specifically in the religious consciousness, but by implication in the world as a whole[101]—Gustafson must suppose that insofar as natural events can be explained, they must be explained as the sciences typically explain them, namely, in terms of efficient material causation. Of course, he never speaks in such terms. Rather he refers, ambiguously, to "secondary causes," as in the following account of his objections to the "inflated claims of religious and theological language and discourse":

> Empirical or experiential claims have to be examined by the means and methods appropriate to them; such means and methods are sometimes scientific in a disciplined sense and sometimes more casual and observational. I have, usually at least, been terribly conscious of the importance of not claiming experiential effects for events and faith which cannot be described in nonreligious terms and explained (at least in part) by "secondary causes." And I have tended to prefer language that limits claims made to what is testable even if this requires careful selection from traditional language or jettisoning some of the language and beliefs that it carries.[102]

Deistic and even some theistic conceptions of God rely upon the distinction between God as primary cause and real world experiences and events as the effects of secondary causes. But a theistic conception of God, such as Gustafson's, calls for some conceptualization of God's continuing activity in the world. One may respect Gustafson for his strong resistance to the easy

---

[98] E.g., *Ethics II*, 55; *Intersections*, 145.
[99] 57–58 above, n. 63.
[100] Cf. Chapter 1, 9–11.
[101] "Response to Rottschaefer, Beckley, and Konner," 223.

imputation of divine activity in human affairs, and yet be simultaneously frustrated by his refusal to give any account of how it might be the case that the God he affirms continues to exercise any ordering, governing, or sustaining influence in the world.

Finally, we cannot say whether, in Gustafson's view, secondary causes are sufficient to provide complete, or only partial, or sometimes complete and sometimes partial, explanations of events. Consequently, it is not clear how far his naturalism goes. Only those forms of naturalism delineated and accepted by Griffin are clearly, if implicitly, accepted by Gustafson[103]. But he does not provide a philosophically coherent conceptual alternative to the still widespread default position of scientific naturalism, which is an essentially atheistic and deterministic materialism.

The other general observation to be made about Gustafson's construal of the world is that, for the most part, he does not have a very sophisticated view of science. I have previously noted that he is susceptible to the charge of naive realism.[104] The basis for the charge is simply that Gustafson often writes as if science consistently provides a more-or-less straightforward, literal description of the way things really are. Perhaps no one has taken Gustafson more seriously to task for "the trusting simplicity with which science is invoked" than John Howard Yoder.[105] Yoder cites a number of passages from the *Ethics* in which Gustafson employs phrases like, "what we know about nature," and "well established data and explanations from the sciences."[106] He protests, "The allusions to information drawn from the sciences are always brief, simple, and in laymen's terms. In addition, Gustafson rarely cites his sources." Yoder continues, with what I think is the most significant of his observations:

> A distinction of level between the firm conclusions of specific empirical disciplines, on the one hand, and the cosmological and philosophical superstructures extrapolated from the practice of the sciences, on the other hand, though visible in Gustafson's vocabulary, is not taken account of when it comes to drawing conclusions about God, yet it is only the former that have relatively clear results and only the latter that offer pertinent theological alternatives. This seems to me to abuse

---

[102]"Tracing a Trajectory," 181–82. See my brief discussion of secondary causes in Chapter 1, 21–22.

[103]Chapter 1, 10–11. It also appears that Gustafson rejects what Griffin calls "sensationism"; cf. *Ethics I*, 271.

[104]Chapter 1, 29.

[105]"Theological Revision and the Burden of Particular Identity," Beckley and Swezey, 72.

[106]Ibid.

rather than respect the methods, the warrants, and the conclusions of the natural sciences.[107]

I am not quite prepared to accuse Gustafson of the abuse that Yoder charges. However, Yoder's distinction between the "firm conclusions" and the "superstructures," or what I prefer to call the particularities of scientific knowledge, on the one hand, and the more general philosophical conceptualizations of the world about which such knowledge is claimed, on the other, identifies precisely where the problem lies with Gustafson's approach.

Yoder appears to be most troubled by the fact that, as a consequence of what he takes to be misappropriations of science, Gustafson's appeals to science routinely trump appeals to the traditional language of piety. In the preceding section in this chapter I have attempted to provide a nuanced account of how that is true only in part. Gustafson's radically monotheistic piety also trumps many traditional theological affirmations. I would state my primary objections to Gustafson's way of appropriating science somewhat differently, though not in ways at odds with Yoder's critique.

First, Gustafson fails adequately to appreciate the extent to which scientific language is itself a language of construal. Scientific language requires the use of analogy and metaphor to construct models for describing the natural world and for formulating theories that explain causal relationships among phenomena and events. To be sure, the models and theories are usually rigorously empirically tested, so that those surviving possess a high degree of descriptive and explanatory power. Scientific knowledge, however, is never simply an account of "how things really are," but always a construal or interpretation of "how things really are."[108] Gustafson knows this, but he seldom writes as if he knows it. His realism is insufficiently critical.

Second, Gustafson's appropriation of science fails to give adequate weight to the increasingly complex, and even mysterious, view of "nature" that is emerging in many fields of science. Perhaps some day it will be possible to construct a single unified theory of the universe, but for the time being, such a theory is becoming increasingly elusive. It is increasingly difficult to conceive of the world in materialistic, deterministic categories. Probability, indeterminacy, and even novelty and freedom, are now categories of thought within some scientific frameworks. I will have more to say about this in Chapter 4 on the work of David Griffin. Suffice it to say here that, quite apart from any considerations of theology and piety, Gustafson's appreciation of

---

[107]Ibid., 73.
[108]Recall the brief discussion of the "constructive" nature of science in Chapter 1, 19.

science does not extend deeply enough to take into account some of the most fundamental issues now being raised about the constitution of the universe, the character of its "laws," and hence the very "nature" of the natural world. His approach is simply not adequate as an account of "nature."

My third objection to Gustafson's appropriation of science, which follows from the two failings just mentioned, lies in a previously noted problem. Gustafson does not have a worldview that is sufficiently informed, scientifically as well as philosophically, to provide an intellectually coherent conceptualization of the relation between God and the world. His approach actually precludes such a conceptualization. This is not an unusual circumstance in theological ethics by any means. Very few theologians or theological ethicists bother to provide an intellectually and philosophically coherent account of just how it is possible for God to "act" in and upon the world of nature and history.[109] But Gustafson is quite possibly unique in the extent to which he takes science seriously.[110] The prominent role of scientific knowledge in his *Ethics*, considered in conjunction with the radical departures that he makes from traditional Christian theology, provokes questions about his method and theology that are seldom raised with respect to more traditional theological approaches. That hardly makes other approaches more adequate. It simply means that Gustafson's work must bear a higher level of scrutiny, and that critics are likely to point out certain failings in his work about which they are silent with respect to the work of others.

Theocentric Ethics in Profile

We must now turn to a summary of the key features of Gustafson's theocentric ethics in terms of their relevance to the theology-ethics relationship. Gustafson provides this summary in the first chapter of volume 2 of the *Ethics*. Here the emphasis shifts from a focus on the more general question of the construal of a theocentric ethics to the more concentrated focus on those major elements of the construal or perspective that shape moral discernment. Ethics, he says,

> includes both a descriptive-analytical aspect and a normative, or prescriptive, aspect. Thus the general question can take this form: How do ideas about God and God's relations to the arenas in which we live and act qualify our valuations of things? What values, principles

---

[109]In fact, this is not a question Gustafson wants to answer. He carefully avoids language about "what God is doing," which he distinguishes from his own language about "what God is enabling and requiring us to be and to do." Cf. Beckley and Swezey, 226.

[110]Cf. Robert Audi, "Theology, Science, and Ethics in Gustafson's Theocentric Vision," Beckley and Swezey, 181.

of conduct, ideals and aspirations, and rules are grounded in, backed by, or based upon our understanding of God and God's relations to the world?[111]

Or, to put the question even more simply, "What difference does a theocentric perspective make in the interpretation of morality?"[112]

The first feature of Gustafson's profile is the theocentric focus as such, which he says is "[t]he most critical difference between ethics as I develop it and most Western ethics."[113] Although much has already been said about this, it is instructive to cite Gustafson's own assessment of the significance of this shift in perspective for his ethics:

> Part of the argument of volume 1 is that in the Western moral tradition there are descriptions of man which, because of the distinctive features of human life, place man at the center of all valuation, or as the ultimate value, and see all things in the service of man. The theological construal of the world that I have proposed fundamentally alters this view. It follows from that construal that there are occasions or circumstances in which a course of action that is apparently beneficial to the well-being of individuals or communities is not necessarily the right thing to be done.[114]

The second feature of Gustafson's profile reflects key facets of his construal of the world. As previously noted, Gustafson finds the natural world to be characterized by "patterns and processes of interdependence."[115] However, it is not just the natural world, but also society, culture, and history that manifest a patterning and ordering that relates human beings to each other and to all things. Human life and activity are to be interpreted within this context, in which we participate and upon which we depend but over which we lack ultimate control.[116] The descriptive becomes basis for the normative in Gustafson's "ecological" construal of the wider world, the ordering of which suggests an objective ground for discerning the right ordering of human life and action in keeping with the purposes of a divine Orderer:

> The "ways" of "nature" are indicators of the ways of God, and inferences are drawn from them to aid human beings to discern how they and all things are to be related to each other in a manner appropriate to their relations to God. . . . The determination of right action, prop-

---

[111]*Ethics II*, 3.
[112]Ibid., 1.
[113]Ibid., 4.
[114]Ibid., 5.
[115]Cf. 51, 56, 59, and 60 above.
[116]*Ethics II*, 8.

er ends, and fitting aspirations for human activity—the subject matter of ethics, that is—has objective referents in this objective ordering of all life. The second feature of the profile, then, is that moral values, principles, ends, and duties are grounded in an objective "reality" of which human life is a part.[117]

We see here evidence not only of Gustafson's moral realism, but also of the affinity between his ethics and classic Christian natural law theories, which hold that all things are properly ordered according to their divinely given natures. Having noted this affinity with respect to the work of Thomas Aquinas, Gustafson observes, "The basic pattern of ethics is the right ordering of things in relation to each other for the sake of the purpose of the whole. And the source for understanding these relations of things to each other is given in the natural ordering of the creation."[118]

The third feature of Gustafson's profile is closely related to the second, and confirms the affinity of his theocentric ethics with natural law ethics. Here the focus is specifically on human nature, its inclinations, impulses, and desires. In much Christian thought, especially among Protestants, the orientation of the human will is seen to be seriously debased and the functioning of human reason is held to be greatly distorted as a consequence of sin. Gustafson does not regard the effects of sin to be so thoroughly debilitating, or human nature so deeply corrupted, or evidences of the orientation of human beings toward their own good so profoundly obscured, that the moral and the rational must be conceived in opposition to our existing natures.

> Rather than perceiving the moral primarily to stand over against the natural and the historical, as an alien force, moral thinking gives direction to our natural impulses and desires as individuals within the context of the arenas of life in which we act. Similarly, in dealing with institutions and policies, moral reasoning attempts to give guidance to the exercise of various forms of power that are occurring.... Moral action involves the ordering and directing of existing powers in accordance with moral principles, values, ends, and ideals. It gives direction to our natural drives for sustenance and sexuality, for example. This does not imply that we do not use reason in some circumstances to restrain our natural drives, but even when we do it is nature that is being ordered and directed by rational activity.[119]

Wide differences in judgment will remain regarding what is "natural" for human beings, and care must be taken not simply to rationalize particu-

---

[117]Ibid. Consider this formulation of the relation between what is and what is right and fitting in light of my discussion of the indicative and the imperative, Chapter 1, 33ff.
[118]Ibid., 45.

lar desires and interests of human individuals and communities. Evidence, argument, and discernment must be employed in the discriminate valuation as well as ordering and direction of existing human powers and inclinations. But such rational activity is continuous with, not contravening of, human desires, affections, and volitions.[120]

The fourth feature of the profile is another that has already been dealt with at length, the significance of piety for the moral life. I have referred to the sense of awe and reverence that is evoked by the experience of God, or the ultimate power, and of nature and its powers.[121] Here Gustafson speaks of "the ultimate power and of powers bearing down upon, sustaining, and creating possibilities for action."[122] The sense of awe and reverence may be thought of as the specifically religious sense that characterizes piety or religious affectivity. Gustafson introduces six other specific senses, however, that he also identifies with this affectivity: the senses of dependence, gratitude, obligation, remorse or repentance, direction, and possibility or hope. Gustafson calls these "fundamental religious affections,"[123] but his discussion throughout the *Ethics* gives the impression that these are universal to the human experience, and not dependent upon identification with or participation in any particular religious tradition.[124] Consequently, some commentators have judged Gustafson to be developing a kind of theory of religion, with a view of piety that is not distinctively Christian.[125]

Nonetheless, Gustafson claims for piety, or religious affectivity, a special role:

> It is a distinctive feature of theocentric ethics to hold piety and morality together; it is a perversion when piety becomes separated from morality as if God were concerned primarily for the salvation of the individual and not the ordering of the creation, and when morality gets separated from piety, as if moral activity were independent of the wellsprings of the human spirit in both their commendable and perverse forms.[126]

---

[119]Ibid., 8–9.
[120]Ibid., 9; cf. *Ethics I*, 78–79; *Ethics II*, 58.
[121]Cf. 62, 63, above.
[122]*Ethics II*, 9.
[123]Ibid., 10.
[124]Gustafson sometimes speaks of a "natural piety," e.g., *Ethics I*, 159, 165, 233, 262; cf. Farley, op. cit., 46.
[125]E.g., Robert Bellah, "Gustafson as Critic of Culture," Beckley and Swezey, 148ff. Cf. Gustafson, "Tracing a Trajectory," 182; Melvin Konner, "Following a Trajectory: On 'Tracing a Trajectory' and 'Explaining and Valuing,' by James M. Gustafson," *Zygon* 30 (1995) 194.

As noted earlier, piety is a kind of religious virtue.[127] It has a central role both in Gustafson's theological construal of God and the world, and in his understanding of moral agency.

A fifth feature of Gustafson's theocentric ethics is the focus of attention on individuals, communities, and events within the context of large wholes.[128] Gustafson distinguishes himself from most Western moral theorists with an expanded view of both the spatial and temporal scope of the whole that ethics must take into consideration in its descriptive, analytical, valuing, and prescriptive tasks. This is not a case for seeing the forest instead of the trees, but for attending to the particularities of individuals, communities, and events in expansive contexts that take into account their extended spatial and temporal relationships to other individuals, communities, and events. The theological warrant for this feature derives from the theocentric perspective:

> If the divine power and powers are, in some sense, providing the conditions of possibility of human action and the ultimate ordering of the creation, the larger context in which individual acts and events take place must be taken into account in morality. Not only do the patterns of relationship ascend in importance as indications of what relationships are right or wrong and what ends of action are good or bad, but also the importance of assessing probable wider and longer-range responses and consequences becomes greater in the determination of particular initiatives.[129]

Integral to this feature is a relational, interactional model for interpreting human life and activity. Gustafson says that H. Richard Niebuhr was correct in his emphasis on interpretation within the context of human action in the development of his model of the "responsible self."[130] For Niebuhr, such interpretation always takes place within a context of relationships in which one is acted upon, responds, and anticipates continuing actions and responses. However, while Niebuhr thought of human agents as "responders," Gustafson thinks of them as "participants." Niebuhr's model understates the "human capacities for self-determination and the determination of courses of events and states of affairs."[131] As "participants," human beings are not mere passive recipients of actions upon them, or spectators of actions around them, but active agents giving shape to the world about them. Nonetheless, as "par-

---

[126]Ibid., 11.
[127]58 above.
[128]*Ethics II*, 11–18.
[129]Ibid., 12.
[130]H. Richard Niebuhr, *The Responsible Self: An Essay in Christian Moral Philosophy* (New York: Harper and Row, 1963).

ticipants," human beings are not radically free agents, but are subject to the material conditions of natural and historical existence.[132] Gustafson wants to avoid too exalted a view of the place of the human being with respect to nature and history. He expresses discomfort, for example, with language that identifies the human being as "co-creator with God." [133]

Gustafson distinguishes his interactional model from the contractual model, on the one hand, and the organic model, on the other. The contractual model is too individualistic, places too great an emphasis on individual autonomy,[134] and tends to favor the rights and interests of the individual over that of the larger natural or social group. The organic model "excessively highlights the processes of mutual determination between persons, between groups, and in some instances . . . between human beings and the rest of nature."[135] It tends to favor the interests of the group over the individual. The interactional model rejects the excesses of each of these other two models, while taking into account what is valid in each of them.[136]

But, with respect to this fifth feature, it is the attention to larger wholes as the contexts for interpretation that most distinguishes—and most complicates—Gustafson's ethics. "The theocentric construal of reality," says Gustafson, "presses us to expand the scope of the wholes that are taken into account in any normative proposal for human action. Such enlargement greatly complicates ethics, and I believe that we have not satisfactorily developed concepts, ways of understanding, and procedures to deal with these complexities."[137] I will not attempt to address these complexities in this book. I simply make two observations. First, attention to larger wholes is consonant with Gustafson's critique of anthropocentrism. An expanded perspective or vision is antidote to the too narrow and often egocentric construals that human beings typically give to their circumstances. These wholes are also to include the nonhuman world, though one cannot say in the abstract how far these relevant wholes may extend in any given circumstance. Second, Gustafson appears here also to be reflecting both the relational value theory

---

[131] *Ethics II*, 13.
[132] Cf. "The powers that bear down on human beings and sustain them . . . shape the 'natures' of the particular individuals—their capacities, their desires and aspirations, and their ways of interpreting life. These particularities are both limiting and the conditions of possibility. They are not merely the conditions of action, they also shape dispositions to act in particular ways"; Gustafson, *Ethics I*, 209.
[133] *Ethics II*, 13.
[134] Cf. "The scope of our 'freedom' is not as vast as it is claimed to be from some points of view"; *Ethics I*, 290.
[135] Ibid., 292.
[136] Ibid., 293.
[137] *Ethics II*, 17.

of H. Richard Niebuhr and the kind of "ecological consciousness" that is increasingly common in contemporary science. In any event, he is moving in a direction similar to what we will see in Sallie McFague and David Griffin.

A sixth feature of Gustafson's ethics is a concern for the common good. He notes that in Western thought the concept has traditionally been used in social and political philosophy. He wishes to extend it to the natural world. This shift in perspective follows directly from the fifth feature's attention to larger wholes, which are not limited to *human* individuals, communities, and events. Gustafson states that there is often tension between the good of the whole and the good of individual parts, even though the relationship between them is reciprocal. In his perspective, there is no *a priori* preference for either the common good or the good of its individual parts, irrespective of the good of the other. Corporatist and anarchist or individualist extremes are to be avoided. Nonetheless, he reports:

> My theocentric construal of the world requires that parts be interpreted in relation to relevant wholes, and that the common good of various wholes is the object of proper concern not only for the sake of the parts but also for the sake of those wholes. It follows from this that theocentric ethics will be weighted more readily, in circumstances of conflict between the claims of parts and the whole, on claims for the common good of a whole.[138]

A seventh feature follows from five and six, namely, an accent on the experience of moral ambiguity and, in particular circumstances, even tragedy. As Gustafson writes in *A Sense of the Divine*, "there is no clear overriding telos, or end, which unambiguously orders the priorities of nature and human participation in it so that one has a perfect moral justification for all human interventions."[139] For Gustafson there are real moral conflicts, and it is not always possible to make non-tragic choices. He sees the controversy over abortion as one that legitimately poses such choices. "The tragic character of many actions resides precisely in the fact that the legitimate pursuit of legitimate ends, or action in accordance with reasonable moral principles, entails severe losses to others."[140] This does not obviate a role for ethics, however. The task of ethics is to clarify what is at stake and give good reasons for decisions and actions, in order to reduce if not resolve the inescapable moral ambiguities of our common life.

The eighth feature of Gustafson's theocentric ethics relates closely to this seventh feature:

---

[138] Ibid., 19.
[139] 72.

[T]heocentric ethics warrants a strong emphasis on self-denial, and in extreme circumstances on self-sacrifice. This is the case whether the "self" involved is an individual person or a human collectivity. Self-denial follows both from theocentric piety and from the ethics grounded in the sovereign ordering of God.[141]

A certain degree of self-control and self-denial is necessary to individuals simply for their own good. Where individual self-interest is in tension with the good of a larger whole, self-denial may be required to maintain or attain sufficient harmony to realize the larger common good. Social groups within the context of the larger society may also be required to forego some measure of their own self-interests in order to contribute to the achievement of the greater good of the society. The good of the natural world may also constrain individuals, groups, and societies in the pursuit of their respective goods.

In secular perspective, the appeal here may be seen as an appeal to an enlightened self-interest or, more nobly, acts of supererogation. In theocentric perspective, however, this willingness to sacrifice interests of the self is motivated and sustained by piety. At this point Gustafson invokes key elements specific to the Christian tradition:

> Most dramatically, the theocentric piety and fidelity of Jesus make clear that the readiness to be concerned for the well-being of others even at cost to onself is a part of Christian morality. The cross, and the way of the cross, are revealing symbols of what is enabled and required of persons who seek to serve and glorify God.[142]

These concluding words of Gustafson's summary profile of theocentric ethics echo dimensions of Gustafson's theological perspective so crucial to his ethics that their importance can hardly be overstated. These must be highlighted in order to complete the profile.

Elements of the Reformed Tradition

In volume 1 of the *Ethics* Gustafson indicates a clear preference for the Reformed tradition in theology.[143] This preference does not extend to ecclesiology, or church order, inasmuch as he counts himself a "Free Church" theologian.[144] Nor does this preference entail an indiscriminate acceptance of every major theological emphasis in the tradition. There are three elements within this theological tradition, however, without which it would be hard to make sense of Gustafson's overall perspective. These are 1) "a sense of a powerful Other"; 2) "the centrality of piety or the religious affections in religious

[140] *Ethics II*, 21.
[141] Ibid.
[142] Ibid., 22.

and moral life"; and 3) "[a]n understanding of human life in relation to the powerful Other which requires that all of human activity be ordered properly in relation to what can be discerned about the purposes of God."[145]

In one way or another, each of these three elements has already been noted. Gustafson explicitly discusses the central importance of piety or religious affectivity, defined here as "an attitude of reverence and awe and respect which implies a sense of devotion and of duties and responsibilities as well,"[146] as a feature of his theocentric ethics in profile. I have noted the six specific "senses" that Gustafson also identifies with that piety. In his view, these senses are widely if not universally shared by human beings irrespective of their religious context. They engender or evoke attitudes and dispositions that shape the moral life. I have also argued above that Gustafson's own commitment to other key elements in the Reformed tradition is significantly a matter of his own piety.[147] This includes the first and third elements of that tradition just mentioned, about which a little more needs to be said.

Regarding the "sense of a powerful Other," Gustafson references the Reformed tradition's central emphasis on the sovereignty of God. Integral to this notion is a strong sense of divine providence and divine omnipotence, and a conviction that God effectively rules or governs all things in power. "With this deep sense of divine providence it is clear not only that are all (sic) things related to God—dependent upon him, intentionally ordered by him, determined in particulars by him—but also that all things ought to be properly related to God's ordering."[148] For ethics the main point is that "there are no spheres of human action that are outside the divine governance and purpose."[149]

But there is a problem in reconciling claims of God's all-pervasive power with those of human freedom. Gustafson interprets both Calvin and Jonathan Edwards to claim divine determination of all particular events. His critique is not a philosophical one, however, but rests on the argument that God is mistakenly understood in anthropomorphic terms by those, like Calvin and Edwards, who claim God's determination in all events. The problem is, first, that God is viewed as "an agent in ways similar to those of a human agent."[150] Second, and more deeply problematic from a theocentric perspective, is "the claim that the divine determination of events occurs for the sake of human well-being, or on the basis of human deserts, or deserving."[151]

---

[143] *Ethics I*, 157–93.
[144] Ibid., 163.
[145] Ibid., 163–64.
[146] Ibid., 164.
[147] Cf. 57ff., 62ff. above. Here Gustafson notes, "Without piety it is relatively meaningless to make a case for the existence or presence of God"; *Ethics I*, 164.
[148] *Ethics I*, 166.
[149] Ibid., 167.

In his appropriation and critique of Reformed theology, Gustafson is telling us what he does and does not mean in identifying God as "powerful Other." It would be easy to misread him here. In much theological parlance, reference to God as "Other" suggests a radically transcendent notion of God. Gordon Kaufman interprets Gustafson to be burdened, perhaps unwittingly, with a Calvinistic conception of God that rests on "radically dualistic metaphysical assumptions"—a conception that seems incoherent in light of Gustafson's overall theological construal of the world and God's relations to the world in generally naturalistic terms.[152] But God is not conceived in stark contradistinction to the world by Gustafson, nor is God thought of as a being or power that stands over against us, as in some theologies where the language of God's "otherness" is employed. That God is "powerful Other" means essentially two things to Gustafson. First, as "powerful," God is related to, and participant in the ordering of, all things. God is in this sense *the* creating, governing, bearing down, and sustaining power of the universe. Second, as "Other," God is not to be understood by analogy to the human, although Gustafson admits the virtual unavoidability of resort to some anthropomorphic language to speak of God.[153] The language of God as "Other" is to resist anthropomorphic conceptions of God and, especially, anthropocentric construals of God's actions and purposes in the world. Thus, Gustafson wants to retain the Reformed tradition's central emphasis on God's providence and power, as well as the piety—the sense of awe and reverence with which it is imbued—but without its "deep strand of utilitarian religion."[154]

The third element of the tradition that Gustafson wants to stress and affirm is simply this: "the chief end of man is to glorify God, to relate to all things in a manner appropriate to their relations to God, in recognition of the dependence of all things upon him, and in gratitude for all things."[155] This is an interesting gloss on the first answer in the Westminster Shorter Catechism, which reads: "Man's chief end is to glorify God, and to enjoy him forever." Gustafson does not hold out hope for life after death, a hope that is rooted in human valuations and egocentric desires for heavenly reward. Indeed, he believes it necessary for theocentric ethics to "develop a position in which life after death is not necessary."[156] Consequently, he must reject the Reformed

---

[150]Ibid., 179.
[151]Ibid., 180; Gustafson later also notes his departure from "a stringent cause-effect view of human action," which he attributes to "the strong determinists of the Reformed tradition," and for which his model of interaction is a replacement; *I*, 187.
[152]In Beckley and Swezey, 24ff.
[153]*Ethics I*, 179.
[154]Ibid., 184.

tradition's claim that the end of human existence is the everlasting enjoyment of God, even while he insists upon its prior claim that God be glorified.

There are two other important themes in the Reformed tradition that Gustafson also wants to retain. One is the notion of sin as an invariable and eradicable presence in human existence. He speaks in terms of the human fault, and of the perception of its depth and persistence.[157] He finds it profitable to draw on the tradition's "astute perceptions of the human condition" regarding such human failures as have traditionally been denoted by idolatry, pride, infidelity, and sloth.[158] But he remains wary of making too much of human sin, due to the ways in which it has been linked to other tenets of Christianity that he rejects, including soteriological doctrines that require Jesus Christ's sacrificial death as payment for the sins of the world, and thus for individual salvation:

> The question to be faced is whether one can take the human fault with deep seriousness, establish some sense of the possibilities of human alternation, and claim some benefits of the divine benevolence, without becoming trapped in utilitarian Christianity's preoccupation with human guilt.[159]

A second and related theme that Gustafson claims from the Reformed tradition is that of conversion, "of significant alteration if not transformation of the perspectives of those who are oriented finally toward God."[160] This theme is so central and so pervasive in Gustafson's *Ethics* that, like the air we breathe or the water in which fish swim, it is easily taken for granted. It is hardly exaggeration to say that conversion is what Gustafson's *Ethics from a Theocentric Perspective* is all about: conversion from anthropocentric and egocentric perspectives, conversion from idolatry and self-preoccupation, conversion from moralistic and fideistic forms of instrumentalism,[161] conversion from all forms of utilitarian religion—to a theocentric perspective, and to that end for which human beings exist: "to honor, to serve, and to glorify (celebrate) God."[162] Gustafson's call to conversion is a call to the most fundamental change in the history of religion, which history, he says, "is the history of human efforts to exercise sovereignty over God."[163]

---

[155]Ibid.
[156]Ibid.
[157]Ibid., 185.
[158]Ibid., 192.
[159]Ibid., 185.
[160]Ibid., 192; cf. Beckley and Swezey, 222.

Theological Ethics in Practice

The practical moral question, with which Gustafson begins volume 2 of the *Ethics*, can now be seen in the light of his most important theological commitments. That question, as he subsequently amends it, is: *What is God enabling and requiring us, as participants in (and through) the patterns and processes of interdependence of life in the world, to be and to do?* The general answer is: *We, as participants, are to relate ourselves and all things in a manner appropriate to our and their relations to God.*[164] Gustafson's theological perspective is crucial to the framing of the question. Most succinctly, the moral question is, "What serves the divine purposes?" But once the theocentric perspective is established and the question is properly framed, how do we discern, in any particular situation or circumstance, what God is enabling and requiring us to be and do? And what does it mean to relate ourselves and all things in an appropriate manner? It lies well beyond the scope of this chapter and this book to provide an adequate account of how Gustafson addresses these questions. I limit my review and comment to those features of his approach that strike me either as most relevant to the articulation of a religiously adequate theological ethics in a Christian context, or as most illuminating for purposes of comparison with the work of Sallie McFague and David Griffin, or both.

Edward Farley has interpreted Gustafson's *Ethics* as an "exploration" of his comprehensive theocentric vision. As such it has no single starting point. It lacks the structure of a deductive system. One cannot categorize his ethics as either teleological or ontological in any strict sense. There is an accent on the primacy of experience, and an orientation toward the complexity of reality.[165] All of this becomes most obvious when one tries to indicate Gustafson's "approach" to any particular question or issue of moral significance. As Farley observes, "his 'beginning' is the concatenation of a great number of elements in the situation of moral experiences and choice."[166] Gustafson's method might best be described as descriptive, empirical, experiential, evaluative, inductive, pragmatic, practically reasoned, and intuitive:

> The final discernment is an informed intuition; it is not the conclusion of a formally logical argument, a strict deduction from a single moral principle, or an absolutely certain result from the exercises of

---

[161] That is, approaches to religion that promise benefit or reward based on right action or right belief.
[162] *Ethics I*, 113; cf. *Ethics II*, 32; Beckley and Swezey, 239.
[163] *Ethics II*, 319–20.
[164] *Ethics II*, 146; the words "and through" do not appear here. Gustafson introduces them without comment in his "Afterword," in Beckley and Swezey, 249.
[165] In Beckley and Swezey, 40–43.

human "reason" alone. There is a final moment of perception that sees the parts in relation to a whole, expresses sensibilities as well as reasoning, and is made in the conditions of human finitude. In complex circumstances it is not without risk.[167]

The features of his theological profile, and the elements he stresses from the Reformed tradition, clearly give shape and form to Gustafson's perspective on matters of moral significance, but they are not strictly determinative of the process of moral reasoning from which a "final discernment," normative judgment, prescription, or choice results. Theocentric piety, and the attitudes and dispositions it evokes and sustains, provide a basic orientation, though no precise prescriptions, for the moral life. Because there are no *a priori* rules or principles one can invoke to prescribe moral action, Gustafson's complex ethics requires careful deliberation and something akin to what philosopher Robert Johann calls "radical choice". It is primarily an activity of practical reason, requiring reasoned choices and practical judgments regarding what sources are relevant to the construction of theological ethics, "but also about which ones are decisive when they conflict, what specific content is to be used from them, and how this chosen content is to be interpreted."[168] The goal of the process of moral reasoning may be some sort of "final discernment," but the task of ethics as such is not necessarily to provide answers. "The practical function of the ethician is not primarily to prescribe and proscribe the conduct of others, but . . . to broaden and deepen the capacities of others to make morally responsible choices."[169]

This is not to say that content is secondary to process, certainly not for any theological ethics that claims to be Christian. The adequacy of any ethics will be judged by the extent to which its development and character, including its principles, rules, values, claims, or commitments, are warranted or authorized by accepted sources. According to Gustafson,

> Christian theological ethics can be tested for their adequacy with reference to four sources: (a) the Bible and the Christian tradition; (b) their philosophical methods and principles; (c) their use of scientific information and other sources of knowledge of the world; and (d) human experience broadly conceived. . . . Four kinds of judgments are involved: about (a) which sources are relevant, and why; (b) which sources

---

[166] Ibid., 43. Employing a rather different and less apt metaphor, Jeffrey Stout calls Gustafson "a most self-conscious practitioner of what I call moral *bricolage*"; op. cit., 169.
[167] *Ethics I*, 338.
[168] Johann, "An Ethics of Emergent Order," in Beckley and Swezey, 100. Cf. Gustafson, *Ethics I*, 158.
[169] *Ethics II*, 315; cf. "Tracing a Trajectory," 184–85.

are decisive when they conflict, and why; (c) what specific "content" is to be used from these sources, and what is to be ignored or rejected, and why; and (d) how this content is to be interpreted, and why.[170]

Gustafson does not provide any systematic account of the place of the four sources, or the criteria for the four judgments, in the development of his *Ethics*. Rather, he illustrates his approach by devoting most of the last half of his second volume to four chapters on four areas of human experience: marriage and family, suicide, population and nutrition, and the allocation of biomedical research funding. "Each of these chapters," he says, "is an exercise in discernment."[171]

Few of Gustafson's interpreters and critics take much exception to his moral reasoning in these four chapters.[172] Gustafson is a knowledgeable, thoughtful, careful, sensitive observer and interpreter of the human experience in its moral dimensions. Criticism is much more likely to be directed at the way in which he conceptually construes the respective characters, weights, and authorities of the four sources that warrant his Christian ethics. I have already noted some objections to the way in which Gustafson regards and appropriates materials from the sciences, including the weight given to scientific knowledge. I have also indicated some of the points at which his Christian critics have been troubled by his departures from theological tradition. And I have discussed some of the problems I see in what I regard as the lack of an adequate philosophical conception of God and God's relation to the world, as well as the ambiguities or obscurities in what he means by "nature" and "naturalism."[173] Two other points at which Gustafson has been subjected to serious criticism involve his understanding of Scripture, or the Bible, and his appeal to human experience. The many comments and criticisms made about his use of his four sources prompted Gustafson to provide a brief but focused discussion of these sources in his "Response" in the volume edited by Beckley and Swezey.[174]

I have already said enough about my reservations regarding Gustafson's appropriation of scientific knowledge in his "naturalistic" construal of the world. In the remainder of this chapter I wish to concentrate on other fea-

---

[170]*Ethics II*, 143–44; cf. *A Sense of the Divine*, 46.
[171]Ibid., 149.
[172]Lisa Sowell Cahill expresses more reservations than most in her essay, "Consent in Times of Affliction," *Journal of Religious Ethics*, esp. 25–26, 31–32. Gordon Kaufman, on the other hand, comments, "I find myself largely in agreement with Gustafson's work; his discussion of concrete issues seems to me extraordinarily wise and insightful. To the extent that the proof of ethics is to be found in its practical applicability, Gustafson's program, in my opinion (at least with reference to these four examples), must receive very high marks"; "How Is *God* to Be Understood in a Theocentric Ethics?" in Beckley and Swezey, 33. And Robert Bellah observes, "These four chapters are among the most impressive in the book"; "Gustafson as Critic of Culture," in Beckley and Swezey, 145.

tures of Gustafson's approach that seem to me to continue to be most problematic. I will note particular instances where I am in basic agreement with Gustafson's perspective, and indicate whether I think his argument can be strengthened. I will also review instances where I differ, and what I think needs to be amended. In this way the agenda will be set for the discussion in Chapter 5, where I will examine together the contributions that Gustafson, McFague, and Griffin each have to make toward a more intellectually and religiously adequate theocentric, naturalistic, theological ethics.

Problematic Issues

Bible

If one knew nothing else about James Gustafson except that he is a Protestant Christian in the Reformed tradition, one might expect him to have a high view of the authority of the Bible. But Gustafson shares "the modern commitment," with its insistence on human experience and reason as the final arbiters of human knowledge.[175] Thus the Bible has no *a priori* claim to authority. On the other hand, the Bible is not just some occasional writing, or collection of writings, of a distinctly religious character. In the first place, the Bible is derivative of human experience, and not just any human experience, but experience of the divine: "the biblical materials are themselves human expressions of and reflections upon human experience of a divine reality."[176]

In the second place, the Bible has had and continues to have an integral place and role in the life of the historic Christian Church and in the lives of individual Christian communities, and thus gives shape and form to the traditions and practices that help nurture, and provide content for, religious piety in the Christian context. Gustafson identifies the Bible, along with Christian tradition, as one of the four sources that serve as criteria for the adequacy of Christian theological ethics.

But critics charge that Gustafson does not accord the Bible its rightful authority, and sometimes seem to wonder if he takes the Bible seriously

---

[173] Gustafson acknowledges in his "Response" in Beckley and Swezey, 212, that "the cluster of questions around the relation of God and nature gave me more intellectual agony than any other part of the work."

[174] 205–10.

[175] Chapter 1, 3.

[176] *Ethics I*, 18. Cf., "One can argue, as I would, that what is given in the Bible is itself reflection on the meanings of common human experience in the light of an experience of the presence of God"; *Ethics I*, 146. Gustafson's discussion of scripture, revelation, and tradition in *Ethics I*, 145ff., is most helpful to understand his position.

at all. Richard McCormick, for example, indicts Gustafson because he does not view scripture as revelation, but only "as a *merely* human source," inasmuch as Gustafson has no notion of divine inspiration. "[T]his is not the Christian . . . understanding of Scripture," McCormick insists.[177] In fact, Gustafson leaves room for a "weak sense" of revelation within his framework, but scripture, or the biblical writings, hold no place of epistemic privilege in his theology. What is called revelation by others is, in his view, (only, but not merely) "reflection on human experiences in the face of the ultimate power and powers."[178] The Bible is a source that provides a historical record of such reflections, but it is not an exclusive source by any means. Gustafson rejects any notion that one can locate God's self-manifestation in the Bible, or in the world of nature, or anywhere else, precisely because this suggests a too personal, and thus anthropomorphized, conception of God.

It would be wrong to conclude from this that the Bible is incidental to Gustafson's thinking and perspective, "deeply informed as it is by the Bible and traditions that flow from it."[179] Harlan Beckley provides the following concise, accurate summation of the role of the Bible and tradition in Gustafson's thought:

> Gustafson's use of the sciences avoids polarizing theology and the sciences and makes possible intelligible communication with scientists who possess a sense of the divine or natural piety, but it does not preclude an important place for the Bible and tradition in theological ethics. Recall, piety emerging from experience, not beliefs derived from the sciences, is the principal basis for consent to the tradition. Moreover, the subjective aspect of this "justification" from piety is mitigated by the authority of religious perceptions and construals because they have met the test of time (*Ethics* I, 234-35). Specific themes, symbols, and ideas of the tradition carry weight in Gustafson's composite rationale because the "tradition is not an ancient bag of irrational nonsense [but] carries a way of relating . . . to God that has been forged by human experiences both similar and dissimilar to our own" (*Ethics* I, 234). It has authority apart from its detailed accordance with our experience (or with the sciences). Participation in the tradition and its rituals is further justified because it is necessary if piety is to become a vital aspect of our religious and moral being (*Ethics* I, 317–25; II, 290–92).[180]

---

[177]"Gustafson's God: Who? What? Where? (Etc.)," *Journal of Religious Ethics*, 66–67.
[178]*Ethics II*, 28.
[179]*A Sense of the Divine*, 46.

Clearly, Gustafson's view of scripture is not that of most of the Christian tradition. If one grants the naturalistic perspective or shares the modern commitment, however, one may conclude that Gustafson accords the Bible all the respect and authority one could expect from someone deeply imbued with the Christian tradition.

Tradition

So far as Gustafson's other departures from the Christian tradition are concerned, they are all warranted by his naturalistic perspective, his theocentric perspective, or both. In other words, he abandons traditional doctrines or beliefs when, in his view, they clearly conflict with what we know from the sciences and human experience, or when they are at odds with theocentric piety, or both. Granting the theocentric, naturalistic perspective, the only question here is whether Gustafson's departures are all entirely justified in light of scientific knowledge and "in piety." Although he is unquestionably unorthodox from a traditional perspective, for the most part I believe that Gustafson rightly divides the essentials of Christian faith from those that have become intellectually untenable in the contemporary context. However, I think he presses the demands of his theocentric piety too far in his rejection of all personalistic conceptions of God and in the extent to which he distances himself from certain theological affirmations that bespeak God's love for humankind.

Given what little we know of the entire universe, it would be the greatest hubris to assume that human beings are the pinnacle or ultimate end of divine creation. Gustafson is certainly right on that score. However, given what we do know of the universe, there is certainly reason to claim a unique and special place for human beings within the currently known scheme of things, and to imagine that the divine solicitude for humankind is not so widely at variance with general human aspirations as Gustafson seems to think. At the very least, it seems to me, the cultivation of a theocentric sense of piety requires a view of God as somewhat more interested, benevolent, and responsive toward humankind than Gustafson is willing to admit.

Let me give a specific example. I agree with Gustafson that theology must not uncritically indulge the human desire to believe in some kind of life after death. Though such a prospect cannot be ruled out entirely by what we know of "how things really are," belief in heaven, or some kind of life hereafter, is an element of the tradition that needs to be seriously questioned. But it remains

---

[180]"A Raft That Floats: Experience, Tradition, and Sciences in Gustafson's Theocentric Ethics," *Zygon* 30 (1995) 205–6.

important to be able to speak of God in ways that affirm divine presence and activity on behalf of creation—including but certainly not limited to human beings—not only in the most general sense that God's ordering, sustaining, and bearing down are manifest in the powers of nature and the larger social order, but in the particularities of our individual circumstances. This does not mean that one can ever say, "Lo, here!" or "Lo, there!" by way of identifying the precise locus and content of divine activity.[181] But it does mean that one is not constrained to think of God as unresponsive to our own or any other particular circumstance. Gustafson would probably counter that such a claim about God reflects the insinuation of human self-interests and aspirations. I would argue that such a claim about God surely also contributes to an understanding of God that is evocative of greater theocentric piety. I will say a bit more about this below, but a fuller statement of the argument will have to wait till Chapter 5.

Human Experience

Although there has thus far been little explicit discussion of the role of experience in Gustafson's thought, numerous indications of that role appear throughout this chapter. I have noted that, for Gustafson and all who share the modern commitment, human experience and reason are the final arbiters of what can be held to be true. We have seen that scientific knowledge, the Bible, and tradition all have authority for Gustafson, an authority that is grounded in certain kinds of human experience. Human experience also gives rise to those six "senses"—dependence, gratitude, obligation, remorse or repentance, possibility or hope, and direction—that are widely if not universally present in human cultures[182] and are potentially constitutive of religious affectivity or piety when "perceived to be ultimately related to the powers that sustain us and bear down upon us."[183] And then there is what he calls "human experience broadly conceived."

Gustafson lays out his basic views on human experience in a section in volume 1 of the *Ethics* titled, "Convictions: The Priority of Experience." He begins and ends that section with the same identical paragraph, where he writes with characteristic care and imprecision:

> Human experience is prior to reflection. We reflect on human experience itself, and on objects perceived, interpreted, and known through our experiences of them and through the experiences of others. Religion and morality are aspects of human experience; theology and ethics are not only articulations of ideas in relation to the ideas others

---
[181]The problematic of any such specification of divine activity is vividly and extensively addressed in *An Examined Life*, 1–4, 18–19, 51, and passim.
[182]*Ethics I*, 129–36.
[183]Ibid., 195.

have expressed but are ideas about aspects of experience. Experience is social; it is a process of interaction between persons, between persons and natural events, and between persons and historical events. Its significance is explained and its meanings assessed in communities that share common objects of interest and attention and share some common concepts, symbols, and theories. Experience is not only socially generated; it is socially tested. And it is experience of others, of "things" objective to human persons. This is the case in the sciences, in ethics, and in theology; it is the case in all ways of knowing and understanding.[184]

Human experience may be prior to reflection, as Gustafson begins by saying, but we reflect both on what we experience and what others experience, and we reflect on human experience itself. Thus, experience is not entirely individual, it is also social. It is socially generated, interpreted, and tested. Moreover, human experience is not primarily experience of ourselves, but of "things," including other persons, external though hardly unrelated to ourselves. Even when one experiences oneself, says Gustafson, one experiences an objectified self. "Because there is this objective pole we can engage in 'reality checks.' We can assess the accuracy and adequacy of our knowledge and understanding of that to which we are responding."[185] In addition, I take Gustafson to be saying at least two things here that merit notice. One is that we reflect on, and are therefore conscious of the fact that we have, experience. In other words, we are not only conscious, but self-conscious. We experience and know ourselves to be experiencers. The other is that the content of our experiences, that is, of what we come to know or to "sense" from our experiences, is mediated by our social and historical existence.

Some of Gustafson's critics seem to worry that he lacks a critical epistemology, or theory of knowing.[186] I think this is right, if by theory one means an abstract or philosophically elaborated account of what one knows and how one knows it. Moreover, it is not clear whether he adequately acknowledges that our very perceptions of the things we experience are shaped by our particular biographies, histories, and cultures. I suspect it depends both on one's own epistemology and on one's reading of Gustafson, who is less than explicit on matters of epistemological distinction, and who argues against "the imposition of sharp distinctions" on experience,[187] whether he is to be faulted here or not.[188]

---

[184]115, 129.
[185]Ibid., 128.
[186]See especially Yoder, op. cit., 72ff.; also Hauerwas, op. cit., 15ff.; Cahill, op. cit., 26–30.

On one level, I do not find Gustafson's "commonsense empiricism" particularly problematic. In a discussion of the epistemological issues that confront Gustafson with respect to his construing of the world, Stephen Toulmin provides an assessment with which I have great sympathy. Recall that what is at stake, for Gustafson, is whether, to what extent, and in what way one can discern "indicators" of the divine in the patterning and ordering of the world. Toulmin observes, in what I take to be a pragmatic vein:

> His approach is, characteristically, level-headed. . . . If we rely on the critical use of our own natural perceptiveness, we shall find ways of making progress *ambulando*, as we go along, without the need to "justify" them in advance. For, apart from getting on with this task, no procedure exists to guarantee us a sure way of correctly identifying the patterns of relationships in which all the constituents of the world stand to God.[189]

It goes without saying that we can never be certain our construals of the world are correct. That is to say, we can never be certain they are wholly congruent with God's ordering purposes. Yet we have no independent, non-experience-based means by which to discern and confirm those purposes.

On another level, however, I believe that Gustafson lacks an adequate and comprehensive understanding of the nature of human experience itself. In particular, he lacks a vocabulary, as well as a conceptuality, to speak about experience and perception that is not sensory-based. For example, when he speaks of the six "senses" that he associates with religious affectivity he intimates the possibility of an awareness of realities, the experience of which is not directly mediated by the human sense organs. These "senses" clearly belong to human experience. However, he regards them essentially as affectivities. "Human experience broadly conceived," as explicated by Gustafson, is "experience of others, of 'things' objective to human persons." The religious affections, on the other hand, are understood to be "generated in response to 'others',"[190] rather than actually being experiences of others. The general character of a more adequate understanding of human experience, one that argues for a more comprehensive notion of perception and knowledge, will be presented in the discussion of the work of David Griffin in Chapter 4.

---

[187] *Ethics I*, 120.
[188] In the course of providing descriptive and analytical accounts of experiences, Gustafson comments that "the complexities of experience resist the divisions which analysis makes for purposes of clear thinking"; ibid., 117.
[189] "Nature and Nature's God," *Journal of Religious Ethics* 13 (1985) 48.

The Descriptive and the Prescriptive

I have previously noted the complexity with which Gustafson himself views the task of giving an adequate descriptive account of "how things really are," especially in the context of large wholes.[191] It is obvious, *ipso facto*, that Gustafson's prescriptive ethics must share this complexity. What is happening in the world is the basis for discerning God's ordering, sustaining, and bearing down, and thus for discerning what God is requiring and enabling us to be and to do.

Gustafson is keenly aware of the challenges not only of the descriptive task itself, but of the possibly even greater difficulties of moving from the descriptive to the prescriptive, or from the "is" to the "ought." In *Intersections* he mentions the issue several times.[192] In his 1995 essay, "Tracing a Trajectory," he makes the following declaration:

> The old "is-ought" question is raised. At issue is not only which description and explanation of an event or circumstance is most adequate, . . . but how one justifies moral inferences or conclusions from the descriptive and explanatory premises being used. Any ethic that has a naturalistic premise, whether a strong one in classic natural law theory or a weaker one, has to find some way of showing relations, both negative and positive, between the descriptive and the normative.
>
> I believe that resolving the is-ought issue one way or another in the abstract does not fully resolve the relations between descriptions and morally desirable outcomes in very specific circumstances. Also, those relations will vary depending upon what sort of moral issue is under consideration.
>
> This has gotten me into very difficult intellectual straits.[193]

In my discussion of the "is-ought" problem in Chapter 1, I indicated the broad outlines of a way to conceptualize this problem that, I believe, clarifies the difficulty.[194] The "is-ought" problem is not a problem of logic but of interpretation. In any particular situation, and given the complexity of the patterns and processes of interdependence of life in the world, the challenge to prescriptive ethics is actually two-fold. On the one hand, one must seek to provide the most adequate account, with respect to possibilities of human action, of all that is going on. On the other hand, one needs to discern the

---

[190] Ibid., 129.
[191] Cf. 59ff., 72–74, above.
[192] Cf. 9, 16, 84, 135; cf. also *An Examined Faith*, 11–12.
[193] 185. In *Intersections*, Gustafson says that "when one is negotiating the claims of disciplines that relate in various ways to theological ethics, general hermeneutical theories, general epistemological theories from extreme realism to extreme relativism, and general theories of facts to values, is to ought, are not very helpful," 135.

moral significance of those possibilities for human action. What one ought to do is always constrained by, as well as indicated by, these possibilities. In Gustafson's terms, what one ought to do is always circumscribed by what God is requiring on the one hand, and enabling on the other. The challenge of discerning from among the possibilities what is most "appropriate" as the way to relate ourselves and all things to God remains. And Gustafson is right in saying the answer cannot be worked out in the abstract. It requires practical moral reasoning and is, as he says, "an exercise in discernment."[195]

God

Much of this chapter has been devoted to identifying and critiquing Gustafson's construal of God. Is there an alternative way of construing God and God's relation to the world that addresses most of what is problematic in Gustafson's construal of God? Is there a way to conceptualize God as both personal and agential as well as purposive? Is it possible that God may be experienced by human beings in ways, and to an extent, that Gustafson does not allow?[196] In Chapters 4 and 5 I will attempt to show how to answer these questions in the affirmative. This does not mean, however, that I think it is necessary, or even possible, to claim that God possesses an ultimate *telos*, if by *telos* one means a final end. After all, God is traditionally thought to be infinite, and infinity has no final end. My goal is not to set forth a conceptualization of God that simply conforms to more traditional conceptions. Rather, my intent is to explore the possibilities of conceptualizing God in terms that are more intellectually *and* religiously adequate than Gustafson's without abandoning either the naturalistic or the theocentric commitment.

Furthermore, a religiously adequate conception of God requires more than a philosophically or intellectually adequate conceptualization of God and God's relation to the world. It also requires language about God, and in reference to God, such that God can be meaningfully understood to be the object of the religious affections. Critics and commentators on Gustafson's *Ethics* note that he does at times resort to anthropomorphic language about God, and that even God as "creator," "governor," "orderer," and "sustainer" who "bears down" and is "requiring" and "enabling" seems to suggest di-

---

[194]Chapter 1, 33-38.
[195]Cf. 81 above.
[196]Although Gustafson can speak of "human experience of a divine reality" (*Ethics I*, 118) and of "an experience of the presence of God" (*I*, 146), these are circumlocutions that should not be equated with the assertion of a direct or immediate experience of God. But Gustafson also carefully equivocates, "We do not have, except perhaps in the case of the true mystic, experiences of God as a distinct and isolated object" (*Ethics I*, 205).

vine activity analogous to the human.[197] Gustafson for his part acknowledges that symbolic language—e.g., God as Creator, Sustainer, Governor, and Redeemer—is necessary within religious communities as means "by which we consciously acknowledge God, and through which we praise God."[198] Gustafson seems to have placed himself in the untenable position of affirming, on the one hand, that anthropomorphic language is essential to the nurturing of piety within religious communities yet, on the other hand, that piety rightly calls us to eschew the use of such language in our theocentric construals of God. I think Gustafson is correct about the need for symbolic language, including language that is clearly anthropomorphic, within the context of worship in the religious community, which is at least one important place where piety is evoked and nourished. Thus we need to explore whether the exorcism of anthropomorphic language from our theological construals is as critical to the anthropocentric critique as he contends. The use of symbolic and metaphorical theological language, including language that is decidedly anthropomorphic, will be a central focus in the following chapter on the work of Sallie McFague.

Could it also be relevant to note in this context that, among the six "senses" identified by Gustafson as constitutive of the religious affections, one of the three cardinal Christian virtues is not mentioned? Hope, conceived primarily as possibility, is included.[199] Faith, which is basically trust, is subsumed under dependence.[200] But love is ignored altogether. Love, usually regarded as the highest of all Christians virtues, surely has an affective dimension, and would seem to be oriented toward an object—something, or more likely, someone—to love. A religiously adequate conception of God, at least for Christians, would seem to be one in which God is understood to be an (though hardly the only) object and recipient of the individual adherent's love, as well as hope and trust.

Moreover, in Christian scripture and tradition, human love of God is generally assumed to be rooted in, and responsive to, God's love for the world: "We love because [God] first loved us."[201] Human love—of God, of one another, and of the world—is predicated upon the divine love. The point is not simply that human love is motivated by the love of God, but that God's love is the very possibility for human love. *Agape*, the distinctive form of love in the New Testament, refers first of all to divine love. The absence of any

---

[197] Cf. Kaufman, 31, and Farley, 50–51, in Beckley and Swezey.
[198] *Ethics I*, 279; cf. 250–51; 317ff.; as previously noted, he also admits the inevitability of some anthropomorphism in theological reflection (77 and n. 153 above).
[199] *Ethics I*, 133.
[200] Ibid., 130.

mention of love in Gustafson's account of the religious virtues, or affections, would seem to implicate his view of God's disposition toward the world. Gustafson rather hesitantly affirms the goodness, or beneficence of God. Of course, he does not want to valorize anthropocentric notions of what that goodness requires. Nonetheless, given the centrality of love within the Christian tradition as a description—even definition—of God's fundamental character, we must again question whether God as construed by Gustafson is sufficiently solicitous and caring, not only toward humankind, but toward all creation.[202] I believe a much stronger argument can be made on behalf of divine love.

More generally, I will argue in the coming chapters, what is needed is a conception of God as One who is worthy of worship, honor, and service. Gustafson writes of "consenting to divine governance."[203] He does not mean resignation, but acceptance and affirmation. But if such consent is to be anything more than a matter of necessity, born of a largely stoic recognition that only God can be God, surely one must have an apprehension of the divine such that those moral qualities and virtuous affections that are called forth from us in our relation to God and to all things do not surpass what we are able to attribute to God.

---

[201] 1 John 4:19.
[202] As I have just argued above, 84–85.
[203] Cf. *Ethics I*, 97, 234, 242, 247, 308, 317.

3

Sallie McFague's Theology of Nature: Metaphor to the Rescue?

Introduction

OVER a period of twenty-five years Sallie McFague has published a half dozen books that have made her one of the best-known theologians in America.[1] Her books have reached a far wider reading public than those of either James Gustafson or David Griffin.[2] Her last four books, especially, as well as many of her other writings, display a strong ethical purpose, as she has addressed herself to such issues as patriarchy, the planetary threats of nuclear and ecological disaster, and the perils of consumerism. She has been called "one of the leading ecological theologians of our time."[3] She is also regarded as a feminist theologian. What is perhaps her best-known book, *Models of God*, has also received the most attention in academic circles. In December 1987, at one of the sessions held during the annual meeting of the American Academy of Religion, the book was the focus of several presentations subsequently published in the Spring 1988 issue of *Religion and Intellectual Life*. In 1988 it also received the Academy's Award for Excellence. *Models of God* has been called "a landmark of feminist theology, a powerful contribution to mainline Protestant theology, and a major contribution to theological discourse whatever one's predilections."[4]

It must be noted, however, that none of McFague's books provides the definitive statement of her theological approach. Each one is better seen as a report of work in progress. She begins the Preface to her latest, *Life Abundant*,

---

[1] *Speaking in Parables* (1975), *Metaphorical Theology* (1982), *Models of God* (1987), *The Body of God* (1993), *Super, Natural Christians* (1997), and *Life Abundant* (2000). McFague has also edited two other books, and earlier wrote one other, *Literature and the Christian Life* (New Haven: Yale University Press, 1966).

[2] This is surely true with respect to the theological writings of these three thinkers. However, David Griffin may become a more familiar figure due to the robust sales of his two recent books critiquing the U.S. administration's official account of the events of September 11, 2001.

[3] Charles Birch, William Eakin, and Jay B. McDaniel, editors, *Liberating Life: Contemporary Approaches to Ecological Theology* (Maryknoll, N.Y.: Orbis, 1990) 201.

by observing, "I have written each of my books in an effort to make up for deficiencies in the last one."[5] This does not mean that her latest book provides the most comprehensive and most adequate statement of her thinking to date. Rather, the statement reflects the fact that certain features of her theological approach are exemplified in her written work.[6] For example, in *Models of God* she writes of the heuristic, or experimental, nature of the theological task as she understands it.[7] The implication is that theological work is constantly subject to examination, testing, and revision.[8] Theological language, in particular, must be seen as provisional and subject to change. In response to others' critiques of her work she stresses that theology is a collaborative effort.[9] Her practical commitment to this is manifest in various ways. Not only does she cite a great variety of sources in the notes and indices to her books, her writings reflect that she has been in active dialogue with these sources. Moreover, one can trace significant changes or shifts in emphasis from one book to another in light of some of these dialogues. In addition, the dialogical character of so much of McFague's work, incorporating insights ranging from literary criticism to the philosophy of science, introduces methodological tensions that are often neither explicitly addressed nor easily resolved, and that thus make it difficult to reach a settled conviction about the adequacy of her approach.

In consequence of her own approach, therefore, it is hardly possible to provide a definitive interpretation of McFague's work. On the other hand, one should avoid an idiosyncratic interpretation. My interpretation will necessarily be selective, for it is not possible here to attend substantively to every significant facet of McFague's theological work. In particular, my interpretation will be shaped by the naturalistic and theocentric commitments and concerns that are central to this book. Nonetheless, it should be possible to

---

[4]Mary Jo Weaver, "A Discussion of Sallie McFague's *Models of God: Theology for an Ecological, Nuclear Age*: Introduction," *Religion and Intellectual Life* 5 (1988) 9–10.
[5]xi.
[6]In the Introduction to *Speaking in Parables*, McFague states, "This essay is, for me, merely 'on the way'; it does not present an example of the kind of theology it calls for" (8). Although none of her books is "more like a parable than a system," as she puts it, there are other respects in which they exemplify her theological methodology.
[7]36; cf. *Metaphorical Theology*, 193–94; *Body of God*, 84.
[8]This theme is also accented, for example, in the Introduction to *Super, Natural Christians*: "This book is about experimenting with the subject-subjects world model. . . . As much as a book of this sort can do, it is meant to be an experience (sic), a test case, of whether a proposal for seeing everything through the lens of subjecthood is helpful and perhaps even necessary for Christians in our time," 9.
[9]"Response," *Religion and Intellectual Life* 5 (1988) 43–44. In *The Body of God*, McFague advocates a "collegial style" of doing theology; 67ff.

render a fair and accurate account of certain key and characteristic features of McFague's theological ethical project.

In the introduction to *Super, Natural Christians*, in a passage where she is reflecting on the theologian's task, McFague says that her book "is the last in a series of four books on religious language."

> *Metaphorical Theology* laid the groundwork with the claim that since all religious language is metaphorical, alternatives to traditional metaphors are possible. *Models of God* experimented with several alternative models: God as mother, lover, and friend and the world as God's body. *The Body of God* attempted a systematic theology through the lens of one of these models. The present book suggests that a Christian nature spirituality should be based on a subject-subjects model of being, knowing, and doing in place of the subject-object model of Western culture.[10]

I wish to make two observations in light of this remark. First, if there is a center of gravity to McFague's work, I take it to be these four books. Moreover, I think the middle two books, *Models of God* and *The Body of God*, may be taken as most characteristic and most substantive for interpreting McFague's theological ethics. As already implied, there are differences in emphasis and approach in these two books, and there are differences between these two books and McFague's other writings. But these two books raise and address most of the core issues that are present in her work and of relevance to my task. Consequently, my interpretation of McFague will concentrate most heavily on these two books, while also looking both backward and forward to assess her overall approach in the broader context of her other writings.

My second observation is that McFague sees her primary work as a theologian to be concerned with "religious language." She may be a feminist theologian. She may be an ecological theologian with a passionate interest in the natural environment. Her work is clearly motivated by pragmatic moral and ethical concerns, and—as will be noted—characterized by a prophetic style. But her distinctive contribution has been what she has called metaphorical theology. Her key insight has been that all religious language—indeed, all language—is necessarily metaphorical.[11] Therefore, all religious language is provisional and never fully adequate. Our allegiance to any particular religious language must be relativized, for it is subject to a kind of pragmatic ethical validation that may change over time. It can never be taken literally, it may be called into question, and it must at times be revised. In the latter sections of this chapter I will explore McFague's metaphorical theology as a strategy for dealing with a number of issues that must be confronted in order

---

[10] *Super, Natural Christians*, 2.

to advance the purpose of this book, namely, to provide a basis for the articulation of an intellectually *and* religiously adequate theological ethics.

However, it must be stressed both that McFague is more than a metaphorical theologian and that, as a theologian, her work cannot adequately be described simply as metaphorical theology. In fact, the way in which she develops her metaphorical theology needs to be seen against the background of the largely implicit underlying worldview that is manifested in our "post-Christian, secularized culture."[12] For the most part, this worldview is to be identified with modern science, which McFague differentiates from what she calls postmodern science.[13] Modern science is objective, mechanistic, atomistic, deterministic, positivistic, and reductionistic, and leaves little room for God. Postmodern science, by contrast, presents us with a view of reality that is relativistic, holistic, organic and relational, open and dynamic. It has occasioned the opportunity for the reformulation of our understanding of the God–world relationship.[14] Perhaps one could say that, for McFague, modern science has made the reformulation of theology necessary, while postmodern science has made it possible.

McFague's enthusiasm for postmodern science notwithstanding, I will argue that the modern scientific worldview has served as more than historical background to her theological project. It has also continued to frame her perceptions of what is methodologically required to engage in the constructive theological task, and it has done so in ways that are conceptually problematic. One result has been her theology of nature, explicitly articulated in her essay, "Imaging a Theology of Nature,"[15] and then in *The Body of God*.[16] In all her major writings, McFague is obviously interested in integrating scientific and religious perspectives. She is also greatly concerned about the social, cultural, political, and moral implications of religious language. She approaches her task as a Christian whose naturalistic perspective obliges her to reinterpret the language of her faith in ways that are both congruent with her understanding of a postmodern scientific worldview and responsive to the moral dimensions of contemporary life in a world of great inequities and looming threats of nuclear and ecological disaster. Her primary contribution to my task in this book lies in her articulation of the

---

[11]*Metaphorical Theology*, 16.

[12]*Speaking in Parables*, 1. Elsewhere she writes of the loss of a sacramental universe; cf. *Metaphorical Theology*, 1ff.

[13]Recall the discussion in Chapter 1, 32, of Griffin's and McFague's uses of the term "postmodern" to refer to a post-Cartesian, non-mechanistic, non-atomistic, non-positivistic worldview. Significant features of postmodern science, as McFague understands it, will be further elaborated on below.

[14]Cf. "Cosmology and Christianity," in *Theology at the End of Modernity*, edited by Sheila Greeve Davaney (Philadelphia: Trinity, 1991) 25; *The Body of God*, 91ff.; *Metaphorical Theology*, 75ff.

metaphorical character of religious language and the recognition of its moral and ethical significance in shaping perceptions and thus contributing to the construction of our social world. I will have much more to say about this later.

McFague also relies on metaphorical language to attempt a reconciliation of scientific and religious perspectives on the world, however. In this she does not succeed, precisely because the tensions that exist between scientific naturalism and Christian theism do not exist only at the metaphorical level. The limitations of her theology of nature are particularly evident whenever she begins to address issues at the conceptual or metaphysical level. One then sees that she still assumes a universe in which the causal relations among events virtually preclude any attribution of divine influence. Her metaphors are intended to express the God–world relation, but conceptually she has no way to make the connection between God and world.

Soon after writing *The Body of God* McFague must have became aware that her theology of nature was problematic, for she makes a subtle shift away from tentative wrestling with conceptual issues and changes her terminology. In her next book, *Super, Natural Christians*, she no longer describes her approach as a theology of nature. There she speaks of her work as "a Christian nature spirituality,"[17] an approach more closely resembling the "creation spirituality" she criticizes in *The Body of God*.[18] The change appears to be partly semantic, but also substantive. The title, *Super, Natural Christians*, is significant not only for its implied alternative to supernaturalism, but more especially for its emphasis, not on God and theology as such, but on the calling of Christians to care for the natural world.

Nonetheless, I find some form of a theology of nature to be implicit in at least a rudimentary way in all of McFague's books, though the outlooks of her two most recent books are certainly less constrained than most theologies of nature by the knowledge of the world coming to us from the sciences. Hence they are less congruent with the realities of our world as the sciences understand them. But now we need to consider specifically what grounds

---

[15]Birch, Eakin, and McDaniel, op. cit., 201–27

[16]"A Theology of Nature," 65–97. Recall the reference to Ian Barbour's typological description of this way of viewing the relation of science and religion in Chapter 1, 8–9. It is not clear whether McFague is indebted here to Barbour, though she later cites his characterization of a theology of nature approvingly; see "Ian Barbour: Theologian's Friend, Scientist's Interpreter," *Zygon* 31 (1996) 23. Rosemary Radford Ruether also writes of a theology of nature in *Sexism and God-Talk: Toward a Feminist Theology* (Boston: Beacon, 1983) 85–92.

[17]*Super, Natural Christians*, 2. McFague defines Christian nature spirituality as "Christian praxis (reflective practice) extended to the natural world," 9. She also claims her position is "distinctively different" both from what she calls "nature 'spirituality'" and from what she previously (*Models of God*) called "creation spirituality but here (*Super, Natural Christians*) calls "creation theology," 13; 180, n. 12.

there are for identifying McFague's theology as a theology of nature, and to what extent that theology of nature bears significance for McFague's overall approach.

McFague's Theology of Nature

In the first chapter I cited Ian Barbour's delineation of a theology of nature as one that "starts from a religious tradition based on religious experience and historical revelation" and argues "that many of its beliefs are compatible with modern science but some beliefs should be reformulated in light of particular scientific theories."[19] It is not clear whether McFague has directly appropriated this characterization from Barbour. In any event, it must be noted, when she outlines the features of her own version of a theology of nature, her first criterion is that "it must be informed by and commensurate with contemporary scientific accounts of what nature is."[20] In another essay she says that theology "must be based in contemporary reality, not the reality of the scriptural world nor of the medieval or Reformation world nor of Isaac Newton's or René Descartes's world but reality as understood by postmodern science."[21] Later, in *The Body of God*, she says that "a theology of nature attempts to reconceive belief in terms of contemporary views of the natural world. A theology of nature does not solicit the help of science to provide a basis for or to confirm faith, but uses the contemporary picture of reality from the science of its day as a resource to reconstruct and express the faith."[22] In other words, a theology of nature is not a natural theology, which claims evidence for and knowledge of God gained through the exercise of reason in light of our experience and examination of the world.[23] Nor is it an attempt at total synthesis or harmonization of theological and scientific belief. It starts from a religious faith perspective, but modifies some of the content and conceptualization of religious belief in light of what is known, or believed to be known, about the natural world.

There are other, more specific, features that McFague attributes to her theology of nature, but let us begin by considering how her work fits this general description. First of all, it is implicit in all her writings that she stands in, and speaks out of, the Christian tradition. For example, McFague never really argues for the existence of God. The reality of God's existence and benevolence is presented in terms of an initial "wager," on the basis of which we

---

[18] *The Body of God*, 69–73.
[19] Chapter 1, 8.
[20] "Imaging a Theology of Nature," 203.
[21] "Cosmology and Creation," 21.
[22] *The Body of God*, 65–66.

can live and act accordingly.²⁴ For McFague, the content of this "wager" is the religious faith of a Christian:

> Christian faith is, it seems to me, most basically a claim that the universe is neither indifferent nor malevolent, but that there is a power (and a personal power at that) which is on the side of life and its fulfillment. Moreover, the Christian believes that we have some clues for fleshing out this claim in the life, death, and appearances of Jesus of Nazareth.²⁵

In her more recent books, we should note, McFague speaks of God in decidedly less personal and agential terms. In her latest book she says that "God is not the supernatural being who can control what happens, either at a natural or a personal level, but rather is the direction toward flourishing for all creatures. 'God' is the belief that hope and not despair, life not death, laughter not tears are deep in the nature of things . . ."²⁶ We will later have to explore the implications of this move away from personal and agential language for God.

In any event, it remains characteristic of McFague's theology throughout that she believes in a benevolent God or ultimate reality.²⁷ This God promotes the flourishing and fulfillment of all life, but not in any way that could be understood as a form of supernatural intervention. She also believes Jesus Christ to be somehow revelatory of the divine nature, and of true humanity, or "what it means to live under God's rule," but makes no special ontological claims regarding his person. Jesus is *a* (not, *the*) "parable" of God, but his identity with God is denied.²⁸ He is the "exemplar" and "root-metaphor" of Christianity,²⁹ and his life is paradigmatic for the Christian's understanding of the God–world relationship,³⁰ but his death on the cross is not understood in the traditional terms of expiation for human sin.³¹

McFague argues for the authority of the Bible, but again, not in traditional terms. The Bible is not, nor does it contain, supernaturally revealed knowledge or truth. Rather, it has "the authority of a classic poetic text," an authority that is "substantial and enduring, both because *its authority is*

---

²³Cf. ibid., 146–47.
²⁴*Models of God*, 192–93, n. 37; 195–96, n. 13; also, "Response," *Religion and Intellectual Life*, 42, and "Imaging a Theology of Nature," 208.
²⁵Ibid., x; the passage also appears almost verbatim in "Imaging a Theology of Nature," 204, and in somewhat revised form in "Cosmology and Christianity," 30.
²⁶*Life Abundant*, 154–55. Nonetheless, she also speaks of God as "agential" in the same chapter, 151.
²⁷ In *Life Abundant* she also says that "God is reality (being-itself)," 183; cf. *Metaphorical Theology*, 192.

intrinsic . . . and because *its interpretation is flexible*."[32] The New Testament writings, in particular, are "foundational," because they provide the paradigmatic account of Jesus. Still, "we cannot say that the Bible is absolute or authoritative in any sense except the way that a 'classic' text is authoritative: it continues to speak to us."[33]

Clearly, Sallie McFague shares the "modern commitment,"[34] or what at one point she calls the "modern sensibility."[35] Hers is what I am calling a naturalistic perspective. Her discussion of the role of scripture and the Christian tradition in her theology indicates that she shares Gustafson's view that these are ultimately derivative of human experience. "Experience," she says, "is the primary category." She does not mean merely individual experience, nor does she privilege religious experience over other forms of experience. She simply means, with respect to religious sources of theology, "that all our texts, including Scripture and the classics of the theological tradition, are 'sedimentations' of interpreted experience."[36] Thus, as with Gustafson, neither the scriptures nor the Christian tradition are claimed to possess extrinsic or *a priori* authority. Moreover, in a discussion of the nature and importance of experience as a source and warrant for her organic model of the world as God's body, McFague explicitly notes that her view of experience as embodied, physically and culturally, has been specifically informed by Gustafson's position.[37]

Given the priority of experience over other epistemic authorities, it is nonetheless clear that McFague wants to move beyond the intellectual and cultural assumptions of the modern period. She most explicitly identifies her approach with a "postmodern sensibility,"[38] which features "a growing appreciation of the thoroughgoing, radical interdependence of life at all levels and in every imaginable way," and "the recognition of the importance of language (and hence interpretation and construction) in human existence." Her postmodern sensibility also includes a gestalt of other features that appear to be correlated with, if not derived from, a worldview marked by rejection of atomistic mechanism and positivistic science in favor of interdependence and

---

[28] *Metaphorical Theology*, 51–52.
[29] Ibid., 111.
[30] *Models of God*, 45–57.
[31] Ibid., 143ff.
[32] *Metaphorical Theology*, 59.
[33] Ibid., 19.
[34] Cf. Chapter 1, 3.
[35] *Metaphorical Theology*, 49. I take her to mean, at least, the absence of any unwarranted presumption of the reality of God, but also a non-sacramental, non-supernatural apprehension of the world. Her general perspective is more adequately denoted by what she calls the "postmodern sensibility," however.
[36] *Models of God*, 42.

creative construction.³⁹ Among those features are "a greater appreciation of nature, linked with a chastened admiration for technology; . . . the acceptance of the challenge that other religious options present to the Judeo-Christian tradition; a sense of the displacement of the white, Western male and the rise of those dispossessed because of gender, race, or class; and an apocalyptic sensibility."⁴⁰ McFague's constructive metaphorical theological work is clearly permeated by this postmodern sensibility.

But while McFague is eager to move from a "modern" to a "postmodern sensibility," it is never entirely clear whether she recognizes the general conceptual or metaphysical implications of such a transition. For example, she clearly rejects conventional notions of supernaturalism, and at one point implies that her metaphorical approach holds promise of transcending the "modern" distinction between the natural and the supernatural.⁴¹ However, she never engages in an explicit attempt to explain how nature or supernature might be reconceived in a postmodern perspective. Thus, one cannot say whether she thinks this "dualism" can actually be resolved at the conceptual level, or whether it is enough that it be dissolved at the metaphorical level.⁴² Judging from McFague's efforts, metaphorical theology can provide a language of religious metaphors and models in which this distinction, as one of the dualisms that characterize the modern period,⁴³ simply does not receive explicit articulation.

As I have already indicated, it appears that McFague develops her metaphorical approach and her theology of nature out of an implicit metaphysical worldview in which certain conceptual difficulties of the modern period are not resolved but largely obscured. She proposes largely personal, imagistic metaphors for *expressing* the God–world relation. She does not develop more general or metaphysical concepts for *explaining* or *understanding* that relation. All the while, her thought seems to be encumbered by residual elements of a basically "modern" view or understanding of the way the world actually works.

---

³⁷*Body of God*, 87; 240, n. 58.
³⁸In the Preface to the Second Printing of *Metaphorical Theology*, x–xi, and in the Preface to *Models of God*, x–xii.
³⁹*Models of God*, x.
⁴⁰Ibid.
⁴¹Cf. *Models of God*, 10–11.
⁴²Sheila Greeve Davaney notes a lack of conceptual clarity in McFague's work due to her focus on metaphors and models to the neglect of conceptual frameworks; Davaney and John B. Cobb, Jr., "*Models of God: Theology for an Ecological, Nuclear Age*," review article, *Religious Studies Review* 16 (1990) 40. Accepting the view that all language is metaphorical, Gordon D. Kaufman distinguishes between metaphors that are conceptual and imagistic and personal metaphors of the sort that McFague primarily employs, and suggests the need for both; "*Models of God*: Is Metaphor Enough?" *Religion and Intellectual Life* 5 (1988) 16–18.

For example, although she eschews an atomistic, mechanistic view of nature, she still seems to assume that the relationships among natural events are to be understood solely in terms of material causation. At least, there can be no divine influence on, or contribution to, the course of natural events. Thus, in a discussion of events that philosophers of religion often refer to as natural evils, McFague can say, "God is not the *cause* of these events and *cannot be* if we take seriously *the* contemporary scientific picture of reality."[44] In the first place, there is no single "contemporary scientific picture of reality," but in the second place, at least some "postmodern" scientific understandings allow for divine influence or causation within natural events in ways that "modern" mechanistic, materialistic scientific understandings have not. This is but a specific instance of a still pervasive indebtedness that one can detect in McFague's work to a "modern" conceptualization of the God–world relationship. The point is *not* that God causes natural events to occur that are injurious to human welfare, but that McFague seems to rule out categorically any direct divine involvement in the sphere of nature. However she proposes to express the God–world relation, it does not appear that she understands God to have much if anything to do with what transpires in the processes of non-human events.[45]

At the same time, one can detect developments in her thought that indicate rethinking of earlier theological formulations that have been rendered problematic by the modern sensibility. For example, in the Preface to *Metaphorical Theology* she writes, "I have not found it possible as a contemporary Christian to support an incarnational christology . . ."[46] Here she is no doubt rejecting a "two natures" christology, that is, Jesus Christ as both human being and God, and therefore God in the flesh. But, in developing her model of the world as the body of God, she has since reconceived the meaning of incarnation, so that she can say, "Jesus Christ is the incarnation of God,"[47] but also, "we are God incarnate."[48] It is important to note, the change is not only metaphorical but also conceptual.

Clearly, McFague's religious beliefs have been profoundly informed by, and reconceived in light of, modern scientific understandings, as well as the

---

[43]In *Models of God*, 10, McFague's list of the "old dualisms" she hopes to transcend includes spirit/flesh, human/nonhuman, objective/subjective, and reason/passion, as well as supernatural/natural. Her metaphors explicitly address some of these dualisms better than others. She mentions other dualisms to be overcome, including culture/nature and mind/body, in "An Earthly Theological Agenda," *Christian Century* 108 (1991) 12.

[44]*Body of God*, 176; my emphasis. She also says, "If one intends to take scientific explanation seriously, then no teleological maneuvers should be considered"; ibid., 76. Cf. her statement regarding biological events that "evolutionary theory tells us can have only local causes"; ibid., 145.

[45]It is less clear whether McFague thinks God influences human events. In *Models of God*, she writes of "experiences of relating to God" (39), and even possibly of experiences of God (192,

critical perspectives of history and the social sciences. She has abandoned most of the same orthodox Christian convictions that Gustafson has abandoned, and largely for similar reasons. One major exception to this should be noted. Her view of the divine benevolence is coupled with a vision of the divine purpose that looks forward to an ultimate healing, harmony, and unity of creation. This vision does not depend on a particular reading of the evolutionary process. Some natural theologies may claim to discern a teleological orientation in evolutionary history, but her claim is a matter of faith. "It is," she says, "a retrospective, not a prospective, claim; it begins with experiences of healing and salvation that one wagers are from God, and reads back into creation the hope that the whole creation is included within the divine healing, liberating powers."[49]

McFague has been criticized for the development of an ecological theology that does not take seriously the conflicts, suffering, and losses of evolutionary struggle, let alone the realities of "tooth and claw" in every ecological environment.[50] Ironically, this is a criticism that she herself makes against creation spirituality in *The Body of God*. In a passage that refers specifically to the work of Thomas Berry, she writes:

> But what Berry and other creation spirituality writers lack is a sense of the awful oppression that is part and parcel of the awesome mystery and splendor. The universe has not been for most species, and certainly not for most individuals within the various species, a 'gorgeous celebratory event.' It has been a story of struggle, loss, and often early death. To see the universe and especially our planet as 'the primary mode of the divine presence,' as Berry does, is to claim implicitly an optimistic arrow in the evolutionary story, a position that Berry's mentor, Teilhard de Chardin, embraced but that few if any scientists are willing to allow. Creation spirituality suggests an ungrounded optimism, based in part on its reading of evolutionary history but also on an illumination model of how human beings change: to know the good is to do the good. If we learn about the common creation story and where we fit into the scheme of things, we *will* change.[51]

---

n. 37), though these would not necessary entail divine influence. However, she also affirms the view that with the emergence of human beings, God begins to provide "direction" to the evolutionary process; *Body of God*, 148. The implicit human/nonhuman dichotomy (dualism?) of such a view is never justified. Cf. my discussion below, Chapter 4.
[46] *Body of God*, viii.
[47] *Life Abundant*, 13.
[48] Ibid., 183.
[49] *Body of God*, 181; cf. *Metaphorical Theology*, 143.
[50] See, e.g., Sideris, op. cit., 60–90.

It is hard to imagine McFague offering this critique after reading her *Super, Natural Christians*. Lisa Sideris, based largely on her reading of that book, argues that McFague's "ecological model is not the 'modern evolutionary, ecological perspective.' It is simply the peaceable kingdom, a corrective to nature as it really is."[52] McFague knows that there is dissonance between Christianity's vision of inclusiveness, which she extends even to the most vulnerable creatures, and "biological evolution, in which millions are wasted . . . and even whole species are wiped out in the blinking of an eye."[53] But already in *The Body of God*, with its metaphor of the world as God's body, McFague seems to regard the planet as "the primary mode of divine presence,"[54] and to harbor an unduly optimistic hope for human change and planetary harmony. Religious faith manifestly trumps ecological and evolutionary science when it comes to McFague's eschatology. But then, McFague never promised otherwise. As she alerted her readers from the very beginning of her major book on ecological theology:

> This book is not about science, although it uses science as a resource for theology. The model of the world or universe as God's body is, I will argue, in keeping with the view of reality coming to us from contemporary science. It is a plausible theological response to that view of reality, a response that ought to make Christian interpretations of the relations between God and the world more credible than interpretations based on out-moded views of reality. This essay is not, however, about shaping theology to science, finding a tight fit between the two areas on particular issues. Rather, it is interested in a loose fit between the contemporary scientific picture and theological reconstruction. This is a *theological*, not a scientific project.[55]

It should be added, McFague's work is not only a theological project, it is also an exercise in moral discourse, with both ethical and prophetic dimensions.[56] Her primary aim is not to be descriptively realistic, but prescriptive, or at least advocational.[57] She seeks to enlist her reader in the restoration and healing of creation, not leaving our environments to the perfidies of human exploitation or the vagaries of "benign neglect."[58]

---

[51] *Body of God*, 71.
[52] Op. cit., 83; cf. *Super, Natural Christians*, 158.
[53] *Body of God*, 171. Scientists believe there have been five great extinctions in the earth's natural history, beginning with the Ordovician extinction, some 440 million years ago, when two-thirds of all species were killed, and as recent as the Cretaceous-Tertiary event that destroyed the dinosaurs and half of all other species about 65 million years ago; *Bloomington Herald-Times*, January 8, 2004, A7.
[54] Ibid., 182.

Indeed, there is a fundamentally ethical purpose in all of McFague's work.[59] If she abandons or significantly reformulates a number of traditional Christian tenets, it is not simply because they have become intellectually untenable from her contemporary (naturalistic) perspective. As I will discuss below, it is also because they function in harmful ways. They are ways of imagining, or construing, the God–world relationship that do not promote right relationships among human beings and other "subjects" in the natural world.[60] That McFague holds on to what appears to be a rather romantic and utopian Christian eschatology, the harsh realities of evolutionary and ecological science to the contrary, may likewise be for moral or ethical reasons. She is in any case convinced we need to imagine the world, and its relation to God, in more hopeful terms that evoke our love and care.

Nonetheless, it remains problematic that this *imagining* of the world is presented as a *re-imagining* in light of the picture of the world coming to us from contemporary science, ecological science in particular. Is there sufficient congruence between the view of the world provided by ecological science and the view of the world in McFague's moral eschatology to lend the latter credibility? It would take us too far afield to explore this question here in much depth. My point in raising it is to illustrate that, even though McFague's approach may be characterized as a theology of nature, she is hardly constrained in her theological affirmations by what can be reconciled with the knowledge of the sciences. This is an important difference in her approach when compared with that of James Gustafson.

In fact, McFague's appropriation of scientific knowledge differs substantially from Gustafson's. As an ethicist, Gustafson makes extensive use of

---

[55]Ibid., ix.
[56]James Gustafson distinguishes among four types of moral discourse, ethical, prophetic, narrative, and policy; cf. *Intersections*, 37–55. The purpose of ethical discourse, in his terms, is "to decide how one ought to act in particular circumstances"; 39. Prophetic discourse tends to view matters in larger perspective, and to take the form of either indictment or utopian vision; 41–42. In these terms, McFague's work would seem to be more prophetic than ethical. However, I think it can still be considered under the rubric of theological ethics.
[57]"Cosmology and Christianity," 19, 21; *Body of God*, 68–69.
[58]For example, with respect to how subjects, human and nonhuman, are to live together in an ecological community characterized by care and justice, McFague writes, "We do not have utopias on earth, but we do have some towns and cities, and even some countries, that are closer to the dream than others. It is our responsibility to work for as close a match to the dream as we can in the places where we live"; *Super, Natural Christians*, 158.
[59]Cf. Rosemary Radford Ruether, "*The Body of God: An Ecological Theology*," review article, *Interpretation* 48 (1994) 316: "Her ultimate purpose is ethical, the very purpose she affirms must be the purpose of all theology."
[60]Cf. *Body of God*, 69.

particular scientific knowledge in exploring and deciding about particular issues of moral significance. At the same time, Gustafson is interested in the larger implications of a scientific understanding of the world, or "how things really are," for his theological construal of the relation of God and the world. McFague makes little appeal to particular scientific knowledge. Her interest lies in the broad features of science, or what she calls "the picture of reality coming to us from the sciences."[61] Unlike Gustafson, she does not think this "picture of reality" tells us "how things really are." Even when Gustafson's realism is not naive but critical, even when he acknowledges that all scientific data are theory-laden and all scientific knowledge is interpretation, he clearly regards the view of the world that comes to us from the sciences to be much more closely congruent, or isomorphic, with reality than McFague ever claims. For McFague, scientific language, like theological language, is highly metaphorical—even imaginative—and model-dependent. Moreover, in the final analysis, McFague's interest in science seems to come down to two primary and related foci. One of these is the nature of the world as viewed by what she identifies as postmodern science. The other is what she calls the "common creation story."[62]

As previously noted, according to McFague, the worldview of postmodern science is no longer the closed, mechanistic, atomistic world of Descartes and Newton, but rather the organic and relational, open and dynamic world of post-Newtonian cosmology, evolutionary biology, and ecological science.[63] The postmodern worldview emphasizes interrelatedness and interdependence, unity and diversity, a high degree of complexity and individuation, and the interplay of chance and necessity. The universe is understood to be multi-leveled, with a correlation between increasing complexification and increasing subjectivity. Several of these themes are captured in a brief paragraph that McFague quotes from Ian Barbour:

> Cosmology joins evolutionary biology, molecular biology, and ecology in showing the interdependence of all things. We are part of an ongoing community of being; we are kin to all creatures, past and present. From astrophysics we know our indebtedness to a common legacy of physical elements. The chemical elements in your hand and brain were forged in the furnaces of the stars. The cosmos is all of one piece. It is multi-leveled, each new higher level was built on lower levels from the past. Humanity is the most advanced form of life of

---

[61] Cf. McFague, "Ian Barbour: Theologian's Friend, Scientist's Interpreter," 23.
[62] Cf. *Body of God*, 27ff.; "Cosmology and Creation," 31ff.
[63] 95 above.

which we know, but it is fully a part of a wider process in space and time.[64]

All things, in this view, have a common origin. Their differences are understood in terms of evolutionary processes of differentiation that do not belie, but bespeak, their ultimate interrelatedness or unity. Causal relationships are not understood in a strictly deterministic way, leaving room for genuine novelty to emerge. This broad-brush view of the character of the universe provides McFague the basis for her organic model of the world as a body, and receives further articulation in terms of the common creation story.

The common creation story is not a story from scripture or religious tradition, but precisely the generalized account of the origins of the universe accepted by the majority of scientific cosmologists today. It all begins with the Big Bang, some fifteen billion years ago.[65]

> From this beginning came all that followed, so that everything that is, is related, woven into a seamless web, with life gradually emerging after billions of years on our planet (and probably on others as well) and evolving into the marvelously complex and beautiful forms we see about us. All things living and all things not living are the products of the same primal explosion and evolutionary history and hence are interrelated in an internal way right from the beginning.[66]

There are three features of this common creation story, as McFague presents it, that I want to highlight at this point. One is the acknowledgment that life probably exists elsewhere in the universe. For the most part, however, this probability does not figure significantly in the language that McFague uses to speak of her "cosmocentric" perspective. Second, McFague observes that the direction of the evolutionary process is toward diversity, but she sees no need to attribute this direction to anything other than natural physical processes.[67] "The common creation story . . . claims that no special entity, principle, or substance needs to be or should be introduced to explain the evolution of the universe from its simple (sic) beginning to its present outcome."[68] In other words, McFague, like Gustafson, apparently sees no need to appeal either to teleological principle or to divine purpose to account for the emergence of all that is. To be sure, McFague is describing or reporting the common creation story, as scientists have constructed it, but she is also taking it to be an adequate account, at least on scientific terms.[69]

---

[64]Barbour, *Religion in an Age of Science*, 147; cited in *Body of God*, 27–28; cf. McFague, *Super, Natural Christians*, 20.
[65]The latest estimates seem to be a billion or so years lower.
[66]"Cosmology and Christianity," 31.

The third point to be noted is that this common creation story, and all the general features of the universe that McFague identifies with it, are regarded as more than simply a "picture of reality." For all practical purposes, she treats this picture of the world as if it tells us what the world is really like. In this respect, she is not far from Gustafson. In terms of her methodology, the common creation story may only provide a model of the universe, but it is a model on which to bet our lives, our fortunes, and the future of this planet:

> The common creation story is more than a scientific affair; it is, implicitly, deeply moral, for it raises the question of the place of human beings in nature, and calls for a kind of praxis in which we see ourselves in proportion, in harmony, and in a fitting manner relating to all others that live and all the systems that support life.

In words reminiscent of themes we have seen accented by Gustafson, McFague continues:

> To feel that we belong to the earth and to accept our proper place within it is the beginning of a natural piety, what Jonathan Edwards called 'consent to being,' consent to what is. It is the sense that we and all others belong together in a cosmos, related in an orderly fashion, one to the other. It is the sense that each and every being is valuable in and for itself, and that the whole forms a unity in which each being, including oneself, has a place. In involves an ethical response, for the sense of belonging, of being at home, only comes when we accept our proper place and live in a fitting, appropriate way with all other beings. It is, finally, at a deep level, an aesthetic and religious sense, a response of wonder at and appreciation for the unbelievably vast, old,

---

[67] *Body of God*, 45.
[68] Ibid., 47; cf. 38–47; 118.
[69] In my judgment, McFague's view of causation, even if not strictly deterministic, rules out any claims of divine agency. Hers is more a modern than a postmodern perspective, as I hope will become clearer in Chapter 4. Interestingly enough, in a recent essay she makes no mention of the "common creation story," writing instead of the "creation-providence story" within Christian tradition; "Sallie McFague," in William C. Placher, editor, *Essentials of Christian Theology* (Louisville: Westminster John Knox, 2003) 101–16. While emphasizing what she takes to be the implications of this story for how we are to live justly and sustainably, she also appears to be deliberately modifying her terminology not only to suggest faith's conviction of God's continuing involvement in the world, but also to allow for the possible conceptualization of divine agency. Inasmuch as the world is God's body and God is incarnate in the world, God presumably may be thought of as having an intimate role in all that happens as "the spirit empowering the universe" (109). McFague also insists, however, that God shares power with the world or creation (114). As elsewhere, she herself offers no account of how the God–world relation is to be conceived.

rich, diverse, and surprising cosmos, of which one's self is an infinitesimal but conscious part, the part able to sing its praises.[70]

The common creation story, and the generalized picture of the nature of reality that McFague associates with it, constitute the major portion of what science has to contribute to McFague's construction of her theology of nature.

I began this section by recounting McFague's first criterion for a theology of nature, that it be "informed by and commensurate with contemporary scientific accounts of what nature is." She proposes three additional criteria, the bases for which should now be at least partially evident: (1) A theology of nature "needs to see human life as profoundly interrelated with all other forms of life, refusing the traditional absolute separation of human beings from other creatures as well as of God from the world." (2) It will also be "creation-centered, in contrast to the almost total concern with redemption in some Christian theologies." (3) Finally, a theology of nature "will acknowledge and press the interconnectedness of peace, justice, and ecological issues, aware that there can be no peace or justice unless the fabric of our ecosystem is intact." McFague pronounces, expansively, "What this means, I believe, is that for the first time in the history of the human race, we see the necessity of thinking responsibly and deeply about *everything that is*."[71] More prosaically, it means that we must think holistically. Gustafson, we saw in the last chapter, argues the need to perceive and think in terms of larger wholes.[72] McFague in effect does him one better. Nonetheless, one hopes she would concede that we cannot think in terms of any whole larger than that of which we can gain enough knowledge, understanding, and perspective to make meaning or sense with respect to whatever matters of value or ethical significance are perceived to be at stake.

Because my aim in this book is to critique and appropriate the work of Gustafson and McFague, as well as Griffin, toward the articulation of a more adequate theological ethics, it is crucial to identify a substantial congruence or "fit" among these three thinkers on a range of issues constitutive of such an ethics. Perhaps the most useful way to provide a further elaboration of McFague's theology of nature is to compare and relate various other features of her theological ethics to those of Gustafson. Once this is done, we will be prepared to examine and assess the role that her metaphorical approach plays in addressing what she perceives to be the most problematic issues for Christian theology, ethics, and life in our time.

---

[70]*Body of God*, 111–12; the same passage appears in "Cosmology and Creation," 39–40.
[71]"Imaging a Theology of Nature," 203.
[72]Chapter 2, 73–74.

McFague's Theological Perspective in Profile

Naturalism

In the foregoing section I have sought to indicate the largely implicit naturalistic assumptions that inform McFague's theology of nature. Like David Griffin, she appears to be a naturalist in rejecting both epistemic and ontological supernaturalism. It is less clear whether she accepts the type of naturalism that Griffin calls "domain uniformitarianism," the view that "religion is to be explained in terms of the same causal categories that are used in other cultural domains."[73] McFague is not a social scientist or historian, and does not discuss or try to explain religion in such terms. To the extent that she does try to explain religion, it is in terms of the language that is used to express religious belief. She repeatedly reveals her conviction that the way we think and perceive affects the way we act and live.[74] To some extent this is surely true. But she simply does not address the question of how the major features of any religion are to be explained. She presents her own religious outlook as a matter of faith, understood as a "wager" regarding the "truth" of one's (metaphorically expressed) religious beliefs, pragmatically confirmed by believing and acting accordingly.[75] This suggests a view of religion—at least her own—that might be explainable in psychological categories, but hardly in sociological, historical, or cultural terms.

It is doubtful that McFague would agree with Griffin's other characterization of naturalism in terms of the notion of "empirical groundedness," the view that religious claims are susceptible to empirical testing just as are scientific claims. She certainly does not think that theological truth claims are as subject to empirical testing as those of scientific theories: "there are no empirical tests of the verifiability or falsifiability of theological statements of the order we find in science."[76] On the one hand, therefore, there is "no way behind our constructions to test them for their correspondence with the reality they presume to represent."[77] On the other hand, theological models, which provide the basis for theological truth claims, are subject to a kind of empirical testing:

> The isomorphism between scientific models and the reality to which they refer is capable of much more careful testing than is the case with theological models. But even for theology such testing is not totally absent. The isomorphism, or similarity of structure, between

---

[73]Cf. Chapter 1, 10.
[74]E.g., *Metaphorical Theology*, xi; *Body of God*, 77, 202; *Super, Natural Christians*, 2, 6; *Life Abundant*, xi.
[75]*Models of God*, 192–93, n. 37; 195–96, n. 13.

our models and the divine-human relationship can certainly never be direct. We do not *know* that our models of father and mother, of liberator and friend, of creator and redeemer, really reflect the structure of the divine-human relationship. At most, we can say that, given our experiences of healing, of liberation, of renewal, and so on, they appear to be apt or appropriate to the most profound dimensions of human existence. Such a statement is, of course, finally a statement of faith, and it can only be made responsibly and convincingly in light of the anomalies, especially the experience of evil in ourselves and in the world, which often, and for some people constantly, appear more real than experiences supporting belief in God.[78]

For McFague's theology of nature, it is desirable that the isomorphism between theological models and human experience that she describes in this paragraph also be corroborated by an isomorphism between the theological models and scientific understandings of the world.[79] But, as we have seen with respect to McFague's eschatology, this is not finally determinative. The validity or "truth" of a theological model is thus not only a matter of "fit." There are two other important criteria. One is the material norm of "demonstrable continuities" with the Christian paradigm.[80] For McFague, the key features of the story of Jesus are his speaking in parables, his table fellowship with outcasts, his death on a cross, and the appearance stories. Based on her interpretation of this paradigmatic Christian story she argues for "a destabilizing, inclusive, nonhierarchical vision of fulfillment for all of creation,"[81] and on this basis she develops her models of the world as God's body and God as mother, lover, and friend.

But there is also a pragmatic criterion for McFague's theological models. "[M]odels are selected and survive because they make sense out of human experience."[82]

> How does one come to accept a model as true? We live *within* the model, testing our wager by its consequences. These consequences are both theoretical and practical. An adequate model will be illuminating, fruitful, have relatively comprehensive explanatory ability, be relatively consistent, be able to deal with anomalies, and so on. . . . [I]n the tradition of Aristotle, truth means constructing the good life for the polis, though for our time this must mean for the cosmos. A 'true'

---

[76] *Metaphorical Theology*, 105.
[77] *Models of God*, 26.
[78] Ibid., 142–43; cf. *Body of God*, 181.
[79] Cf. *Metaphorical Theology*, 141.
[80] Ibid., 41, 44ff.

model of God will be one that is a powerful, persuasive construal of God as being on the side of life and its fulfillment in our time.[83]

In sum, McFague's theological perspective is only partially conformed to naturalistic scientific understandings of the world. She agrees with Griffin and Gustafson in rejecting epistemic and ontological supernaturalism. We may perhaps also attribute to her weak versions of the forms of naturalism identified by Griffin as "domain uniformitarianism" and "empirical groundedness," though her views on the former are mostly unstated and on the latter significantly qualified. What she thinks regarding the forms of naturalism that Griffin rejects is even harder to determine.[84]

We have seen where McFague seems to reject the notion that God "causes" natural events to happen. She also acknowledges that she accepts "scientific reductionism" as a methodology, though not as a metaphysics.[85] That is to say, she thinks it is a legitimate research strategy for scientists to try to explain everything they can with a given theory, so long as they do not presume that everything can be so explained.[86] But does this mean she thinks some events can be fully and adequately explained on materialist assumptions? If so, then what distinguishes those events from other events that are not susceptible to such explanation? If not, then are there additional grounds on which some events can be fully and adequately explained? Or are full and adequate explanations simply not to be had?

If McFague thinks it is possible, in principle if not in fact, for natural events (at least those that are non-human) to be accounted for solely in terms of their material causes, then it is not clear that God makes any difference in the world. In *The Body of God* she does seem to view God as the world's primary cause,[87] and in that limited sense as the world's "creator and sustainer."[88] Moreover, with—and only with—the emergence of human beings, she attributes *direction* to God,[89] a peculiar claim for one who wants to overcome the dualism of the human/nonhuman. Clearly, McFague rejects metaphysical reductionism because she does not want to say that the cosmos consists

---

[81] Ibid., 49. In *Super, Natural Christians* the paradigm is reformulated as Jesus' "destabilizing, inclusive solidarity with the poor and the oppressed," 16.
[82] Ibid., 143.
[83] "Imaging a Theology of Nature," 208. On the same page McFague says, "The 'truth' of a construal of the God–world relationship is a mixture of belief (Ricoeur calls it a 'wager'), pragmatic criteria, and what Philip Wheelwright terms a 'shy ontological claim'." If one thinks of belief in terms of the Christian tradition, and the ontological claim in terms of an isomorphism of theological and scientific models, we have a corroborating identification of her three bases for theological truth claims. See also McFague, "Response," 43–44, for a brief discussion of the importance of pragmatic criteria for justifying ontological claims.
[84] Cf. Chapter 1, 10.
[85] *Body of God*, 92–93.
[86] Cf. ibid., 241, ns. 68, 69.

only of physical or material entities. She wants to speak of God as an agential reality. However, if she takes the natural world to be comprehensible without any assumption of divine influence in nonhuman events, then, apart from dogmatic assertions or claims of faith regarding divine influence in human culture, it is not clear that she has any grounds for rejecting those forms of naturalism Griffin identifies with atheism and materialism.[90]

On the other hand, her whole project would appear to be at odds with the form of naturalism that denies personal causation. Morever, the kinds of experiential claims she makes in her latest book, *Life Abundant*, would seem to be at odds with the view that all experience derives from sensory stimulation, the form of naturalism that Griffin calls "sensationism."[91] My conclusion is that McFague is no more a scientific materialist than Gustafson. But, very much like Gustafson, the extent and limits of her naturalism are fuzzy. This is largely because she lacks a conceptualization of the relation of God to the world that would provide some basis for understanding how it is, or could be, that God is active in the causal nexus of events as an effective power or presence in the world. In short, McFague does not tell us anything about how God—not just human conceptions, images, or metaphors of God—might conceivably make a real difference in what transpires in the cosmos.[92]

Theocentrism

McFague apparently regards her theological perspective as theocentric, though she also wants to denote it as life-centered and cosmocentric.[93] Each of these three terms, she notes, "highlights a somewhat different focus on a set of interrelated entities: God, life, and the total environment that both supports and includes life."[94] Each of these terms provides an alternative to a human-centered, or anthropocentric, perspective.

McFague is clearly familiar with Gustafson's *Ethics from a Theocentric Perspective*, and makes common cause with him in critiquing anthropocentrism. But while Gustafson's attack on anthropocentrism derives much of its passion from his theocentric piety, McFague is much more oriented by a passionate concern for the planet and its life-sustaining ecosystems. It may only be on account of Gustafson's *Ethics* that she speaks of theocentrism at all. She professes to be theocentric,[95] however, she does not invoke it all that often. The

---
[88]Ibid., 148. Recall the discussion of God as primary cause in Chapter 1, 21–22.
[89]Ibid.
[90]Atheism being the view that there are no causal powers beyond the totality of finite causes, and materialism the view that denies the existence of any other than physical or material entities; cf. Chapter 1, 10.
[91]Cf. *Life Abundant*, 8ff.
[92]In *Models of God*, 73, McFague states, "If the entire universe . . . is God's body, then God acts in and through the incredibly complex physical and historical-cultural evolutionary process

point to a *cosmo*centric perspective, however, is to emphasize the new picture coming to us from the sciences regarding who we human beings are in relation to the whole of creation, or the cosmos.

In one of her most focused critiques of anthropocentrism McFague observes, "Traditionally, theological anthropology, by constructing the human image after the divine image, as a reflection of it, has separated human existence from its empirical, cosmic setting."[96] Although science must not dictate theological anthropology, according to McFague, science must be taken seriously as a resource for reconstructing our central theological doctrines. Science does not speak to us about theology, but it surely tells us something about reality, including the interrelatedness and interdependence of all things. Moreover, when we take in view the whole of existence as we are coming to understand it through science, we implicitly enlarge our view of God, insofar as God is understood to be the Creator of the universe, whose concerns are not limited to our human well-being. So there is a theological warrant, as well as an empirical one, for a more cosmocentric perspective. McFague summarizes her case against anthropocentrism:

> My thesis has been that whatever more one wants to say about who we are, to be credible and persuasive, as well as on the side of life and its fulfillment for our planet, it must be in keeping with the broad parameters of the view of reality coming from postmodern science. . . . Once one accepts this view of who we are in the scheme of things there can be no return to anthropocentrism. Once the scales have fallen from our eyes, once we have seen and believed that reality is put together in such a fashion that we are profoundly united to and interdependent with all other beings, everything is changed. One sees the world differently, not anthropocentrically, not in a utilitarian way, not in terms of dualistic hierarchies, not in parochial terms. One has a sense of belonging to the earth, of having a place in it, and of loving it more than one ever thought possible.[97]

---

that began eons ago. This does not mean that God is reduced to the evolutionary process, for God remains as the agent, the self, whose intentions are expressed in the universe." What could this possibly mean, given how McFague develops her model of the world as God's body, as well as her rejection of divine causation, in *The Body of God*? As we have seen above (107), McFague finds no need to invoke God's presence or activity to account for the whole of evolutionary history.

[93]"Imaging a Theology of Nature," 202, 203, 219–20, ns. 2, 3; *Body of God*, 167.
[94]Ibid., 220, n. 3.
[95]Cf. *Body of God*, 68, 144; cf. *Life Abundant*, 7, 30.
[96]"Cosmology and Christianity," 22.

A scientific view of humanity's place in the universe informs and provides warrant for McFague's critique of anthropocentrism, just as it does Gustafson's. But, as suggested by this passage, it is not really *theo*centrism, nor even *cosmo*centrism, that animates McFague's critique. What really counts is being "on the side of life and its fulfillment for this planet," which calls for loving the earth "more than one ever thought possible." If an *anthropo*centric perspective is one in which *human* interests, values, and aspirations are uppermost, because human beings are regarded as the "measure of all things," then McFague's perspective approaches being an *earth*-centered, or *geo*centric one. For her, it seems to be all about the continued flourishing and fulfillment of life on this planet. She appeals to science and the "common creation story" to de-center human beings in the scheme of the universe, only to place planet Earth at the center instead.

This judgment needs to be qualified in one significant respect. In *Models of God* McFague develops the metaphor of the world as God's body, and in *The Body of God* this image becomes the central metaphor for her understanding of the God–world relation. The metaphor implies a kind of re-sacralization of the world: "The world in our model is the sacrament of God, the visible, physical, bodily presence of God."[98] This means, on the one hand, that the world is a source of divine grace, or blessing. It mediates to all creatures and living things God's gift of life. But it also means, on the other hand, that loving the world is tantamount to loving God's body, and thus of loving God. Inasmuch as Earth is a part of the world, it is a part of God's body, so that loving the Earth is a way of loving God. Or, as McFague later puts it, "we are created to give God glory by loving the earth."[99] Even more recently she writes, "In our model, the body of God is the entire universe; it is all matter in its myriad, fantastic, ancient, and modern forms, from quarks to galaxies. More specifically, the body of God needing our attention is planet Earth, a tiny piece of divine embodiment that is our home and garden."[100]

Pragmatically speaking, does it not make sense to limit the scope of one's moral and ethical concerns to life on Earth? Not entirely, if one's perspective is scientifically informed. The possibility that some forms of life may exist even on other bodies within our solar system has led scientists in the United States space program to take steps to avoid contaminating the environments of these other solar bodies with microorganisms from Earth. A truly cosmocentric perspective that exercises solicitude for all life need look no further for reason to extend its sphere of interest and moral concern beyond our planet.

---

[97] Ibid., 38.
[98] *Body of God*, 182.
[99] *Life Abundant*, 54.

We may never discover other life in our solar system or the rest of the universe, but the possibility that such life, including intelligent life, exists is one reason for keeping the Earth as the penultimate, not the ultimate, focus of our concern. A second reason, explicitly articulated by Gustafson, lies in the knowledge that some day all life will be extinguished on our planet regardless of the stewardship we exercise over our global environment.[101]

Conversion

Another way to compare and contrast McFague's cosmocentric theocentrism with Gustafson's more radically theocentric perspective is to examine what she has to say about conversion. No less than Gustafson's *Ethics*, her writings are a call to conversion, although for the most part, like Gustafson, she avoids the language of conversion. For Gustafson, the conversion needed is couched in terms of a turn from anthropocentrism to theocentrism. But for McFague, again, the call is for conversion from anthropocentrism to cosmocentrism[102] or, as she puts it, following Rosemary Ruether, a "conversion" to the earth.[103] In a somewhat autobiographical article written between *Models of God* and *The Body of God*, McFague contends:

> The enemy—indifferent, selfish, shortsighted, xenophobic, anthropocentric, greedy human beings—calls, at the very least, for a renewed emphasis on sin as the cause of much of the planet's woes and an emphasis on a broad and profound repentance. Theology, along with other institutions, fields of study and expertise, can deepen our sense of complicity in the earth's decay. In addition to turning our eyes and hearts to an appreciation of the beauty, richness and singularity of our planet through a renewed theology of creation and nature, theology ought also to underscore and elaborate on the myriad ways that we personally and corporately have ruined and continue to ruin God's splendid creation—acts which we and no other creature can knowingly commit. The present dire situation calls for radicalizing the Christian understanding of sin and evil.[104]

In the same article, as well as in the opening chapter of *Life Abundant*, McFague actually attributes her own conversion to this changed perspective to her reading of a 1982 address by theologian Gordon Kaufman.[105] The resulting "cosmocentric" perspective clearly informs her four subsequent books, as well as her other writings. But in *Life Abundant* she also describes another personal con-

---

[100] Placher, op. cit., 111.
[101] *Ethics I*, 83.
[102] *Life Abundant*, 7.
[103] "Imaging a Theology of Nature," 202.

version, a conversion that, while not away from cosmocentrism, seems to be more aptly spoken of in terms of theocentrism than her previous perspectives. "Finally, after years of talking *about* God," she confesses, "I am becoming acquainted *with* God."[106] As becomes evident, the focus of McFague's perspective has shifted. She has become much more explicit about linking her moral concerns to God:

> Theology *is* about God; if it isn't, it's not theology. I will suggest that North American theology should be about economics and politics, consumerism and its alternatives, global warming and diversity, but *as they* contribute or diminish to giving glory to God by loving the world. A cosmocentric theology—or any other—must be theocentric: theology is about *God* and the world. . . . Nothing else matters except God or, to phrase it differently, everything else matters as it is related to God. God is not an object or abstraction added *to* the world, but the ground and source *of* the world. God is not a being in whom we should believe, but the breath of life in every being that exists. God is not a possibility within reality, but reality itself. To say yes to God is simply to trust reality; it is to acknowledge that reality is good.[107]

It is possible that in this much more direct language about God we are seeing nothing more than a shift away from the personal and imagistic metaphors of earlier writings—a shift that is already evident in *The Body of God*—to a more conceptual metaphor of God as "reality" or "being-itself," a conception that shows indebtedness to theologian Paul Tillich.[108] But I think we can also take McFague at her word and conclude that God has become more real to her, not as a personal being but as a reality within personal experience. That is to say, the ultimate with whom, or with which, she has to do (and with whom, or with which, we all have to do) calls forth a response that can no longer be adequately expressed only in terms of "loving the earth." Setting aside any question regarding the adequacy of her conception of God, I think her latest book goes much further than her previous writings in making good on her stated commitment to a theocentric perspective. The call to conversion away from an anthropocentric perspective is now not only a call to a cosmocentric perspective, needed to change human thinking and acting in order to avoid planetary disaster, but to a life in which loving the world is conceived to be the means of giving glory to God.

---

[104]"An Earthly Theological Agenda," *Christian Century* 108 (1991) 15.
[105]Ibid., 13 (the date stated in the article, 1983, is incorrect); "Christianity and Cosmology," 19, n. 1; *Life Abundant*, 6–7.
[106]Ibid., 8.
[107]Ibid., 39, 127.
[108]So far as I can tell, McFague's ontological view of God is basically Tillichian, despite her assertions that we cannot know God's "nature"; cf. *Metaphorical Theology*, 96–97, 119, 192;

Sin

We saw in Chapter 2 that James Gustafson wants to retain but also reformulate the emphasis on human sin in the Reformed tradition. Thus he writes of human sin in terms of "fault."[109] Sin runs deep in the human condition, and there is no prospect for its eradication. Profound insights into the human condition are captured by some of Christianity's traditional language about sin. Gustafson and McFague agree in rejecting the notion that the work of salvation accomplished by Jesus of Nazareth's death on the cross was an expiation for human sin. Both understand salvation less in terms of redemption from human sin and more in terms of the greater realization of the actual possibilities that are given to us and all life in the creation. For Gustafson, the conversion from anthropocentrism to theocentrism entails a conversion from self-centeredness to a much wider sphere of interest and concern. It also implies an acceptance of human finitude rather than the implicit denial of such finitude in prideful human efforts to be the measure of all things, in effect, usurping the place of God.

Although McFague is even less inclined than Gustafson to use traditional language about human sin, there is substantial congruity between her view and his. We have seen her indictment of human beings as "the enemy," and her call for a radicalization of the Christian understanding of sin and evil. Basically, she calls for recognition of the threat that human beings pose to themselves and to the continued existence of all life on the planet. We need "to understand human beings and all other forms of life as radically interrelated and interdependent."[110] This is really not a radicalization of the Christian understanding of sin as such. It is rather a re-interpretation of our circumstances in the face of the potentially momentous consequences of our increasing technological powers to pursue selfish, self-protective, self-aggrandizing, and prideful ends.

McFague acknowledges "the profoundly tragic character of existence,"[111] which denotes the inescapable realities of suffering and evil in the world quite apart from human perfidy. She also recalls the traditionally Christian view that "human beings are responsible for sin, for refusing to accept their place, for wanting to be like God," a temptation so constant and attractive "that it appears inevitable that we succumb."[112] But her main concern is to address the sense of responsibility we feel for the harms that we have inflicted on one another, on other life, and on the environment we share. Sin, in this context, is "the refusal to be the special part of creation, of God's body, that we are called to be."[113] "Sin is

---

Life Abundant, 183. In one of her most recent statements she says, "When we say 'God' . . . we mean . . . the power and source of all reality"; in Placher, op. cit., 113.
[109]Chapter 2, 78.
[110]"An Earthly Theological Agenda," 15.

the refusal to realize one's radical interdependence with all that lives; it is the desire to set oneself apart from all others as not needing them or being needed by them. Sin is the refusal to be the eyes, the consciousness, of the cosmos."[114]

Where Gustafson emphasizes our failure to accept our human finitude, reflecting his critique of anthropocentrism, McFague emphasizes our failure to accept our interrelatedness and interdependence, reflecting her concern for remedy of the ecological crisis. But the difference is one of emphasis, not disagreement. For both, an enlarged perspective and recognition of the ways in which we are interrelated and interdependent is integral to our salvation, or the greater realization of the actual possibilities that are given to us and all life in the creation. In McFague's words, "we shall understand salvation to be the making whole or uniting with what is attractive and valuable, rather than the rescuing of what is sinful and worthless."[115] For Gustafson, the goal is discernment and action in accordance with "the necessary conditions for life to be sustained and developed."[116]

Both Gustafson and McFague call for a re-ordering of our relations with one another and with the natural world. Where they do differ significantly, is in the degree to which they attribute the extent of evil and suffering in the world to remediable human actions, and thus in the degree to which they consider it possible to overcome the elements of suffering and loss in existence. In keeping with our observations regarding her eschatology as compared to Gustafson's,[117] McFague holds a relatively optimistic soteriology. Human beings can change their ways, address the planetary crisis, and provide for the continued flourishing of life. For Gustafson, on the other hand, the conditions of finitude make the human prospect obscure, and all existence is subject to the realities of the tragic. In any event, we are fitted, not for our own individual salvation, or even for species survival, but for the service of God.

Critical Realism

One of the primary convictions underlying McFague's theology of nature is that the metaphors by which we express the God–world relationship are also the means by which the realities of that relationship are to be at least partially understood. In other words, these metaphors should be, on the one

---

[111] *Models of God*, 137; cf. 148.
[112] Ibid., 138–39.
[113] Ibid., 136; cf. "Cosmology and Christianity," 38.
[114] "Imaging a Theology of Nature," 217.
[115] Ibid., 130.
[116] *Ethics, I*, 339.
[117] 103ff. above.

hand, "isomorphic" with our own experience and, on the other hand, also "isomorphic" with the picture of reality coming to us from the sciences.[118] McFague claims that, epistemologically speaking, this position is one of critical realism. She first articulates her view of critical realism in a discussion of the use of models in science:

> It is evident . . . that scientists who believe that certain models reflect the way things are do not do so without evidence. The evidence need not be conclusive and it is never absolute; such models are not literal descriptions but they have been proven to carry explanatory power for the phenomena in question. Moreover, they are supported because they generate further discovery. . . . They also continue to provide connecting links with other theories and models in the overarching purpose of science to explain how phenomena work. Such an epistemological position on models may be called critical or modified realism and it owes its success, as Mary Hesse says, "both to fidelity to nature as revealed in experiments, and to the fertile imagination which selects appropriate analogies from familiar experiences and familiar types of language, and thus exhibits relations between one aspect of experience and another." Both experimentation and imagination are ingredients of this perspective.[119]

McFague proceeds to argue that a form of critical realism is also appropriate for theology. In both fields, models and theories are inescapably metaphorical, therefore relative and partial, and never literal. But presumably "some models 'fit' reality better than others,"[120] and it is incumbent upon theologians as well as scientists to make the case for that fit.

Clearly, McFague can be described as an ontological realist. She never questions the existence of a reality independent of human perceptions and constructions. Clearly, she is also an epistemological relativist and—to invoke a term used by Robert Audi to describe Gustafson's position—"fallibilist."[121] That she thinks it is important for our models and metaphors to possess significant congruence with reality, a congruence that she sometimes speaks of in terms of isomorphism, defines her critical realist position:

> Constructive thinkers in any field . . . are critical realists to the extent they believe that all perception and interpretation is metaphorical—that is, indirect (seeing or interpreting "this" as "that")—and who also hold that their constructions are not heuristic fictions but discoveries of some aspect of the structure of reality. Moreover, all critical realists will claim

---

[118]Cf. *Metaphorical Theology*, 133.
[119]Ibid., 101.
[120]Ibid.

that their metaphors and models are not merely a matter of personal preference, but can be better substantiated than the alternatives.[122]

This description of critical realism seems tailor-made to describe McFague's position, as she outlines it in *Metaphorical Theology*. But by the time she writes *The Body of God* she seems to have stopped calling herself a critical realist. The term still appears in a footnote that identifies her position in *Models of God*,[123] and in her 1988 essay, "Imaging a Theology of Nature."[124] References to "reality" abound in *The Body of God*, confirming her ontological realism, but I find no reference to critical realism. Her next book, *Super, Natural Christians*, explicitly asserts that the subjects-subjects model she develops there is not a realist account.[125] In a footnote to that assertion, however, she describes her current position in terms not all that different from what she has said all along.[126]

Is McFague a critical realist or not?[127] It may be as much a matter of definition as it is of change in her position.[128] Perhaps she abandoned the term in light of critiques of her work that find her claim of critical realism misleading.[129] Perhaps she recognized that her pragmatic criterion of "truth," namely, "what is good for the planet and its life forms," is just as important, if not more so, than her critical realist claims.[130] In any event, a critical realist epistemology seems to suggest a higher degree of congruence than McFague is able to assert between theological statements and models on the one hand, and the nature of the reality to which these statements and models are taken to refer on the other.[131] The same perhaps may be said with regard to her view of scientific theories and models. It nonetheless remains the case that McFague regards both God and the world as realities that exist independently of human constructions, and that both theological and scientific language seek to be referential. Theological language, especially, must be seen as only partially and mostly indirectly referential.

---

[121] Chapter 1, 33, n. 69.
[122] *Metaphorical Theology*, 132.
[123] *Models of God*, 193, n. 43; cf. 26.
[124] 208. The essay, though published in 1990, was delivered at a 1988 consultation on ecological theology.
[125] *Super, Natural Christians*, 9.
[126] Ibid., 179, n. 6.
[127] David J. Bromell, in "Sallie McFague's 'Metaphorical Theology'," *Journal of the American Academy of Religion* 61 (1993) 485–502, finds her stated commitment to critical realism compromised by inconsistencies between her methodological and epistemological claims.
[128] Avoiding the term "critical realism," Terrence Reynolds interprets her position in *Models of God* as "realist" inasmuch as she has what Jeffrey Stout calls a weak (or "good") correspondence theory of truth, "which affirms that . . . theological discourse does refer, in some way, to transcendent reality"; see "Two McFagues: Meaning, Truth, and Justification in *Models of God*," *Modern Theology* 11 (1995) 295ff.; 310, n. 6.

Although she frequently reiterates that the sciences provide us a picture of reality, not a literal description of things as they are, it remains crucial to her approach that certain features of that picture of reality are regarded as true.[132] And whatever else it may mean to say that they are true, it means that they constitute the basis on which life is to be lived. "We are profoundly interrelated and interdependent with everything living and nonliving in the universe and especially on our planet," she avers. Therefore, "[w]e must become who we really are, neither the possessor nor principal tenant of planet Earth," but the only species that knows our planetary predicament and can bear the responsibility of doing something about it.[133]

For McFague, a lot is at stake in what she initially called her critical realism, however she might now denote it. The following passage is particularly revealing:

> [A]dvocational theology, the kind of theology needed in our time, cannot be either merely heuristic, playing with different imaginative possibilities, or merely utilitarian, insisting that God and nature be seen as benefiting (sic) human existence. Rather, this theology—as is true of all theology—must, I believe, be rooted in the sense of reality current in our time.[134]

The passage is noteworthy, first of all, for its implied critique of heuristic theology, precisely the kind of theology that McFague herself advocated in *Models of God*.[135] More will be said about this shortly. McFague makes two implicit claims that are most relevant here. One is that theology needs to communicate a sense of reality. The reason for this is surely that it will not otherwise be credible and persuasive.[136] It will not be able to accomplish what it advocates.[137] The other implicit claim pertains to McFague's case against anthropocentrism. We do not want a theology that is merely utilitarian, that is, construed to serve merely human ends. A realistic theology, one that presumably identifies humanity's true or proper place in the universe, is needed as an antidote to anthropocentrism. In sum, the sense of reality is needed in theology for moral or ethical reasons, namely, to make a persuasive case on behalf of all life and its fulfillment on planet Earth.

---

[129] E.g., Sheila Greeve Davaney, "Models of God: Theology for an Ecological, Nuclear Age," review article, *Religious Studies Review* 16 (1990) 39.

[130] Cf. McFague, "Ian Barbour: Theologian's Friend, Scientist's Interpreter", 2; also, *Super, Natural Christians*, 179, n.6.

[131] At times McFague sounds positively agnostic about God. For example, in *Models of God* she says, "how language, any language, applies to God we do not know; what religious and theological language is at most is metaphorical forays attempting to express experiences of relating to God," 39; cf. xii, 61. She also writes of the "unknowability of God"; ibid., 97.

[132] Cf. "Cosmology and Creation," 36–37.

[133] Ibid.

[134] Ibid., 21.

Metaphorical Theology: Necessity and Virtue

There are at least three reasons for someone like McFague to develop a *theology of nature*. The first is a matter of intellectual integrity for anyone who shares the modern commitment, with its reliance on experience and reason. Theological statements that make explicit or implicit "truth" claims about God, the world, and human nature should take serious account of what is known, or at least believed, about the way things are, based on the empirical investigations of the sciences. Theologians and theological ethicists are not free from the need to warrant their substantive claims, nor are they exempt from the demands of critical thinking. A theology of nature recognizes the critical contributions to the reformulation of theology that the sciences can provide.

The other two evident reasons for constructing theology of nature relate to the discernment and motivation of right action in the world. We have just seen that a "sense of reality" is important to indicate the proper place and role of human beings in the world. We have also seen that a "sense of reality" helps to make a credible and persuasive case for action in keeping with that place and role. Human beings need to be adequately and, so far as possible, accurately informed about themselves, their world, and the place they occupy in that world, if they are to attain and act upon a realistic perspective of their own actual significance in the world. By taking seriously the picture of reality that comes to us from the sciences, a theology of nature can provide that sense of reality. Why, then, also a *metaphorical theology*?

A metaphorical theology commends itself in a number of ways. In the first place, if all language is metaphorical, then theological language is necessarily so as well. In this sense, all theology is metaphorical. But McFague hardly lets matters go at that. She also suggests that there is something uniquely appropriate about a *Christian* metaphorical theology. "If it can be established that the critical form of Jesus' teaching, the parables, is metaphorical, and further, that the life and death of Jesus himself is a parable of God," she writes, "then a case can be made that modes of interpretation founded on

---

[135] Also in her essay, "Imaging a Theology of Nature," 203ff.

[136] As McFague states in *Models of God*, 31: "What our time lacks, and hence a task that theology must address, is an imaginative construal of the God–world relationship that is credible to us."

[137] In a footnote McFague approvingly quotes physicist and theologian Arthur Peacocke: "Any affirmation about God's relation to the world, any doctrine of creation if it is not to be vacuous and sterile must be about the relation of God to the creation, and this creation is the world that the natural sciences describe. Theology really has no other choice unless it wants to retreat to a ghetto where people just talk to themselves and not to the rest of the world"; ibid., n. 3.

these sources should also have metaphorical characteristics."[138] Of course, McFague proceeds to make that case. But there are additional reasons for her approach that require us to review, briefly, McFague's account of the character of metaphor itself.

What is a metaphor? "Most simply, a metaphor is seeing one thing as something else, pretending 'this' is 'that' because we do not know how to think or talk about 'this,' so we use 'that' as a way of saying something about it."[139] Language is filled with dead and live metaphors, according to McFague. Dead metaphors appear to us to be literal, direct forms of speech, but that is only because they have become familiar and conventional. We no longer recognize their metaphorical character. As McFague says, "it is not the case that anything can be known or thought of directly or literally; rather, we have simply acquired a way of looking at it which is acceptable to us."[140] There is an important epistemological assertion here, namely, that we do not have any direct access to reality. This means that "metaphor is a way of knowing, not just a way of communicating."[141]

The capacity of the metaphor to refer, yet refer indirectly, means that it also has the character of "is" and "is not."[142] Metaphors do not assert identity with that to which they refer; rather, they are ways of talking about that which we cannot talk about directly. This is especially important for theological language. To say that God is Father, or Jesus Christ is Son, is not to claim an identity between God and Father, or between Christ and Son. Neither statement is to be taken literally. Each is a way of trying to think and talk about something ("God" or "Christ") in terms that have particular meanings that are regarded as somehow appropriate for that to which they refer.

Models, according to McFague, are metaphors with "staying power."[143] In Christianity, "Father, Son, and Holy Spirit are models of the divine life that inform the tradition's most central concept, the trinity."[144] The fact that such models have been around for virtually the whole two thousand years of Christian history does not mean, however, that they are unimpeachable. There are models in science that have had to be abandoned or modified as new insights, discoveries, and even new scientific paradigms have arisen. The same may be true for Christian theology, insofar as we come to new or revised

---

[138] *Metaphorical Theology*, 44.
[139] Ibid., 15.
[140] Ibid., 16.
[141] *Speaking in Parables*, 4. In *Models of God*, 34, and in "Imaging a Theology of Creation," 207, however, McFague says that "*in certain matters* there can be no direct description" (my emphasis); the implication seems to be that perhaps in some matters direct description is possible.
[142] *Models of God*, 33.

understandings of ourselves, our world, and the relationship of God and the world.

McFague begins and concludes *Metaphorical Theology* with the claim that her metaphorical theology is a response to two serious issues facing religious language in our time.[145] On the one hand, there is the plague of idolatry and literalism, which is evident wherever particular theological language is regarded as absolute and inviolable. Idolatry, for McFague, means substituting a particular model of God, such as God as Father, for the mysterious and ultimately unnameable reality that is God, and then regarding that model as indispensable and irreplaceable. On the other hand, there is the problem of irrelevance, occasioned at least in part by the use of language that excludes, or tends to devalue, persons due to gender, race, or other worldly condition. A patriarchal or monarchical model of God, for example, God as Father, Lord, Sovereign, or King, appears to privilege males over females while at the same time giving a kind of implicit sanction to hierarchical social arrangements that tend to be oppressive of certain racial, ethnic, or social groups. The problem of irrelevance is also evident in the disjuncture that exists between the sort of world envisioned in theological language and the secular, non-sacramental sense of reality that prevails in modern period.[146]

Stressing the nonliteral, indirect, "is" and "is not" character of metaphorical language gives McFague the warrant she needs for subverting the hegemony of particular theological language:

> McFague assists us in internalizing this "is/is-not" perspective by highlighting both the accuracy and the inaccuracy, both the insights and the limitations of Christianity's commonly used images for God. She assists us initially by distinguishing between the dominant metaphor of father and the root-metaphor of patriarchalism. God-as-Father can serve as a meaningful example of divine-human relationship for many people, as it did for Jesus, McFague maintains. But patriarchalism is a perversion and abuse of the father metaphor. Insofar as patriarchalism is a system that fosters male superiority at all levels of personal and public life, it is fundamentally opposed to the gospel criticism of all worldly hierarchies. To the extent that the patriarchal grasp has restricted images used to convey one's relationship to God, patriarchalism furthers idolatry. It weights one image more heavily than any single image can ever bear.[147]

---

[143] Ibid., 34.
[144] Ibid.
[145] *Metaphorical Theology*, ix, 193.
[146] Cf. *Metaphorical Theology*, viii, 1–2.

McFague's answer to the problem of literalism, or idolatry, is first of all a plurality of images, metaphors, or models for God. Since no metaphor or model alone is adequate, many are needed. Indeed, many are available from within the Christian tradition itself. Moreover, "[s]ince no language about God is adequate and all of it is improper, new metaphors are not necessarily less inadequate or improper than old ones."[148] The reappropriation of older, neglected metaphors, and especially the introduction of new ones, constitutes a challenge to "creedal control and the formulations of orthodoxy," and is therefore destabilizing,[149] a feature that links this approach with the parabolic, paradigmatic, destabilizing, inclusive, nonhierarchical ministry of Jesus. In other words, this is what Christian theology should look like.

A metaphorical theology that is pluralistic, appropriating a variety of metaphors and models, also addresses McFague's concern about the relevance of religious language. For one thing, this opens up the possibility of "identifying and elucidating primary metaphors and models from contemporary experience which will express Christian faith for our day in powerful, illuminating ways."[150] However, the key to interpreting McFague's approach here is to recognize that the metaphors and models she proposes are not presented simply as differing metaphors about God, as if a mere piling up of such metaphors by itself would engender the more adequate understanding of God that we need. Our primary theological metaphors, she claims, are "principally adverbial, having to do with how we relate to God rather than defining the nature of God." Therefore, "no metaphors or models can be reified, petrified, or expanded so as to exclude all others."[151] Thus, the "models of God" that McFague refers to in her best-known book are really to be understood as models (or perhaps only metaphors) of the God–world relationship.[152] As McFague noted already in *Metaphorical Theology*, "*many* models will be necessary both to express and to interpret the complexity and richness of the divine-human relationship" (and, she should have added, the divine–world relationship).[153] But, again, a mere profusion of metaphors or models is not all that is required.

Although McFague is quite prepared to look elsewhere for the images and metaphors required for a relevant metaphorical theology in our time, at first she finds the needed root-metaphor within the Christian tradition. That root-metaphor is not the patriarchal one that has given rise to the dominant

---

[147]June O'Connor, "*Metaphorical Theology: Models of God in Religious Language*," review article, *Religious Stujdies Review* 12 (1986) 204.
[148]"Imaging a Theology of Creation," 207; cf. *Models of God*, 35.
[149]Ibid.
[150]*Models of God*, 2.

model of God as father. Rather, it is the metaphor of the kingdom or rule of God, "a relationship between the divine and the human that *no* model can encompass. The divine-human relationship, therefore, demands both the limitation of the fatherhood model and the introduction of other models."[154] As McFague interprets this root-metaphor, it is about "a way of being in the world—in permanent tension with accepted or conventional ways"—a way that is under the rule of God and is exemplified in Jesus as parable of God.[155] "Jesus is inextricably linked with the new root-metaphor as both the proclaimer of the kingdom and the way to the kingdom."[156] McFague also identifies Jesus as the root-metaphor "without which Christianity would not be the religion it is."[157]

In *Metaphorical Theology* McFague declares that "Christianity will be lost if another root-metaphor is substituted" for the kingdom of God and "the relationship of a certain kind" that it expresses.[158] The implication seems to be that Christianity has been diminished insofar as the dominant model of God the father has failed appropriately to express the divine-human relationship. Thus, feminist theologians who critique this model are not deviating from Christianity but actually calling it back to its roots. However, when we turn to McFague's next book, *Models of God*, we find that she herself is no longer prepared to embrace the kingdom of God metaphor, and in fact engages in an explicit critique of the monarchical model of God as king.[159] The problem with kingdom of God language, apparently, is that the king-servant relationship it implies is not the sort of relationship McFague wants to valorize.[160] Without ever explicitly saying so, McFague attempts to extricate Jesus from the kingdom of God metaphor:

> To see God's relationship to the world through the paradigm of the cross of Jesus is illuminating of salvation for our time if neither the servant nor the king is a major model but some other highly significant and very rich metaphors are investigated for their potential as expressions of the destabilizing, inclusive, nonhierarchical vision in an ecological, nuclear age. That is my thesis.[161]

---

[151] Ibid., 39; "Imaging a Theology of Creation," 206.
[152] Cf., "religious metaphors and the models that emerge from them are not pictures of God but images of a relationship," *Metaphorical Theology*, 166.
[153] 127; cf. 125.
[154] Ibid., 146.
[155] Ibid., 108
[156] Ibid., 10; this root-metaphor is judged to be "new" for Jesus' time, not for ours. In *Metaphorical Theology*, 164ff., McFague also identifies herself with those feminist reformers who, she says, regard human liberation as the root-metaphor of Christianity.
[157] Ibid., 111.
[158] Ibid., 110.

It is noteworthy that in the process of changing the language and shifting the focus, if not the substance, of her root-metaphor away from the kingdom of God to Jesus and his destabilizing, inclusive, nonhierarchical ministry McFague no longer speaks only of the divine-human relationship but of the relationship of God to the world.

The God–World Relationship

The central feature of McFague's metaphorical theology is her preoccupation with the question of how the God–world relationship is to be construed. I believe she is, implicitly, in agreement with Gustafson that this is the most critical element of any theological ethics. I find her to be more agnostic than Gustafson regarding what we can actually profess to know of God. In her interpretation of real-world possibilities, she is less constrained than Gustafson by what may be regarded as scientific knowledge about "the way things are." In both respects she appears to be more of an epistemological skeptic. But she seems no less convinced than Gustafson that the most decisive issue to be addressed in her work is that of the construal or metaphorical expression of the God–world relationship.

In the first place, it is crucial that she be able to employ theological language that implies the existence of a significant relationship between God and the world. Moreover, it is important that the nature of this relationship be seen as continuous with the Christian tradition. Thus, on the one hand, there are intellectual or philosophical and theological issues that require attention in her metaphorical approach. On the other hand, the God–world relationship must be imagined and expressed in terms that are responsive to major obstacles to life and its fulfillment in our time, in particular, patriarchy, the threats of nuclear and ecological disaster, and the exploitative and destructive effects of consumerism. Thus, McFague's metaphorical theology is also an undertaking of decidedly moral and ethical dimensions.

How is the God–world relationship to be construed, according to McFague? I have emphasized that, at least within the context of her theology of nature, McFague holds to certain "modernist" notions about God and the world that preclude the possibility of divine causation. God cannot be the cause of natural events, nor is it to be asserted that God initiated the "Big Bang," according to McFague.[162] What can it mean, then, to speak of divine purposes? How can God possibly make any difference in the world? McFague

---

[159] 63–69; cf. "Imaging a Theology of Nature," 208ff.
[160] Cf. *Models of God*, 55–56.
[161] Ibid., 56.

seems to concede that, within a scientifically informed perspective on the world, there is no place for a personal, agential God.

But of course Christianity does have a personal, agential understanding of God. Moreover, that God is claimed to be the Creator of the universe, which must mean at the very least that God had something to do with getting it all started. Thanks to metaphorical theology, we can be delivered from this predicament. Since all language is metaphorical, and therefore not *directly* referential according to McFague, we can still use language that is personal and agential for God without ever claiming that this is what God is really like. McFague seems surprisingly unabashed in revealing that this is just what she is doing. For example, when she begins to introduce her metaphor of the world as God's body in *Models of God*, she raises the question whether this metaphor is pantheistic, and thereby reduces God to the world. The clear implication is that a pantheistic understanding of God is not compatible with Christianity, and therefore must be avoided. She argues, however, that her metaphor distinguishes between God and the world, without introducing a new dualism. Rather than being pantheistic, her view is panentheistic. "[I]t is a view of the God–world relationship in which all things have their origins in God and nothing exists outside God, though this does not mean that God is reduced to these things."[163]

It is always a puzzle what to make of McFague's arguments when she speaks about God in such terms, if all language about God is presumably metaphorical and not directly referential. Is this language that informs our understanding of the actual relation between God and the world, or does it merely construct for us an imaginative picture of that relation? In any case, the picture is important, and it would not do to think of God in terms that fail to distinguish God from God's body:

> On this model, God is not reduced to the world if the world is God's body. Without the use of personal, agential metaphors, however, including among others God as mother, lover, and friend, the metaphor of the world as God's body would be pantheistic, for the body would be all there were.[164]

---

[162] Cf. above, 101, n. 44; 107, n. 68; *Body of God*, 236–37, n. 32. But also cf. above, 112, n. 87; 112–13, n. 92. In a recent article McFague continues to recognize, and largely dismiss, the conceptual difficulty of claiming divine influence in the world; "Intimate Creation: God's Body, Our Home," *Christian Century* 119 (2002) 41.
[163] *Models of God*, 72.

The metaphor, however, requires an understanding of divine agency in which God's action is understood to be interior, rather than external, to the world:

> If the entire universe, all that is and has been, is God's body, then God acts in and through the incredibly complex physical and historical-cultural evolutionary process that began eons ago. This does not mean that God is reduced to the evolutionary process, for God remains as the agent, the self, whose intentions are expressed in the universe.[165]

Here we have an understanding of divine agency that seems potentially congenial with traditional theological claims regarding God's role in the cosmos. The question continues to nettle, however: how is this metaphorical view of God to be reconciled with McFague's metaphysical assumptions, attributed to the scientific view of the world, that deny any place for divine participation in the causal nexus of events?

McFague's insistence on the need for a personal, agential understanding of God shows up again in *The Body of God*. In the chapter where she presents her theology of nature she engages in a brief critique of natural theology, an approach to the reconciliation of scientific and theological perspectives in contradistinction to which she develops her own approach. Natural theology allows for the possibility of both deistic and mystical understandings of God, she admits, but "[w]hat does not seem possible is the personal God of the Jewish and Christian traditions."[166] On this basis natural theology is rejected.

Later in the same book McFague reviews five major models of God and the world that she finds in Christianity. One is deistic: God is seen as fashioning the world and getting it started, but lacking any on-going relationship with the world. Another is dialogic: God speaks, and we respond, as in an I-Thou relationship, but there is no articulation of God's relation to the rest of the natural and social world. A third is monarchical: this dominant model in Christianity sees God as an absolute sovereign or king, but at a distance, who exercises power in ways that raise problematic questions of human freedom and theodicy. McFague's fourth and fifth models are the agential and the organic, and it is these two, she says, that she wants to continue and develop at the metaphorical level.[167] Neither the agential nor the organic model alone is adequate. The one preserves divine transcendence, the other underscores divine immanence.[168] The organic model is quite evidently McFague's pre-

---

[164]Ibid., 71–72; cf. "Imaging a Theology of Nature," 213.
[165]Ibid., 73.
[166]*Body of God*, 77.

ferred way of imagining God. Not only does she devote an entire chapter to this model, it is clearly the model that is most fully appropriated in her model of the world as the body of God. "However," she notes,

> apart from the agential model, which suggests a center of being not exhausted by or completely identified with the world or universe, the organic model is pantheistic. The world is, becomes, divine. Christian thinking, with its ancient commitment to a transcendent deity who created a world distinct from himself has had, as we have seen, a highly ambivalent relationship to the organic model.[169]

As this statement and many others make clear, whatever McFague may actually believe about the relationship of God and the world, one of her chief criteria for constructing models of the God–world relationship remains its continuity with the Christian tradition. Metaphorical theology is thus a strategy, intended as such or not, for being able to continue to use much of the traditional language of Christianity, and especially its language of divine person and agency, in order to invoke the Christian tradition and evoke the responses of people who are responsive to the language of that tradition, on behalf of all life and its fulfillment.

In *Life Abundant* McFague clearly acknowledges her view that God is not a person or being.[170] Though I cannot identify any equally explicit self-disclosure in her earlier writings, I take it that has been her view of God throughout most of her professional life. What seems new in her latest book is her affirmation that God, though not a person, is personal. The basis for this affirmation does not appear to be a new theological insight or re-conceptualization of the God–world relationship, however. It is not at all clear how such an affirmation is to be understood, conceptually, if God is not a person. For McFague it appears to be simply a matter of experience: "I believe God is personal because I have experienced God this way in prayer; I am conscious of being with a Presence, a Thou, not an It."[171]

What are we to make of this affirmation, especially in light of McFague's rejection of the dialogic model of the God–world relationship? At the least, it helps raise an interesting question. What criteria must be met to warrant the use of personal metaphors for God and the God–world relation? For the most part, McFague has appealed to the Christian tradition's understanding of God as personal and agential to warrant her own use of such metaphors, without ever

---

[167] Ibid., 136–41; these same five models are reviewed in *Life Abundant*, 138ff., and "Intimate Creation," 38–41, with the same conclusion.
[168] Ibid., 141.
[169] Ibid., 140.
[170] 18, 183.

claiming that God is actually a personal being. In my view, this is not a sufficient warrant for the use of such metaphors, which clearly intimate the possibility of a personal relationship with God that is more than a unilateral projection of personal qualities onto some aspect of our experience.[172] Personal metaphors need not be taken to imply that God is some kind of "Big Person," a view that only the most literal-minded would claim, but surely these metaphors intimate qualities of subjectivity and responsiveness. Is it, then, possible not simply to construct a metaphorical image but to articulate a metaphysical conceptualization of God, and God's relation to the world, such that God is understood to be personal, possessing subjectivity and responsiveness?[173] And if this is possible, would this be sufficient warrant for the use of at least some personal metaphors for God? I will be taking up these questions in Chapters 4 and 5.

McFague's metaphorical theology appears to be a self-conscious strategy both for claiming continuity with Christian tradition and for getting past certain conceptual theological difficulties having to do with the nature and being of God and God's relation to the world. However, McFague plainly advocates for her approach primarily in terms of its moral and ethical implications. The acid test of a theology is not its ability to resolve intellectual or philosophical puzzles. "We should stop fretting about 'theodicy'," she adjures, "and consider the increasing and appalling extent to which we are" responsible for evil.[174] "The goal of theology," as McFague sees it, "is to be *functional*, that is, to actually work in someone's life. It is meant to be an aid to right living."[175]

In a recent essay McFague again makes clear that her primary interest is not in resolving conceptual theological issues but in engendering concern for the world:

> While there have been efforts on the part of some theologians and scientists to internalize divine action within the cosmic processes and thus retain a notion of divine intention and design in nature, these efforts are mainly aimed at satisfying why, not where, questions; that is, to allow us to believe in both the existence of God and the truth of science. They are not oriented toward helping us learn about and pay attention to the world for its own flourishing.[176]

---

[171]18.

[172]To say that God, or any other entity, is personal is to say more than that one can have a personal relationship with that entity. In the movie, "Cast Away," the Tom Hanks character establishes a personal relationship with "Wilson," a volleyball. But "Wilson" is neither a person, nor personal, in the sense of exhibiting a responsive subjectivity.

[173]Recall the brief discussion of imaging vs. conceptualization earlier in the chapter, 100ff. The question is not simply one of how, metaphorically, to express the God–world relation, but of how, more generally or metaphysically, that relation is to be conceptualized or understood.

[174]*Life Abundant*, 201.

This statement is far too dismissive of the conceptual theological work that is necessary to give intellectual integrity to any theological claims regarding divine action or influence in the world.[177] How can one reject supernaturalism, yet invoke *theological* sanction for one's moral or ethical claims, without some notion of how God's will is made known or God's influence is made manifest in actual events? However, the statement does invite us to acknowledge the real strength of McFague's approach, which lies in the power of her metaphorical theology to challenge, critique, and re-shape our perceptions regarding the God–world relationship and the ways in which we human beings properly "fit" into the overall ecology of the natural world.

Specific Metaphors Considered

A thorough treatment of any of McFague's metaphors for the God–world relation lies beyond the scope of this chapter. Her primary metaphors include the world as God's body and God as parent/mother, lover, and friend.[178] She provides much more cursory treatments of such metaphors of God as creator, liberator, and sustainer.[179] McFague also acknowledges the possibility of impersonal metaphors for God, but argues that attractive, personal, agential metaphors are needed to overcome the triumphalist royal metaphors of the tradition.[180] A brief review and critique of two of her metaphors, God as mother and the world as God's body, as well as some of the trinitarian metaphors McFague employs, will help indicate the potential contribution I believe her metaphorical theology can make to a more adequate theological ethics in our time.

God as Mother

In the latter half of *Models of God* McFague devotes three chapters to her experiment in imagining God as mother, lover, and friend. Her chapter on "God as Mother" also appears in an abbreviated and slightly revised version in a collection of feminist writings.[181] The metaphor of God as mother is particularly important to McFague's critique of patriarchalism in Christianity.[182]

---

[175]Ibid., 15. Cf., "The common creation story gives us a functional, working cosmology. It gives us a way of understanding where we fit"; *Body of God*, 112.
[176]"Intimate Creation," 41.
[177]In their reviews respectively of *Models of God* and *The Body of God*, both Sheila Greeve Davaney and Kathryn Tanner note how unresolved conceptual issues undermine the coherence and persuasive power of McFague's metaphors; Davaney, "*Models of God*," *Religious Studies Review* 16 (1990) 40; Tanner, "*The Body of God*," *Modern Theology* 10 (1994) 418.
[178]See in particular *Models of God*, 59–180; *The Body of God*.
[179]Cf. *Life Abundant*, 143ff.

But her purpose is not simply to provide a counter to patriarchalism, nor to supplant the model of God as father with her own model of God as mother. In the first place, she emphasizes, a multiplicity of metaphors for God, none of which is entirely fitting, is needed to underscore "the unknowability of God." The model of God as father must be critiqued and supplemented, if only because otherwise "it becomes idolatrous, for it comes to be viewed as a description of God."[183] In the second place, imagery of God as mother is necessary to provide balance to God as father, in keeping with the central biblical and theological view that human beings have been created in the divine image. "[S]ince human beings are male and female, if we seek to imagine God 'in the image of God'—that is, ourselves—both male and female metaphors should be employed."[184] And in the third place, McFague wants to provide an alternative interpretive context for the model of God as father, one that is no longer primarily patriarchal, or even paternal, but rather parental. Her rationale is to investigate the potential of the maternal model in such a way that both God as mother and God as father can be seen as complementary, with the accent on the parental rather than either the maternal or paternal.[185]

McFague also argues for using female imagery for God as a way of unmasking the sexual nature of male images of God. Since female metaphors for God are typically seen as blatantly sexual, their use makes evident the sexuality of both male and female metaphors and "jolts us into awareness that there is no gender-neutral language if we take ourselves as the model for talk about God, because we are sexual beings. Hence, traditional language for God is not nonsexual; on the contrary, it is male."[186] It is also to be hoped that the deliberate use of metaphors for God that have an overtly and obviously sexual character will help gain a greater openness and acceptance of human sexuality as a human good.[187]

However, the model of God as mother, or as parent, falls short in one significant respect, says McFague. Parental love is invariably limited and partial. It is preferential even if not exclusive. But "God as parent wants *all* to flourish." God's love, an agapic love, is to be understood as impartial and inclusive. It is a love that desires all life to flourish.[188]

---

[180]*Models of God*, 39; 79ff.; cf. 204, n. 6.
[181]"God as Mother," in *Weaving the Visions: New Patterns in Feminist Spirituality*, edited by Judith Plaskow and Carol P. Christ (San Francisco: Harper and Row, 1989) 139–50.
[182]In her earlier critique of patriarchy in *Metaphorical Theology*, McFague proposes and briefly develops the metaphor of God as friend as a counter-alternative; see 177–94.
[183]"God as Mother," 139; *Models of God*, 97.
[184]Ibid.
[185]Ibid., 142; *Models of God*, 101.

It is not hard to see that McFague thinks of human language, and especially our language about God and the God–world relation, in terms of how it shapes our perceptions of, and relations to, others and the world. Religious language is not primarily descriptive. Certainly our language about God is not descriptive, in her view. Rather, such language is constructive—though McFague allows that her theological construals are also responsive to a very modest but unspecified degree. That is to say, she does not regard her language about God to be mere projection, but a way of bringing reality to language. The metaphors she employs "are offered as 'redescriptions' (in place of God as monarch and patriarch) of God's relationship to the world."[189] They make "shy" ontological claims, but these cannot be proven.[190] The main focus is always on the ethical implications of the theological metaphors we employ. "God as mother" is a metaphor that exposes idolatry, subverts patriarchy, implicitly affirms the differentiation of male and female and blesses human sexuality, and (imperfectly) images a parental divine love for all creation. "God as mother" enlarges and enriches our thinking about the divine love, creativity, and justice, thus informing our understanding of how we are to relate ourselves to all that exists.[191]

The World as God's Body

Although McFague claims that all our theological metaphors are imaginative construals of the God–world relation, and none is sufficient, the metaphor or model of the world as God's body best serves her purposes and is most integral to her constructive theological position. She introduces this model in her chapter on "God and the World" in *Models of God*, develops it further in her essay, "Imaging a Theology of Nature," and "attempts to look at everything through [the] lens" of this one model in *The Body of God*.[192] The model continues to be integral to the arguments of her two subsequent books as well.

What warrant is there for this model? First, McFague presents this model as a way to interpret the significance of the appearance stories that constitute one of the "distinctive features of the paradigmatic story of Jesus of Nazareth."[193] She writes:

> How should one understand the presence of God to the world in order to empower [the Christian gospel's destabilizing, inclusive, non-

---

[186]Ibid., 140; *Models of God*, 98.
[187]Ibid.
[188]Ibid., 148; *Models of God*, 108.
[189]"Response," *Religion and Intellectual Life* 5 (1988) 42; cf. *Models of God*, 21–28.
[190]Ibid.
[191]Cf. *Models of God*, 101.

hierarchical vision of fulfillment for all of creation]? In some way, the surprising invitation to the oppressed, to the last and the least, expressed in the parables, the table fellowship, and the cross needs to be imaginatively perceived as permanently present in every present and every space: it needs to be grasped, in the most profound sense, as a worldly reality. . . [W]hat if we were to understand the resurrection and ascension not as the bodily translation of some individuals to another world—a mythology no longer credible to us—but as the promise of God to be permanently present, 'bodily' present to us, in all places and times of our world?[194]

The world as God's body, then, is a way to capture the sense of God's permanent and ubiquitous presence to us. Moreover, the "body" language of this metaphor is aptly expressive of Christianity's traditional theology of embodiment or incarnation.[195] McFague is quick to point out that this is an imaginative depiction of God's relation to the world, not a definition or description, and therefore it must not be absolutized.[196] Nonetheless, she first commends it in light of Christian tradition.

A second warrant for the model of the world as God's body seems to be the "common creation story" and the picture of reality that McFague says is coming to us from postmodern science. As we have observed, McFague claims that a mechanistic view of the world is now being replaced by a more organic and relational view of the world as multi-leveled, highly complex and individuated, open and dynamic, encompassing difference and unity. This view of the world, in which all things are complexly interrelated, clearly suggests the appropriateness of the body metaphor. Thus, there is a congruity, or isomorphism, between this image of the God–world relation and the picture of reality attributed to postmodern science.[197]

A third warrant for the world as God's body metaphor is its ethical significance. On the one hand, McFague takes pains as she develops this model to critique what she regards as the dominant model of God in Christian tradition, the monarchical model.[198] We have seen that she later employs her model to critique other models as well. The failures of the monarchical model are threefold.[199] First, God is seen as distant from the world, such that

---

[192] *Body of God*, vii.
[193] *Models of God*, 59.
[194] Ibid., 60.
[195] Ibid., 62. Cf., "Christians should, given their tradition, be inclined to find sense in 'body' language, not only because of the resurrection of the body but also because of the bread and wine of the eucharist as the body and blood of Christ, and the church as the body with Christ as its head," 71.
[196] Ibid., 63.

the world is empty of God's presence. Second, God relates only to the human world, thus there is no concern for the rest of creation or the cosmos. Third, God rules either through domination or benevolence, undercutting human responsibility for the world. Moreover, "the imagery of sovereignty supports attitudes of control and use toward the nonhuman world."[200]

On the other hand, the world as God's body metaphor is highly responsive to the ecological sensibilities of our time and, as such, provides a strong counter-vision to that of the monarchical model in particular. First, God is seen as intimately related to the world, such that the world is filled with God's presence. Second, God is related to all of creation, exercises care and compassion toward all of creation (which, after all, "is" God's body), and seeks the flourishing and fulfillment of all life everywhere. Third, God is not seen as imperiously powerful and in control, but vulnerable and "at risk" to the extent that any part of the world is subject to suffering and destruction. Much of this suffering and destruction, in McFague's view, currently derives from human activities. Because of our unique capacities, we must assume the responsibility and challenge of restoring and healing the creation.

More generally, the imagery of the world as God's body underscores the conviction that bodies matter. The substance of McFague's Christian faith is not about saving souls out of the world, it is not about life hereafter, and it is not about coming to know the perfect truth about God and the world. "Our model helps us to keep theology earthly," she says; "it helps us to avoid abstraction, generalization, and spiritualization.... [A]n incarnational theology always insists that both sin and salvation are earthly matters."[201] It is about the flourishing and fulfillment of this bodily life, for all creatures.

As serviceable as McFague finds the metaphor of the world as God's body to be, she recognizes that it is neither a personal nor an agential metaphor. Consequently, it cannot stand alone. In *Models of God* she explicitly introduces her models of God as mother, lover, and friend not only to avoid pantheism, but to provide a personal, agential view of God.[202] She argues, further, that a personal model for the God–world relationship is needed in order to "move people to live by it and work for it."[203] In *The Body of God*

---

[197] Cf. *Body of God*, ix.
[198] *Models of God*, 63–69; "Imaging a Theology of Nature," 208ff.
[199] "Imaging a Theology of Nature," 209–11.
[200] Ibid., 211. I find each of these to be over-simple characterizations of the monarchical model of God's relation to the world, more accurate regarding what is asserted about God than in what is claimed to be the consequent implication. The monarchical model is also problematic for other reasons. It acutely raises the theodicy issue, which McFague mostly ignores. It construes divine power as basically unilateral and coercive, further problematizing the conceptualization of divine agency.

and her subsequent writings, however, McFague largely neglects the more imagistic personal metaphors for God. But she still recognizes the need for an agential view of God, inasmuch as the Hebrew and Christian traditions are "indelibly agential."[204] She recognizes in process thought and the work of Teilhard de Chardin two credible and persuasive attempts to combine agency and organism in re-thinking the God–world relation. Her own work, she says, "is a continuation of these projects at the metaphorical level."[205]

McFague's metaphorical solution is to propose that "God is related to world as spirit is to body."[206]

> We are suggesting, then, that we think of God metaphorically as the spirit that is the breath, the life, of the universe that comes from God and could be seen as the body of God. Both of these terms, spirit and body, are metaphors: both refer properly to ourselves and other creatures and entities in our experience of the world. Neither describes God.[207]

As McFague further elaborates this conjunction of metaphors, she undermines her stated intent to provide an agential view of God. For "God is not primarily the orderer and controller of the universe but its source and empowerment, the breath that enlivens and energizes it":

> The principal reason, then for preferring spirit to alternative possibilities is that it underscores the connection between God and the world as not primarily the Mind that orders, controls, and directs the universe, but as the Breath that is the source of its life and vitality.[208]

When McFague says that God is "not primarily" orderer, or Mind, she apparently means "not at all"—or at least, "not as a final or an efficient cause"—for she rejects the claim that "the divine mind is the cause of what evolutionary theory tells us can have only local causes."[209] It is ironic here that McFague is constrained by this essentially materialist view of evolutionary theory, given that she criticizes James Gustafson and Gordon Kaufman for retreating from personal language for God on grounds that their retreat gives "too strong a control of science over theology."[210]

[201] *Body of God*, 114.
[202] *Models of God*, 71–72; also "Imaging a Theology of Nature," 213.
[203] Ibid., 80; McFague's other claims on behalf of personal metaphors are less convincing; see 82ff.
[204] Ibid., 142.
[205] Ibid., 141.
[206] Ibid.
[207] Ibid., 144. However, the implication that spirit and body are descriptors with respect to human beings, but only metaphors with respect to God, seems problematic. When is a metaphor not a metaphor? Or only a metaphor?

In any event, McFague's notion of divine agency seems to amount to little more than vitalism. God provides no direction or purpose *until* the emergence of self-consciousness, at which point evolution is not only biological but also historical and cultural.[211] There is a mixing of the body and spirit metaphors here that is confusing, to say the least. Human beings, as part of the world, are part of God's *body*. Once this part of the body has come to self-consciousness, however, we are to think of God, as *spirit*, exercising a previously non-existent direction and purpose. Conceptually, the metaphors as elaborated by McFague do not work. In her view, divine agency, to the extent that it is meaningfully present, is contingent on the emergence of human agency. This turns Hebrew and Christian tradition on its head. Her further elaboration of the world as the body of God metaphor along procreative-emanationist lines seems consistent with an organic model, but hardly restores a meaningful sense of divine agency.[212] If the metaphor of the world as God's body is going to be credible and persuasive within a Christian context, it will require an alternative elaboration, a matter to be explored in the remaining two chapters.

Trinitarian Metaphors

Most of Christianity attempts to understand God in trinitarian terms. Although McFague gives us no reason to suppose that God is actually a triune being, her metaphorical theology has the "virtue" of being able to speak of God in such terms. It is important to keep in mind that her trinitarian metaphorical language does not describe God, nor even refer directly to God, but is primarily a way of imagining and imaging the God–world relation, a relation that no single metaphor can even begin adequately to express. I make no attempt here to assess the relative adequacy of her trinitarian metaphors. My main point is that McFague's metaphorical approach provides this important way to remain in continuity with the language of the Christian tradition. Indeed, since traditional trinitarian language tends to be concrete and imagistic, rather than abstract and philosophical, one tends to focus on

---

[208] Ibid., 145.
[209] Ibid.
[210] Ibid., 142. McFague bases this assessment on her reading of Gustafson's *Ethics from a Theocentric Perspective*, Vol. 1, and Kaufman's *In Face of Mystery: A Constructive Theology*; ibid., 251, n. 14.
[211] Ibid., 148.
[212] Ibid., 151–56. McFague's discussion of her procreative-emanationist model reminds me of a lecture I heard in 1971 by the behavioral psychologist, B. F. Skinner, entitled, "On Having a Poem." Having a poem, as Skinner knew, is not the same as creating a poem. Neither is God being the source of a world that emanates from God quite the same as God purposefully creating the world.

the particular content of her specific metaphors and their capacity to capture in new ways essential dimensions of the God–world relation that are regarded as integral to traditional trinitarian thinking. The absence of any speculative philosophical or theological conception of the Trinity hardly seems to matter.

Briefly, among the trinitarian metaphors employed by McFague are God as mother, lover, and friend. Each of these is elaborated in ways that are suggestive, respectively, of God as parent or concerned creator, God as savior, and God as sustainer. They may thus be seen as corresponding in important ways to the traditional Trinity of Father, Son, and Holy Spirit. In *The Body of God* McFague briefly proposes another trinity of metaphors, the mystery of God, the physicality of God, and the mediation of the visible and the invisible. Again, there is at least a rough correspondence with the traditional trinitarian identities.[213] And in *Life Abundant* we find her returning momentarily to the somewhat more personal metaphors of God as creator, liberator, and sustainer.[214] "The trinity, so understood," she says, "is a way of speaking of creation, incarnation, and deification; that is, our beginnings from God, our salvation in God, and our movement toward God."[215]

Whatever one makes of McFague's particular choices of metaphors, her ability to employ trinitarian metaphorical language for God, or the God–world relation, has surely been advantageous in gaining reception for her theological perspective within a Christian context. To the extent that such metaphors can also be readily elaborated in terms of their implications for how human beings are to live and act in the world, a metaphorical theology—trinitarian or otherwise—surely commends itself in the articulation of an adequate theological ethics.

Prospects for a Metaphorical Theology of Nature

In the preceding section on "The God–world Relation," I find McFague to be in basic agreement with Gustafson that the construal of the God–world relation is of critical importance for theological ethics.[216] This matter of agreement should not blind us to major differences in how they go about this construal. Neither one of these thinkers has a single, fixed starting point for theological reflection. Nonetheless, one may distinguish between them in terms of how they understand the relation between theology and ethics. For Gustafson, the theocentric perspective is the touchstone, if not the actual starting point, for his ethics. Theology has a kind of integrity of its own that

---

[213] *Body of God*, 193.
[214] *Life Abundant*, 143ff.
[215] Ibid., 144.

is prior to ethics, and the direction of influence is primarily from theology to ethics. For McFague, beginning with *Models of God*, the moral concern for planetary life and its fulfillment serves as the interpretive lens for her theology.[217] God is largely unknowable, but we human beings now know that we are facing a global ecological crisis. Indeed, one way to interpret McFague's wager of faith is as an affirmation that God surely must share our commitment and concern for all life known to us. In any case, the ethical implications of our theological metaphors and models of the God–world relation are largely determinative of their adequacy and acceptability. The direction of influence is primarily from ethics to theology.

The second, and related, major difference between Gustafson and McFague in their approaches to construing the God–world relation reflects striking differences in their judgments regarding what can be said with sufficient warrant, and how it can be warranted. For McFague, theology is an experimental and imaginative exercise, the justification for which is partly a matter of "fit" between theological metaphors on the one hand and Christian tradition, experience, and the scientific picture of reality on the other. But, as we have seen, her most important criterion for judging the adequacy of theological metaphors is pragmatic and ethical. It is a matter of whether the metaphors contribute positively to the flourishing and fulfillment of all life on the planet.[218]

For Gustafson, in contradistinction, theology is primarily an endeavor to discern and articulate, so far as possible, the truth about God. In his chapter on "God in Relation to Man and the World" he writes, with respect to his argument in that chapter:

> It lacks the philosophical-theological refinement of those more adept than I in speculative matters. It does, however, form the basis of a theological ethics which I believe bears continuities with the Christian tradition and can be warranted by many human experiences and by data and explanations from some well-established sciences. It has not been developed as an ad hoc rationale to sustain a prior view of morality or a prior view of the Christian faith and religion. Its goal has been to find *what can be most truly claimed about God* rather than to defend traditional Christianity.[219]

Gustafson and McFague obviously approach the theological task with significantly different epistemologies and strikingly different mindsets.

---

[216]127 above.
[217]Cf. *Life Abundant*, 7
[218]Cf. "Response," 143.

Gustafson regards the construal of the God–world relation as a matter of trying to get as close as possible to the truth about the way things really are without over-stating the case. For McFague, on the other hand, the construal of this relation can never be anything but an imaginative construction. However much (or little) it bears congruence with what experience and science purport to tell us about reality, it must above all be responsive to the needs of a planet in crisis. This places McFague in an awkward epistemological position. Professing not to know much if anything about God, reality, or the God–world relation as such, how can she be so sure about the nature of the crisis that faces our planet, the required remedies, or their prospects for success? A great deal hangs on the wager of faith that she makes as a Christian, and the hope that she holds for the future of our planetary existence. She finds sufficient reason in her own experience to confirm her faith and sustain her hope, but for anyone who does not share that experience the epistemological warrants that might justify such faith and provide empirical grounds for such hope are lacking.

In terms of the two views of interpretation described by Wayne Proudfoot and outlined in Chapter 1,[220] the pragmatic and the hermeneutical, Gustafson's approach is clearly pragmatic and referential. On the other hand, McFague's approach is an often confusing mixture of the pragmatic and referential with the hermeneutical and expressive. Her metaphorical language is presumably always at least indirectly referential, and the referents presumably always possess ontological status. But her understanding of the pragmatic validation of her metaphors is tied less to a descriptive account of how things are than to a prescriptive vision of the place and role of humankind in relation to all things. Her theological metaphors, as she herself insists, do not describe the God–world relation. They are, rather, imaginative constructions that provide expressive interpretations and prescriptive construals of that relation. "Images of God do not *describe God*," she says, "but express ways, experiences, of relating to God."[221] These images are "productive of reality." Novel constructions offer new and presumably better possibilities in place of those they replace. Thus, by means of such metaphors "we create the reality in which we live."[222]

In remains important to McFague, nonetheless, that our metaphors and models for the God–world relation are not perceived to be mere fictions. I suspect that is why, after *Models of God* and "Imaging a Theology of Nature," she no longer describes her metaphorical theology as "a kind of heuristic construction."[223] In her earlier book, *Speaking in Parables*, she characterizes

---

[219] *Ethics*, I, 278; my emphasis.
[220] 28–29 above; cf. *Religious Experience*, 43–45.

the theological task as hermeneutical, not in Proudfoot's specific sense but in the general sense that it requires the re-interpretation and re-appropriation of the tradition.[224] And in *Metaphorical Theology* she contrasts heuristic fictions with her critical realist assumptions.[225] But with *Models of God* she repeatedly claims to be engaged in a heuristic theology, emphasizing that her metaphorical approach is, on the one hand, less tied to the interpretation of traditional texts than hermeneutics and, on the other hand, "more experimental, imagistic, and pluralistic" than most constructive theology.[226] The same claims appear, often verbatim, in "Imaging a Theology of Nature."[227] In her 1991 essay, "Cosmology and Creation," however, we find only one brief and dismissive reference to theology that is "merely heuristic," as she writes of the need for "hermeneutical reconstruction" in theology.[228] As noted above,[229] an advocational theology needs a "sense of reality," not "heuristic fictions," to provide a credible and persuasive vision that will motivate and inspire.

It seems to me that this approach to theology and theological ethics should give us pause. One can appreciate the fact that McFague has been responsive to various critiques of her work, and made modifications accordingly. In significant ways her thought exemplifies the evolutionary process that she sees as characteristic of all existence. But the instrumental character of her theological formulations, and their sometimes ad hoc rationalizations, are troublesome, especially from a theocentric perspective. Granted that she does not believe we can know the "truth" about God, or for that matter, the God–world relation, it often seems as if she revels in this circumstance and exploits it as an opportunity for reconstructing God in our own image.[230] I do not criticize McFague for using personal and anthropomorphic metaphors for God. I think she is correct that these are necessary within a Christian context, and that they are not irredeemably anthropocentric. But I often sense that, in her appropriation of these metaphors, she is helping to promote a perspective labeled *cosmocentric*, articulated mainly in *geocentric* terms, that really is *anthropocentric*.[231]

---

[221]"Models of God for an Ecological, Nuclear Age," *Vanderbilt Divinity School Spire* (Summer 1987) 15.
[222]*Models of God*, 26.
[223]Ibid., 40; cf. "Imaging a Theology of Nature," 203ff.
[224]29ff.
[225]*Metaphorical Theology*, 132.
[226]*Models of God*, 37.
[227]"Imaging a Theology of Nature," 205.
[228]"Cosmology and Creation," 21, 30.
[229]121–22.

One indication of this we have noted is McFague's rather romantic and utopian eschatology of earthly harmony, justified in terms of personal experiences of healing. Here she fails to attend sufficiently to the empirical realities of existence in the world of nature (or the historical world, for that matter). A truly cosmocentric, or even geocentric, perspective, characterized by love for the earth, would seem to require a greater and more sober appreciation of actual conditions within nature, including their realistic limitations as well as possibilities for the flourishing and fulfillment of life. McFague sometimes seems to love the earth as one loves an idea, an idea that is integral to one's own continued existence.

Not long after McFague stopped referring to her approach as heuristic she also stopped referring to her epistemology as critical realism. Her latest work appears to rely for its acceptance primarily on its resonance with the ecological sensibilities that are widespread in the culture. She also makes more frequent use of the language of Christian tradition. For the most part I believe her critique of our society's treatment of women, glorification of military violence, degradation of the environment, and economic exploitation of nature, including human nature, are on the mark. Looking at the broad picture, rather than the details, she stands in faithful continuity with Christianity's prophetic tradition. But what is lacking is precisely the "sense of reality" that she claims is necessary for an account of the God–world relationship to be credible and persuasive. A truly compelling theological construal needs to be able to claim a greater congruity between theological metaphors and their referents, including both God and the world as it really is, or even as it possibly could be. The articulation of some possibilities for such a theological construal is one of the primary tasks remaining in this book.

These criticisms notwithstanding, McFague's metaphorical theology represents a distinctive creative contribution to the articulation of an intellectually and religiously adequate theological ethics for our time. Much traditional theological language simply fails to express a contemporary understanding of the nature of God and God's relations with the world. McFague provides a basis both for critiquing existing theological language and for seeking new metaphors that better express what may be believed about the God–world relation. In particular, it would seem that her metaphor of the world as God's body can be articulated in ways that are more congruent with the dynamic, complex, organic, processive, relational, interdependent, but never entirely

---

[230]Cf. *Metaphorical Theology*, 20; *Models of God*, 76, 97.
[231]As previously noted (116 above), McFague's stance in *Life Abundant* may be seen as more theocentric, and thus as something of an exception to this criticism.

harmonious ecological worldview that increasingly characterizes much of today's science.

Unfortunately, McFague's metaphorical theology does not authorize her to speak of God as constant and active presence in nature and history in the way that most Christians would think essential. This is precisely because she lacks an adequate conceptualization of the God–world relation. Nonetheless, she makes a compelling case for the revision of traditional theological language out of concern for the world of nature and history. Although her particular vision of what is possible and necessary is compromised by a kind of theological utopianism, it remains a matter of moral urgency that we learn to see the world differently, and act differently, if human and all other life is to continue to flourish on our planet.

Finally, if would not be enough to articulate an adequate conceptualization of the God–world relation, nor does it suffice to image that relation in ways that change perceptions, without a language capable of evoking affective religious response. Abstract metaphysical concepts are hardly adequate to this purpose. Personal images or metaphors for God continue to be necessary, at least for Christianity and the major Western religious traditions in general. Such images are also necessary for continuity with religious tradition. But they can be new images, emerging out of a critical reappropriation of the insights, values, and relationships deemed central to the truth of the tradition, rendering the possibility of re-imaging and re-presenting God and the God–world relation in the light of a new day. The conceptual deficiencies of McFague's theology of nature are not overcome by her metaphorical approach, but her metaphorical approach may yet have much to offer.

4

David Ray Griffin's Case for Reenchantment: Apprehending God and Nature?

Introduction

David Griffin, recently retired professor of philosophy of religion and theology at the Claremont School of Theology and co-director of its Center for Process Studies, has become today's foremost proponent of a process philosophy of religion.[1] In an academic career now spanning some thirty-five years, he has written or edited over twenty-five books and dozens of articles. With Donald Sherburne he edited the definitive "corrected edition" of philosopher Alfred North Whitehead's major work, *Process and Reality*, published in 1978. His most important work as a philosopher of religion, *Reenchantment without Supernaturalism: A Process Philosophy of Religion*, has been called by one reviewer "the clearest and most comprehensive statement of what philosophy of religion looks like from a process perspective."[2]

Griffin is a theologian as well as a philosopher. He has co-authored *Process Theology* with John Cobb and also written books on Christology, theodicy, the nature of evil, and postmodern theology, all from a process perspective.[3] As theologian Robert Neville has noted, "The overall contribution of process theology has been to make clear the necessity of thinking through the categorical assumptions about our concepts of God, world, and evil. Griffin's work is the most original and fully developed of all the process theologians' in this regard."[4] No one has done more to exploit the possible implications of process thought for philosophical and theological purposes than Griffin. He has also written and/or edited works on spirituality, art, politics, science, and the mind-body problem.[5] He has even taken up issues like parapsychology and life after death that most academic philosophers and theologians studiously avoid. At the same time, he demonstrates a broad acquaintance with contemporary scientific theory and knowledge. As another theologian,

---

[1] Griffin's teacher and, since 1973, senior colleague, John Cobb, owns the distinction of being the foremost process *theologian* of the past three decades or more.
[2] Kevin Schilbrack, "*Reenchantment without Supernaturalism: A Process Philosophy of Religion*," book review, *Journal of the American Academy of Religion* 70 (2002) 639.

William Dean, has observed, "Griffin stands out as one of the very few natural theologians in America today who is scientifically informed and theologically exploratory."[6]

Griffin's naturalistic perspective, as well as his theological explorations, make his work particularly relevant to the purposes of this book. He is not an ethicist, however, nor one whose primary work could be characterized as moral discourse.[7] Nonetheless, he clearly understands himself to be engaged in a task of critical moral and ethical significance. He says,

> Most of my work is on issues that I think are of central importance in a world-view capable of sustaining a sense of the meaning and importance of life, and an ethical stance adequate to the needs of the present and future situation of the world, with its hunger, diminishing resources, and potential ecological disaster. I have found the "process" view of reality suggested by Alfred North Whitehead to be the most adequate, so my work revolves around his vision.[8]

Griffin's close identification of his work with Whitehead's vision is also evident in his remark, previously noted, that Whitehead's "entire philosophy is intended to provide support for the moral life."[9] Griffin clearly sees his own work in a similar vein.

For the purposes of this book, however, the most significant feature of Griffin's thought is his articulation of a worldview that specifically addresses the question of the God–world relation as it has been formulated within the history of Western thought and, in particular, within Christianity. In this

---

[3]John B. Cobb, Jr. and David Ray Griffin, *Process Theology: An Introductory Exposition* (Philadelphia: Westminster, 1976); Griffin, *A Process Christology* (Philadelphia: Westminster, 1973); *God, Power, and Evil: A Process Theodicy* (Philadelphia.: Westminster, 1976); idem, *Evil Revisited: Responses and Reconsiderations* (Albany: SUNY Press, 1991); idem, *God and Religion in the Postmodern World: Essays in Postmodern Theology* (Albany: SUNY Press, 1989); with Huston Smith, *Primordial Truth and Postmodern Theology* (Albany: SUNY Press, 1989).

[4]Back cover of *Evil Revisited*.

[5]Most of these are in the SUNY Series in Constructive Postmodern Thought, of which he is the general editor. A notable exception is his *Unsnarling the World-Knot: Consciousness, Freedom, and the Mind-Body Problem* (Berkeley: University of California Press, 1998). In the long run, Griffin's work as a scholar of process thought may be overshadowed by the work he is doing as a critic of the U.S. government's official accounts of the events of September 11, 2001, including *The New Pearl Harbor: Disturbing Questions About the Bush Administration and 9/11* (Northampton, Mass.: Interlink, 2004), and *The 9/11 Commission Report: Omissions and Distortions* (Northampton, Mass.: Interlink, 2004).

[6]"*God and Religion in the Postmodern World: Essays in Postmodern Theology*", book review, *Process Studies* 18 (1989) 209.

[7]See my brief reference to moral discourse in Chapter 3, 104, and n. 56. In some of his most recent and as yet unpublished writings, however, Griffin is explicitly addressing moral issues, including the moral need for global democracy.

chapter I will review some of the substantial congruities that exist between Griffin's thought and that of Gustafson and McFague, as well as points of significant departure or alternative emphasis. I will also note, in this connection, some of the evident implications of his thought for theological ethics, implications that he has yet to explore thoroughly in his own work. The initial and primary focus, however, will be to set forth and examine the core philosophical ideas and conceptions that, taken together, constitute the view of God, the world, and the God–world relation in Griffin's process theology. I will argue that, however Griffin's work be judged as a resource for theological ethics, he (along with other process thinkers) has provided the best—and in the contemporary situation, perhaps the only viable—conceptualization of the God–world relation that affirms the most essential of the traditional attributes of God, as understood within the major Western religious traditions, while also cohering with assumptions that are indispensable to current thought and conduct in the natural sciences.[10] This is not to say that Griffin's conceptualization of the God–world relation is indistinguishable from currently prevailing scientific worldviews. It is rather to say only that his conceptualization coheres with what is essential to these worldviews. As we will see, his work actually challenges some of the implicit assumptions of science, as widely understood, by offering an alternative metaphysics to the philosophically and scientifically unwarranted, essentially deterministic, and largely atheistic assumptions of scientific materialism.

The Call for a New Worldview

Griffin shares with Gustafson and McFague what we have been calling, following Gamwell, the modern commitment.[11] There is no mistaking his rejection of both epistemic and ontological supernaturalism. One has only to note the title of his major recent book, *Reenchantment without Supernaturalism*. This book is the most comprehensive statement of his philosophy of religion and, along with another major recent book, *Religion and Scientific Naturalism: Overcoming the Conflicts*,[12] will serve as the primary basis for what is to follow.

---

[8]*Contemporary Authors Online*, Biography Resource Center (Farmington Hills, Mich.: Gale Group, 2003); checked at the following URL address on October 20, 2005: [http://www.galenet.com/servlet/BioRC?vrsn=149&OP=contains&locID=iuclassb&srchtp=name&ca=2&c=1&AI=36634&NA=David+Griffin&ste=12&tbst=prp&tab=1&n=10&docNum=H1000039758&bConts=41].
[9]*Reenchantment without Supernaturalism*, 285.
[10]Griffin also wants his perspective to be understood as one that is compatible with major non-Western and even non-theological religious traditions. See esp. *Reenchantment without Supernaturalism*, 271–84, and *Deep Religious Pluralism* (Louisville: Westminster John Knox, 2005) 3–66.

Indeed, the titles of these two books are suggestive of the two major foci of Griffin's work.

On the one hand, Griffin's work is motivated by the intellectual challenge of overcoming the perceived conflicts of religion, and more specifically theology, and science. He accepts the need for a certain kind of naturalism in science. He observes that it is generally assumed that religion, to the contrary, is based on supernaturalistic claims. These claims are both epistemic, having to do with scriptural or other divine revelation, and ontological, asserting the reality of divine intervention in the affairs of nature and history. Thus, religion and science are widely thought to be unavoidably in conflict, especially from the side of science. Like Gustafson and McFague, he seeks to reconcile science and religion by taking an integrationist approach, to invoke Ian Barbour's typology once more.[13] "If there is to be a real reconciliation," says Griffin, "it will require the kind of basis proposed by Whitehead: *a scientific-religious naturalism, supportive of the necessary presuppositions of the scientific and religious communities.*"[14] Whereas the approaches taken by Gustafson and McFague may each be characterized primarily as a theology of nature, Griffin's approach is basically that of process philosophy, although he has also recently incorporated significant elements of natural theology.

On the other hand, the desire for a coherent intellectual conception of the relation of science and religion reflects Griffin's perceived need for a coherent conception of the God–world relation. A coherent conception of the God–world relation is needed for what Griffin calls the reenchantment of the world. And the reenchantment of the world is needed to provide a sufficient sense of meaning and importance to human existence to inspire and undergird human efforts to address the current threats to life on our planet.

Harking back to Max Weber, who first wrote of the disenchantment (*Entzauberung*) of the world, Griffin asks, "What does the 'disenchantment of nature' mean?"

> Most fundamentally, it means the denial to nature of all subjectivity, all experience, all feeling. . . Without experience, no aims or purposes can exist in natural entities, no creativity in the sense of self-determination or final causation. With no final causation toward some ideal

---

[11]Griffin never invokes this particular terminology, but he clearly he identifies with what he calls "the liberal method, by which I mean the method that makes reason and experience—with their criteria of self-consistency and adequacy to the facts—crucial for determining truth"; *Evil Revisited*, 2.
[12]Albany: SUNY Press, 2001.
[13]Cf. 6–9 above.
[14]*Reenchantment without Supernaturalism*, 9.

possibility, no role exists for ideals, possibilities, norms, or values to play . . . With no self-determination aimed at the realization of ideals, no value can be achieved. With no experience, even unconscious feeling, there can be no value received: the causal interactions between natural things or events involve no sharing of values. Hence, no intrinsic value can exist within nature, no value of natural things for themselves. Also, unlike the way our experience is internally affected, even constituted in part, by its relations with its environment, material particles can have no internal relations. Along with no internalization of other natural things, no internalization of divinity can occur.[15]

The alternative to this state of affairs is what Griffin calls panexperientialism. It is an integral element of process metaphysics, to be examined shortly. The immediate point here, however, is that Griffin sees it to be one of the chief purposes of philosophy in our time to pursue the reenchantment of nature in order to provide *"cosmological support for the ideals needed by contemporary civilization."*[16] He explicitly notes that this practical aim of process philosophy complements the more theoretical one of *"the integration of science and religion into a single worldview."*[17]

What is needed, then, is a worldview that integrates science and religion *and* that is capable of sustaining 1) "a sense of the meaning and importance of life," and 2) "an ethical stance adequate to the needs of the present and future situation of the world."[18] This way of stating the matter, however, does not do full justice to Griffin's methodology. It suggests that the worldview is warranted primarily on instrumental grounds, in order to undergird a meaningful, morally significant existence. Griffin also argues in the other direction. He claims that the universal sense of the meaningfulness and moral significance of human existence, expressed in terms of certain "hard-core commonsense notions,"[19] provides epistemological warrant for the metaphysical worldview. Far from being simply an instrumentally motivated construction, the worldview Griffin proposes must meet the two primary tests of truth, namely, adequacy to the facts of experience and logical coherence.[20] In a passage that refers to Whitehead, Griffin writes:

> What is needed for the pursuit of truth . . . is an "unflinching determination to take the whole evidence into account." This is what he has tried to do in his attempt to devise a scheme of ideas applicable to all the dimensions and data of human experience. The attempt to

---

[15] *The Reenchantment of Science* (Albany: SUNY Press, 1988) 2; cf. *Reenchantment without Supernaturalism*, 285ff.
[16] *Reenchantment without Supernaturalism*, 7.
[17] Ibid., 5; cf. 20–21.
[18] Cf. above, 146–47, n. 8.

include the parts of this evidence that have been left out in the late modern period involves, primarily, the effort to include our hard-core commonsense ideas, especially those rooted in our aesthetic, ethical, and religious intuitions.[21]

What is involved here is a certain kind of metaphysics, which, as Griffin notes, Whitehead "understood as 'the science which seeks to discover the general ideas which are indispensably relevant to the analysis of everything that happens'."[22] So understood, this metaphysics is not a kind of speculative, presumptively foundational, "first philosophy," but rather an experientially derived "last philosophy." In a footnote, Griffin reports that Whitehead understood metaphysics as "the endeavor to construct a coherent scheme of ideas 'in terms of which every element of our experience can be interpreted,' adding that the 'elucidation of immediate experience is the sole justification for any thought'."[23] For Griffin, as for Whitehead, metaphysics deals with "the elements common to all experience and with the presuppositions involved in all practice."[24]

There are two primary sources, then, for the interpretation of reality that is Griffin's (and, for the most part, process philosophy's) worldview. One of these is the knowledge of the sciences, the other is human experience, understood both broadly and specifically in terms of the hard-core commonsense notions. Griffin knows that this worldview is an interpretation and, as such, has a somewhat tentative and experimental status. It is, strictly speaking, underdetermined.[25] Nonetheless, it is an attempt to offer a truthful account of reality. It rests largely upon a notion of truth as correspondence. Indeed, as Griffin argues, "[i]t belongs to our hard-core commonsense notions . . . that to say that a proposition is true is to say that it corresponds to the reality to which it refers."[26] Griffin undertakes a Whiteheadian defense of truth as correspondence that I will not attempt to recapitulate here.[27] Suffice it to

---

[19]This is Griffin's term for what Whitehead called the inevitable presuppositions of practice; *Reenchantment without Supernaturalism*, 29.
[20]Ibid., 355; cf. 170–71; *Primordial Truth*, 203.
[21]Ibid., 50. Later, Griffin reiterates, "Modern cosmology has been based almost entirely upon scientific ideas, in distinction from ideas rooted in aesthetic, ethical, and religious experience, whereas Whitehead emphasizes the need to retain 'the whole of the evidence in shaping our cosmological scheme,'" 295.
[22]Ibid.
[23]Ibid., 51, n. 3. Cf. Griffin: "The central task of philosophy . . . is to develop a position that shows how the various notions that we inevitably presuppose in practice can all be true"; *Religion and Scientific Naturalism*, 101.
[24]Griffin, "Values, Evil, and Liberation Theology," in *Process Philosophy and Social Thought*, edited by John B. Cobb, Jr., and W. Widick Schroeder (Chicago: Center for the Scientific Study of Religion, 1981) 185.

say that he rejects any merely functional, utilitarian, instrumental, expressivist, or other view of language in which either the referential character of the language, or the reality of that to which it refers, are categorically denied. The truth of any propositional statement, assuming it meets the test of logical coherence, is precisely a measure of its adequacy in corresponding to the reality to which it refers.

In the previous chapter we saw how Sallie McFague emphasizes the creative character of science as an imaginative undertaking employing metaphors and models to construct a picture of the world that possesses interpretive and explanatory power, as well as normative significance. I do not know that Griffin would reject this view of science, but he certainly places the emphasis elsewhere. After a brief critique that focuses on the materialist and dualist assumptions he identifies with science in the modern period, Griffin writes:

> A description of science for a postmodern world must be much looser than the modern descriptions (which were really *pre*scriptions).

Any activity properly called *science* and any conclusions properly called *scientific* must, first, be based on an overriding concern to discover truth. Other concerns will of course play a role, but the concern for truth must be overriding, or the activity and its results would better (sic) called by another name, such as *ideology*, or *propaganda*, or *politics*. Second, science involves demonstration. More particularly, it involves testing hypotheses through data or experiences that are in some sense repeatable and hence open to confirmation or refutation by peers. In sum, science involves the attempt to establish truth through demonstrations open to experiential replication.[28]

In this statement Griffin simultaneously affirms the rigor of science as a disciplined, empirical search for truth, and challenges the narrowness of recent methodologies and the implicit, or explicit, epistemologies and ontologies by which have been supported. He notes that he is not including in his description the claim that science is "restricted to the domain of things assumed to be wholly physical, operating in terms of efficient causes alone, or even to the physical aspects of things, understood as the aspects knowable to sensory perception or instruments designed to magnify the senses."[29]

---

[25]Griffin states, "I believe that all interpretations are, to use the current jargon, 'underdetermined.' That is, interpretations are never strictly dictated by observations, but always involve a creative surplus. Alternative interpretations that also 'save the appearances' are always possible. I present my interpretation, my philosophical theology, not as the one and only plausible way of showing the coherence among the inevitable presuppositions of practice, but as the most plausible way known to me among past and present options"; *Primordial Truth*, 196.
[26]*Reenchantment without Supernaturalism*, 321.
[27]Ibid., 324–43.

He regards such restrictions in the past as reflective of a now-impermissible materialism or metaphysical dualism. Those restrictions also presume that experience derives primarily if not exclusively from sensory perception. It is central to Griffin's project, and to process philosophy as a whole, that this presumption be rejected.

Also excluded from Griffin's description of science is the specification of any particular type of repeatability or demonstration, such as the laboratory experiment. For example, there are many types of phenomena, from comets to animal wildlife, that cannot be studied under laboratory conditions. The larger issue for Griffin is the rejection of a tendency in science to regard things as essentially independent of their environments, or to regard complex wholes as little more than sums, and thus capable of being comprehended on basically the same terms as their constituent parts.[30]

Griffin also leaves out of his description of science any particular contingent beliefs, that is, any unnecessary metaphysical assumptions about the nature of things. Examples include the belief that the laws of nature are eternal, or that all causation is upward.[31] On the other hand, there are certain beliefs that science must presuppose. Two of these, we have already seen, are the traditional principles of correspondence and noncontradiction, or logical coherence.[32] Griffin proposes three other principles that are related to "the crucial issue of causality."[33] The first of these is that "every event is causally influenced by other events." The second is that "neither human experience nor anything analogous to it is wholly determined by external events." And the third is that "every event that exerts causal influence upon another event precedes that event temporally." Griffin's claim is not that these beliefs are theoretically incontrovertible, but rather that they must be presupposed by scientific thought and practice, precisely because they are presupposed by human thought and practice.[34]

What we have with Griffin, then, is a *pragmatic metaphysics*[35] that takes its cues from particular notions in human experience. One of these hardcore commonsense notions is the belief in causal influence, or causal efficacy. Another that Griffin consistently mentions is the belief in an external world, or ontological realism. He is careful to say that these beliefs may be denied,

---

[28] *Reenchantment of Science*, 26.
[29] Ibid.
[30] Ibid., 27.
[31] Ibid., 28. Every event is to be understood in terms of both upward or efficient causation and downward or final causation.
[32] Ibid., 29.
[33] Ibid., 28.

verbally, but they are of such a nature that they cannot be consistently denied in practice. Indeed, they are of such a nature that the very attempt to deny them involves one in self-contradiction:

> To illustrate this point, we can use the two beliefs already mentioned—the belief in an external world and in causality. If I announce to an audience, or write on my computer, that I am a solipsist, doubting the existence of an actual world beyond myself, I show by my act (of speaking *to the audience* or writing *on my computer*) that I do not doubt this at all. Likewise, if I try to convince some colleagues that there is no such thing as causal influence, I prove by my very attempt to cause them to change their minds that I know otherwise. The same kind of self-refutation would be involved in denials of any of the other hard-core commonsense beliefs to be mentioned later, such as our beliefs in the past, in purposive causation, and in freedom.[36]

In *Primordial Truth and Postmodern Theology* Griffin identifies several other such beliefs. These include:

> time (that there is a difference between the past, which is settled, the present, which is being settled, and the future, which is still in part to be settled), . . . axiological realism (some things are better than other things), evil (some things happen that are worse than other things that could have happened), and ultimate meaning (somehow what happens is ultimately meaningful). We could not deny any of these ideas without presupposing them.[37]

Unfortunately, the various hard-core commonsense notions identified by Griffin do not serve as a major organizing theme in any of his books. Consequently, we do not get an extended, systematic treatment of how these notions actually inform and shape the pragmatic metaphysics, or worldview. To be sure, all of these notions are taken into account by Griffin in the development of his process philosophy. If one accepts this philosophy, then one will likely judge Griffin to have made good on his claim "to develop a position that shows how the various notions that we inevitably presuppose in

---

[34] Ibid.
[35] *Reenchantment without Supernaturalism*, 51, n. 32; 31, n. 12.
[36] Ibid., 33; cf. 46–47. In *Religion and Scientific Naturalism* Griffin notes, "This type of contradiction between theory and practice is called a 'performative self-contradiction' by Jürgen Habermas and Karl-Otto Apel," 99. In the same work he identifies the following commonsense beliefs about ourselves: "(1) that we have conscious experience; (2) that this conscious experience, while influenced by our bodies, is not wholly determined thereby, but involves an element of self-determining freedom; and (3) that this partially free experience exerts efficacy upon our bodily behavior, giving us a degree of responsibility for our bodily actions," 137.

practice can all be true."[38] The problem is that the argument does not proceed in a fashion that demonstrates as explicitly as one might wish why Griffin's particular worldview is the one most strongly supported by these notions. The metaphysics of process thought would surely be more persuasive, because more evidently warranted, if the connections with the hard-core common sense notions of human experience could be more clearly and thoroughly traced.[39]

A related issue is whether the hard-core commonsense notions identified by Griffin are to be accepted without question. Are all of them coherent? universal? infallible? It is one thing to recognize that, *if true*, these notions are implied even by their denial. It is another to claim that these notions truly and accurately express beliefs that are universally valid and cannot be shown to be either incoherent or conceivably falsifiable.[40] I am inclined to agree with Griffin, both in terms of the existence of hard-core commonsense notions, and in terms of the particular notions he identifies, although I think the crucial role that he claims for these notions calls for further demonstration. Furthermore, it would be helpful to know if there are any non-definitional criteria that can be employed to identify those notions that fall in the category of hard-core common sense. As it is, Griffin seems to regard those hard-core commonsense notions that he identifies as self-evidently true—a sort of "I'm convinced of it when I think about it" approach to what is most certainly the case.

With respect to the constructive task of theological ethics, it would also be helpful to know if there are hard-core commonsense notions that can serve as bases for moral or ethical principles or rules. At one point, in fact, Griffin states that "moral notions . . . belong to our hard-core commonsense notions."[41] However, it does not appear that Griffin is saying much more than that there is a universal sense of "better" and "worse." There is this element of objectivity in moral experience, this conviction that there is some sort of moral order in the world, but it remains unclear whether there are any

---

[37]133. Elsewhere, Griffin also identifies the existence of other minds as another hard-core commonsense notion; *Reenchantment without Supernaturalism*, 378.
[38]*Religion and Scientific Naturalism*, 101.
[39]In a chapter in which he makes a natural theology case for God's existence, however, Griffin invokes "arguments from fundamental aspects of human experience." With one exception (193), he does not speak of these as hard-core, common sense notions, though they bear striking resemblances; *Reenchantment without Supernaturalism*, 189ff.
[40]Kevin Schilbrack renders this critique of these notions, to which he then adds, "These disagreements on the fine points, however, do not take away from the important point that Griffin is identifying a criterion for philosophy to which the majority of modern and postmodern criticisms of metaphysics do not apply," op. cit., 640.

specific principles or rules, for example, that are necessarily derivative of this moral sense.

The philosopher Bertrand Russell, despite claiming himself to be a moral subjectivist, once observed, "I find myself incapable of believing that all that is wrong with wanton cruelty is that I don't like it."[42] Would Griffin perhaps argue that the statement, "wanton cruelty is wrong," expresses a hard-core commonsense notion that can be formulated as a general moral principle? If so, are there other moral principles that could be similarly derived? A related issue concerns the clarity with which such principles might be stated. It is not readily obvious what constitutes "wanton cruelty," for example. Moreover, there are some people who seem capable of engaging in acts that others would regard as wanton cruelty who, themselves, express no remorse or guilt. They hardly seem to be captive to the notion that wanton cruelty is wrong, indeed, they may even revel in their own acts of cruelty. Their behavior would appear to confute any claim that "wanton cruelty is wrong" could be, strictly speaking, a hard-core commonsense notion. In any event, the more general problem is simply that it remains unclear how one might go about providing a comprehensive or definitive account of those notions that belong to the category of hard-core common sense.

Despite such ambiguities, Griffin provides ample argument to show how it is that, given the worldview he presents, the various notions he identifies as those we inevitably presuppose in practice can be true. To state the matter in terms of scientific categories, while he does not demonstrate that his theory (worldview) is the most decisively indicated by his data (the hard-core commonsense notions, as well as all the knowledge of the sciences), he makes a thorough and compelling case for the theory as one that gives a coherent account of the data as he finds them.[43]

The Makings of the Worldview

I began the previous section by pointing to Griffin's rejection of epistemic and ontological supernaturalism. It is time now to set forth his alternative epistemology and ontology. Near the beginning of *Reenchantment without Supernaturalism* Griffin identifies two basic types or meanings of naturalism. Both reject supernaturalism, but only one is acceptable from both scientific and religious points of view. The problematic form of naturalism, which Whitehead called scientific materialism, is denoted by Griffin as naturalism$_{sam}$, where s stands for sensationist, a for atheist, and m for materialist.

---

[41] *Reenchantment without Supernaturalism*, 299.
[42] "Notes on *Philosophy* January 1960," *Philosophy* 35 (1960) 146–47.

Griffin finds the roots of this naturalism$_{sam}$ in the rejection of supernaturalism with the emergence of modern science in the seventeenth century:

> As this naturalistic worldview developed concretely . . . it contained other elements that went far beyond [the] mere denial of supernatural interventions. It retained the sensationist doctrine of perception, which had been adopted in the seventeenth century. It also retained that century's mechanistic doctrine of physical nature while rejecting its doctrine of a non-physical mind or soul, with the result that everything in the world, including human behavior, was to be understood in terms of a mechanistic materialism. Finally, in rejecting the *interventionist* supernaturalism of the early modern scientific worldview, it did so, after a brief interlude of *deistic* supernaturalism . . . , in favor of a completely atheistic worldview.[44]

As already noted in Chapter 1, Griffin rejects naturalism understood in sensationist, atheistic, and materialistic terms. As an alternative to naturalism$_{sam}$, he argues for a form of naturalism with a non-sensationist view of perception called *prehension*. Instead of atheism, his naturalism calls for a form of theism called *panentheism*. And instead of a materialist ontology he develops his doctrine of *panexperientialism*. The result is a type of naturalism that he denotes as naturalism$_{ppp}$. We must now consider the three major features of Griffin's naturalistic worldview.

Perception as Prehension

It is important, first of all, to note that Griffin does not question the existence of sensory perception. He simply does not regard sensory perception, as it is generally understood, to be the primary form of perception. In addition to sensory perception, understood to consist of "perception in the mode of presentational immediacy," there are two major forms of nonsensory perception.[45] Perception in the mode of presentational immediacy refers to all that is mediated to us by our bodily sense organs—all that we can see with our eyes, hear with our ears, smell with the olfactory receptors in our nostrils, taste with the taste buds on our tongues, or feel through the nerve endings throughout our bodies. Moreover, it is that which we experience *consciously*

---

[43]It is well to keep in mind that Griffin never claims his philosophical perspective is the only one that could conceivably account for the breadth of phenomena to which process philosophy attends (cf. above, 151, n. 25). However, I am not aware of any alternative comprehensive theory that is in serious contention.

[44]*Reenchantment without Supernaturalism*, 22.

through these sense organs. But, in Griffin's view, as in Whitehead's, we experience much more than this.

For example, Griffin argues that a full-fledged view of sensory perception recognizes the more fundamental mode of perception that Whitehead called "perception in the mode of causal efficacy." In this mode, he says, "we perceive other things as *actual* and as *exercising causal efficacy on us*."[46] Drawing on Whitehead's critique of Hume's epistemology, Griffin explores what it means to say that one sees something "*by* the eyes." What is perceived surely includes the object or datum that we see—an object of a certain size, shape, and color, let us say. But the complete datum of visual perception includes not just what is seen, but the means by which it is seen, that is, the eye that is experiencing what is seen. "The datum, in other words, includes *the eye as exerting causal efficacy* on the percipient (the 'momentary ego') by causing it to see those sights."[47]

Therefore, sensory perception always involves both "perception in the mode of presentational immediacy" and "perception in the mode of causal efficacy." However, the actual awareness of our body's causal efficacy for our experience, says Griffin, is a nonsensory perception:

> I do not see my eyes or hear my ears. My capacity to enjoy sights and sounds through my eyes and ears depends upon my more basic perception of my body through which I receive the information these sensory organs have brought in from the world beyond my body. My most direct perception of my body, furthermore, is not my perception of these organs but my perception of my brain. . . . I indirectly perceive my eyes and ears, then, by directly perceiving my brain.

We are not, to be sure, consciously aware of this perception of the brain. We are consciously aware of the causal efficacy only of those bodily organs, such as the eyes and the skin, in which physiological processes of transmission originate, not of that central organ in which they culminate. We know from physiology, however, that our sensory perceptions depend directly upon the brain. . . . Accordingly, by combining what we know from immediate experi-

---

[45]Griffin notes that Whitehead's view of sensory perception is more encompassing than that of empiricist philosopher, David Hume, for whom sensory perception was limited to perception in the mode of presentational immediacy. For example, Whitehead argued for the more fundamental mode of "perception in the mode of causal efficacy," as well as for "perception in the mode of symbolic reference." In addition, Whitehead argued for two major forms of nonsensory perception, the perception of one's own body and one's own past; cf. ibid., 60ff. The brief review here can provide no more than a very general sense of how a Whiteheadian process epistemology differs from a merely sensationist one.
[46]Ibid., 60.
[47]Ibid., 61.

ence with what we know from science, we must conclude that it is primarily by means of a nonsensory perception of the brain that we perceive the causal efficacy of various parts of the body, and through them of external things, for our experience.[48]

A second and perhaps even more compelling form of nonsensory perception has to do with memory, "which involves one's perception in the present of one's own experiences in the past."[49] The word "memory" itself explains nothing. Moreover, it fails to connote that "each act of remembrance is an instance of perception." Griffin proposes that a more transparent term for memory might be "past-self-perception."[50] Furthermore, we tend to think of memory in terms of the distant or perhaps recent past, and thus associate memory with self-identity over time. But for Whitehead what is even more significant is memory of the "immediate past," that is, of that portion of time between one-tenth and half a second ago.[51] Such memory, or nonsensory perception, is necessary to make sense of an on-going experience—for example, listening to someone speaking. As Griffin observes, "our whole lives depend upon the continuity afforded from moment to moment by the direct perception of the immediately past moment of experience."[52]

It lies beyond my purposes and competence to attempt a full account and thorough evaluation of Griffin's theory of perception, which is drawn largely from Whitehead. Perhaps what has been said and cited is sufficient, nonetheless, to indicate the empirical basis of Griffin's (and Whitehead's and process philosophy's) argument for an understanding of perception that is much more robust than the sensationist view of "perception in the mode of presentational immediacy." Griffin's comments regarding the nonsensory perception of the brain also provide an instance of how process philosophy warrants many of its key concepts by appeals both to human experience and the knowledge of science.

On reflection one may thus be persuaded of the existence of certain *nonsensory* perceptions. But what about *unconscious* perceptions? The very idea of perception seems to connote conscious awareness. Here more must be said about what is meant by experience in a Whiteheadian conception. First, as Griffin notes,

> One of the keys to Whitehead's version of empiricism is his dictum . . . that 'consciousness presupposes experience, and not experience

---

[48] Ibid., 62–63.
[49] Ibid., 63.
[50] Ibid., 64.
[51] Ibid., 65.
[52] Ibid., 66.

consciousness.' This doctrine means that the primary elements in experience are generally not the elements of which we are most clearly conscious.[53]

If consciousness were prior to experience, Griffin argues, then there would be no way to account for the emergence of consciousness. This is the dilemma posed by the mind-brain problem. How can mind emerge from matter—if matter is thought to be wholly insentient, without experience? The problem, says Griffin, "is *insoluble in principle*."[54]

But suppose there is a way of understanding experience that does not presuppose consciousness? In fact, in a Whiteheadian metaphysics, all actual entities or occasions are "occasions of experience."[55] In this view, the elemental units of existence are not particles or bits of matter, but rather events. To understand how they can be said to be occasions of experience, however, we must introduce the notion of prehension. Prehension, as Griffin notes, is Whitehead's more general term for perception. It is "meant to indicate a grasp that could be either conscious or unconscious."[56] Prehension may also be either physical or mental. A physical prehension is a prehension of a prior actuality.

> "Physical prehension" is, in fact a synonym for "perception in the mode of causal efficacy." The data of *mental* (or *conceptual*) prehensions, by contrast, are mere possibilities or universals (which Whitehead calls "eternal objects"), such as the color *white* and the shape *round*. Perception in the mode of presentational immediacy consists entirely of mental (or conceptual) prehensions.[57]

Moreover, each occasion of experience begins, not with a mental prehension or perception, but with physical prehensions This provides a basis for the further claim that "each moment of experience begins with an *affective* or *emotional* response to things prehended."[58] Whitehead actually employs the word *feeling* as a virtual synonym for prehension. Clearly, the language here must be understood analogically, in reference to human experience, which is taken as paradigmatic. The experience of human beings is of a much higher level than that of animals and, as Griffin emphasizes,

> [e]ven the kind of experience enjoyed by a living cell is already a fairly high-level experience, compared with that of macromolecules, ordi-

---

[53]Ibid., 60.
[54]Ibid., 45; cf. Griffin, "Whitehead's Deeply Ecological Worldview," in *Worldviews and Ecology: Religion, Philosophy, and the Environment,* edited by Mary Evelyn Tucker and John A. Grim (Maryknoll, N.Y.: Orbis, 1994) 193.
[55]Cf. ibid., 63–64.
[56]Ibid., 79.

nary molecules, atoms, and subatomic entities such as protons and electrons. The experience of such entities must be assumed to be very trivial. The point remains, however, that they should be thought to be only different in degree from us, however greatly, not wholly different in kind.[59]

The idea of prehension, then, suggests a kind of sympathetic appropriation by each event of those antecedent events that are its causes.[60] In contrast to a billiard-ball image of causation, in which an event is affected only in some external way, this view of causal relations holds that "the causal influence of the past upon the present is in-fluence, a real in-flowing, which affects the present experience internally."[61] It is causation as understood from the perspective of the "effect." Prehension refers to the internal appropriation of causal influences from the past.[62]

The following summary helps to put this epistemological doctrine into perspective:

> At the root of Whitehead's nonsensationist doctrine of perception, therefore, is the idea that our most fundamental perception of the world is not a conscious, sensory perception of it, in which it is represented by barren, unemotional sense data, but a preconscious feeling of it, in which other things are felt sympathetically. . . This doctrine, based on the priority of feeling, involves a complete inversion of the Humean brand of empiricism. . . The traditional doctrine of perception, in other words, has regarded the derivative elements as primary and the truly primary elements as derivative.

The mistake behind this traditional doctrine involved a confusion between two kinds of priority: "The order of dawning, clearly and distinctly in consciousness," Whitehead points out, was assumed to be the same as "the order of metaphysical priority," meaning the order in which the elements arose in an act of experience. "[T]he opposite doctrine," Whitehead contends, "is more nearly true."[63]

---

[57] Ibid.
[58] Ibid., 80.
[59] "Whitehead's Deeply Ecological Worldview," 194.
[60] Griffin explicitly defines it elsewhere as "the *nonsensory sympathetic perception of antecedent experiences*"; *Primordial Truth and Postmodern Theology*, 143.
[61] Ibid., 197.
[62] "Prehension is indeed simply the reverse side of causal influence and is therefore synonymously called 'perception in the mode of causal efficacy'"; Griffin, "Introduction: Sacred Interconnections," *Sacred Interconnections: Postmodern Spirituality, Political Economy, and Art* (Albany: SUNY Press, 1990) 7.

Griffin's reference here to "an act of experience" reflects the conviction that all occasions possess duration and process. In process philosophy time is literally of the essence, constitutive of what it is to exist. That is, it takes time to exist. There is no "nature at an instant."[64] A particular occasion of experience may last less than a billionth of a second, as in the case of photonic events, or perhaps a tenth of a second in the case of an occasion of human experience.[65] Additionally, each actual entity, as an occasion of experience, exists in two modes:

> It exists first as a subject of experience. In this mode, it prehends prior experiences, then makes a self-determining response to them. (This element of self-determination may be more or less significant.) After existing as a subject, its subjectivity perishes; it then exists as an object for subsequent subjects.[66]

Nothing, therefore, exists as an entity unto itself. "That is, far from requiring nothing else to be, it is the very nature of an actual entity to prehend previous actual entities into itself," and then to become such an entity, i.e., an object, to be prehended by subsequent entities or actual occasions.[67] Consequently there are no self-existent actual entities or occasions of experience that, in Descartes' account, "need nothing but themselves in order to exist."[68] All entities or occasions are constituted by their relations, insofar as "each actual entity by definition arises out of its prehensions of a multiplicity of prior actual entities and contributes itself to future actual entities."[69] Human beings are understood to be not single entities, but compound individuals, or personally ordered societies of actual entities, "each of which is constituted out of its relations to prior actual entities." A thoroughly relational conception of the self is necessarily entailed, a feature that has made Whiteheadian philosophy attractive to many feminist philosophers of religion.[70]

The concept of prehension also provides a way to reconcile final and efficient causation. Keeping in mind that all actual entities are to be understood as "occasions of experience" that possess duration, rather than occurring in an instant, Griffin explains:

---

[63]*Reenchantment without Supernaturalism*, 81–82.
[64]Ibid., 43, 107; Griffin sees this as implied by physics.
[65]"Whitehead's Deeply Ecological Worldview," 196.
[66]Ibid., 197–98. Process philosopher Lewis Ford reportedly defined time as "the indeterminate future becoming the determinate past"; personal conversation with David Cockerham, to whom Ford gave this definition.
[67]Ibid., 197; although Whitehead and other process philosophers often speak of entities, they clearly do not regard these entities as "things," let alone "things-in-themselves," as would be the case in a materialistic or atomistic ontology. Cf. 29, n. 60 above.

An actual occasion begins by receiving efficient causation from the past; this is the occasion's physical pole or phase. It then, *without letting in any more influences from without*, exercises its self-determining final causation; this is the occasion's mental pole or phase. Then, after this process of final causation is complete, it exerts efficient causation upon subsequent occasions.[71]

This way of conceiving and reconciling final and efficient causation avoids the problem of materialism, which has no way of dealing with final causation, here identified with the mental pole or phase of every occasion. It also avoids the problem of dualism, which must somehow conceive of final and efficient causation as occurring simultaneously, with final causation supervening and effectively modifying if not nullifying efficient causation. Final causation is thus coherent within a non-dualistic naturalistic worldview.

Panexperientialism

This brief account of Griffin's process view of perception as prehension has required that I introduce some of the ideas that also characterize what he calls panexperientialism.[72] This is the view that "the ultimate units are to be understood as occasions of experience." They are not "vacuous actualities," but "spacio-temporal events."[73] We have already seen how these ideas are integral to the notion of prehension. Panexperientialism is the ontology that complements the epistemology of perception as prehension.

Griffin contrasts panexperientialism specifically with a materialistic metaphysics. He defines materialism as a combination of two doctrines, a mechanistic doctrine of nature, "according to which the ultimate units of nature are entirely devoid of experience and self-determination," and a non-dualistic doctrine, "according to which there are no other actualities, different

---

[68]Cited by Griffin, ibid., 196.
[69]*Reenchantment without Supernaturalism*, 119.
[70]Ibid. I will not attempt to give an account of the organizational duality that characterizes the Whiteheadian view regarding all *enduring* individuals. Suffice it to note that all *enduring* individuals are regarded as spaciotemporal societies of actual entities or occasions of experience. These temporally ordered societies of momentary events may or may not possess a dominant member. Following Hartshorne, Griffin identifies those that possess a dominant member as *compound individuals*, in contradistinction to aggregational societies. The most obvious examples of compound individuals are human beings and other animals with a central nervous system. Although comprised of temporally ordered societies of occasions of experience, each compound individual can nonetheless be considered as one experiencing subject; ibid., 119–22; n. 15. The concept of a compound individual is also integral to Griffin's revision of Whitehead's understanding of God; cf. 166ff. below.
[71]Ibid., 113.

in kind from the ultimate units of nature."[74] Process philosophy also claims a non-dualistic ontology, but it does so on the basis of panexperientialism rather than mechanism. Griffin argues, rightly I believe, that a non-dualistic materialism is necessarily mechanistic. He sees no way to account for non-mechanistic phenomena, such as experience, consciousness, or freedom, based on a purely materialistic ontology. In other words, stripped of metaphysical dualism, materialism is simply Cartesian mechanism.

Why was a materialistic view of nature so widely adopted in the seventeenth century, even by many scientists of religious conviction? Griffin has a fascinating and persuasive explanation. Sociological and theological motivations were more important, he says, than empirical reasons. "The idea that the ultimate units of nature are bits of insentient matter, wholly devoid of experience and spontaneity, was useful in arguing for an omnipotent deity, supernatural miracles, and the immortality of the human soul."[75] The sharper the line drawn between the material and the spiritual, the more the autonomous reality of the spiritual was presumably secured. "The acceptance of a totally ordered world, devoid of self-moving powers and occult forces, was regarded as a natural consequence of the Reformation view that monotheism, in the true sense, means belief in a single, all-directing Providence and thereby a disenchanted world."[76] However, with the subsequent demise of belief in the supernatural and the metaphysical dualism that it entailed, all that remained was the scientific materialism. The disenchantment of the world was complete. Griffin's account of the rise of scientific materialism, which cannot be adequately reviewed here, is especially important because he invokes it to corroborate his argument that there are no compelling empirical warrants to support a materialistic worldview. To the contrary, he claims, there are better empirical grounds for his panexperientialism.

There are various thrusts to Griffin's argument. On the one hand, however speculative panexperientialism may appear to be, at least "we have direct knowledge that 'experiencing actualities' can exist because we are examples of

---

[72]The term is Griffin's. Charles Hartshorne, whom Griffin considers the second founder of process philosophy, introduced the term *panpsychism*, which he later replaced with *psychicalism*, to refer to what Griffin denotes in this way. Neither of Hartshorne's terms is satisfactory in Griffin's view; cf. *Reenchantment without Supernaturalism*, 97.

[73]*Religion and Scientific Naturalism*, 98, 169, 172.

[74]*Reenchantment without Supernaturalism*, 94; in *Religion and Scientific Naturalism* Griffin further characterizes the mechanistic theory of nature as one "according to which the basic units of nature . . . can exercise only efficient causation, being wholly devoid of any capacity for spontaneity, self-determination, or final causation, and . . . can only receive causation from and exert causation on *contiguous* things, meaning that they are incapable of receiving or exerting influence at a distance," 107.

[75]Ibid., 98. See *Religion and Scientific Naturalism*, chapter 5, for an extended account.

such. In supposing that the ultimate units of nature are experiencing actualities, therefore, process philosophers are merely speculating that these entities are further exemplifications of this mode of existence."[77] The materialist position, on the other hand, requires the assumption that "vacuous actualities" or actualities devoid of experience, of which we have no direct experience, are nonetheless a metaphysically possible mode of existence.[78] Thus Griffin sees the materialist ontology as more speculative than his panexperientialism.

If the logic of Griffin's argument fails to convince here, one suspects it is because extrapolating from human experience to claim experience for all other events may seem a bit of a stretch. Moreover, there seems to be a preponderance of indirect evidence on behalf of the materialist position. For the most part, science seems to get along quite well with materialist assumptions. But Griffin presses his case precisely in terms of the shortcomings of a sensationist epistemology:

> Many dualists and materialists, to be sure, seem to think they can tell, just by looking at things, that they are devoid of experience. The assumption implicit in this conclusion is that sensory perception, especially visual perception, involves a direct observation of nature. As Whitehead has emphasized, however, it is a very indirect way of perceiving nature. The fact that visual perception reveals no experience in nature, accordingly, may tell us more about the nature of sensory perception than it does about the nature of nature. In any case, because we have no direct knowledge that the phrase "vacuous actuality" even names a possible type of thing, the idea that the ultimate units of nature are vacuous actualities is far more speculative than the panexperientialist idea that they are experiencing actualities.[79]

Griffin marshals additional arguments on behalf of panexperientialism. The most important of these pertain to the inadequacies of materialist assumptions for physics and the natural sciences, on the one hand,[80] and the indirect evidence from physics and more direct evidence from the natural sciences in support of the panexperientialist view.[81] For example, Griffin briefly references research on bees, single-cell organisms, bacteria, and even macromolecules and elementary particles, claiming that there are forms of behavior that resemble something like experience, perception, and/or memory of a very rudimentary sort at all these levels. These behaviors lend themselves to explanation in terms of his panexperientialism.

---

[76] *Religion and Scientific Naturalism*, 126.
[77] *Reenchantment without Supernaturalism*, 98.
[78] Ibid., 99.

Whether or not one finds such evidence and argument on behalf of panexperientialism compelling, there certainly seems to be growing empirical evidence that weighs against a strictly mechanistic view of nature. Although Whiteheadian metaphysics has not been widely accepted despite its empirical grounding—or perhaps because of it—neither has it been refuted. Rather, there has been a general neglect of metaphysics in philosophy and theology.[82] The view here is that we are not at a total loss regarding knowledge of what is real and enduring, and that some metaphysical claims in fact are necessary to warrant significant human loyalties and the sorts of aspirations and life-demanding commitments that the moral life requires. This brings us to the third major feature of Griffin's naturalistic worldview.

Panentheism

As this term panentheism suggests, process thought sees all things as existing "in God." "All worldly occasions are said to be prehended by, and thereby included in, the divine experience (which Whitehead calls the 'consequent nature' of God . . .)."[83] At the same time, it must be said that God is in all things. In other words, process thought regards the world as immanent in God in addition to holding the traditional theistic view that God is somehow immanent in the world. Moreover, God is also understood to be transcendent with respect to the universe "in the sense that God has God's own creative power, distinct from that of the universe of finite actualities."[84] Panentheism is to be distinguished from pantheism, for which God is essentially immanent in the world and not transcendent, as well as traditional theism, for which God is essentially transcendent and only accidentally immanent. God is necessarily immanent. Although this particular world, or universe, may be regarded as contingent on the divine creativity, there is no God without a world in pro-

---

[79]Ibid. In *Reenchantment without Supernaturalism*, Griffin asks, "how can we think of causality in nature: we can do so by thinking of actualities as passing on their experiences to other actualities," 106.

[80]Cf. ibid., 101–2; *Religion and Scientific Naturalism*, 168–73.

[81]Cf. ibid., 107–8; *Religion and Scientific Naturalism*, 105.

[82]Griffin charges, with some exaggeration, "Modern liberal theology . . . has avoided affirming anything that would conflict with the worldview of modern scientists by hardly affirming anything whatsoever of a distinctively religious nature"; *Religion and Scientific Naturalism*, 108. Fundamentalist, evangelical, and many neo-orthodox theologies, on the other hand, have typically continued to make distinctively religious claims without resort to metaphysics by ignoring critical features of the world as understood by science in preference for an explicit or implied supernaturalism. Postliberal theology attempts to sidestep metaphysics without resort to supernaturalism by adopting an implicitly non-realist perspective that mostly ignores the question of the ontological status of the referents of its theological language.

cess thought. "[I]t belongs to the very nature of God to be related to *some* world embodying this metaphysical order."[85]

Perhaps the most helpful metaphor to describe the God–world relation, provided by philosopher Charles Hartshorne, is that of God as "'the soul of the universe,' being related to the universe somewhat in the way in which the human soul, as the dominant member of the human being, is related to the body."[86] The God–world relation is merely analogous to that of the human mind and body, however:

> Referring to God as the soul of the universe . . . does not imply that God's existence is dependent upon our particular world or even that God's existence is in any sense contingent. One thing it does imply, however, is that being related to a realm of finite actualities is part and parcel of the very nature of God.[87]

Thus, process thought can also speak of the world as God's body, very much as we have seen McFague do in the preceding chapter. God cannot be conceived of apart from some world.

Following Whitehead, Griffin explains that God is the chief exemplification of the metaphysical principles.[88] In what is perhaps his most significant departure from Whitehead, however, he follows Hartshorne and theologian John Cobb in arguing that Whitehead had an insufficiently developed and inconsistent concept of God. The chief problem lies in Whitehead's view of God as a single actual entity, rather than a "serially ordered society of divine occasions of experience."[89] One of Whitehead's metaphysical principles is that "all *enduring* things are temporally ordered societies of actual entities."[90] In other words, in process thought, all other enduring entities are constituted by successive occasions of experience. By conceiving of God as a single, everlasting actual entity, Whitehead had no conceptual way to ascribe temporality to God, thus making God an exception to the metaphysical principles, inasmuch as the "temporal process belongs to the metaphysical nature of things."[91] For God—as an everlasting actual entity—there could be "no transition from divine occasion to divine occasion, as there would be no such occasions."[92]

---

[83] *Reenchantment without Supernaturalism*, 141.
[84] Ibid., 142.
[85] Ibid., 138.
[86] Ibid., 140. The term "soul" here could be replaced with "mind" or "conscious individual," as Hartshorne does in *Omnipotence and Other Theological Mistakes* (Albany: SUNY Press, 1984) 52–56. Griffin notes that "Whitehead said that God 'is not the world, but the valuation of the world'"; "Whitehead's Deeply Ecological Worldview," 206, n. 14.
[87] Ibid.
[88] Ibid., 140.

Griffin points out that Whitehead himself acknowledged he had not worked out a clear doctrine of God, nor had Whitehead made a strong argument for defining God as a single actual entity.[93] Griffin's solution is to reconceive of God as a living person, that is, "as an everlasting personally ordered society of divine occasions of experience."[94] He proceeds to show how understanding God as a living person is consistent with other Whiteheadian metaphysical principles in ways that Whitehead's conception of God is not.

It is possible here to note only the most sweeping implications of the panentheistic view that Griffin presents. There is, first, the claim that this is a naturalistic view of God. Griffin acknowledges that there is a very restricted sense in which process theism might be regarded as a type of supernaturalism. If naturalism is "the doctrine that 'nature is all there is,' with 'nature' understood to be the totality of finite agents, processes, and relationships, including the energy embodied in them," then process theism is not naturalistic, for it does regard God as distinct from this totality.[95] However, it would be very misleading to refer to process theism as a form of supernaturalism, for it assumes no exceptions to the world's normal causal processes, or to the metaphysical principles that pertain to all events.[96] Thus, it is simply important to be specific regarding the form of naturalism that process theism represents.

The chapter in *Reenchantment without Supernaturalism* in which Griffin begins the explication of his panentheism is actually titled "Naturalistic, Dipolar Theism."[97] As he reports, there is in fact a double dipolarity in the process understanding of God. One of these dipolarities, the one more important to Whitehead, parallels the relation we have already identified between the physical and mental poles of all actual occasions. The other dipolarity, emphasized by Hartshorne, relates to the changing and unchanging attributes of God.

Griffin points out that the dipolarity between the changing and unchanging attributes of God is not to be equated with the distinction between the mental and the physical poles of an actual occasion:

---

[89]Ibid., 151–52.
[90]Ibid., 157.
[91]Ibid., 150.
[92]Ibid., 152.
[93]Ibid.
[94]Ibid., 157.
[95]Ibid., 136.
[96]Griffin states, "Because God's way of influencing the world is grounded on the necessities of the (metaphysical) nature of the world as well as upon the necessities of the (metaphysical) nature of God, it cannot occasionally reflect a different modus operandi. The term *naturalistic theism*, accordingly, means that the basic God–world relationship lies in the very nature of things"; ibid., 139.

> Rather, this dipolarity can be described as the distinction between, in Hartshorne's terms, the "abstract essence" and the "concrete states" of God. The abstract essence of God is analogous to what we call the 'character' of a human being, meaning that set of characteristics that remains virtually the same day after day, month after month, while the person lives through millions of experiences, these occasions of experience being the 'concrete states' in which the abstract essence is exemplified now in this way, now in that. The difference, which is why we have here only an analogy, is that a human being's personality can change whereas the abstract essence of God is strictly immutable. One example of God's essence, for example, is omniscience, the characteristic of knowing everything knowable at any given time. God's concrete *knowledge* grows, insofar as new events happen which add new knowable things to the universe. But the abstract attribute of *omniscience*—the attribute of always knowing everything that is (then) knowable—is exemplified in every concrete state of the divine existence.[98]

The other dipolarity, which parallels the relation between the mental and physical poles of all actual entities or occasions, expresses the "dipolarity between God as influencing the world and God as being influenced by the world."

> [It] can be understood simply in terms of the distinction between concrescence and transition, or subjectivity and objectivity. A divine occasion begins its moment of subjectivity, its process of concrescence, by being influenced by all actual occasions that have reached satisfaction. When this divine occasion's concrescence is completed, so that it has reached satisfaction, it becomes a superject and thereby an object for, meaning an efficient cause on, subsequent actual occasions. The dipolarity of God as influencing and being influenced involves, accordingly, not different aspects or natures of God but simply the distinction between the two modes in which a divine occasion exists. The divine individual, therefore, involves the same perpetual oscillation between efficient and final causation that occurs in worldly individuals.[99]

Perhaps the most important implication of this naturalistic, dipolar theism is its capacity to account for *variable* divine influence in the world. As Griffin points out, the medieval view saw God as primary cause of all events, necessary to account for the fact that there is a world at all, and perhaps also for the fact that it is continually being sustained. Given God as primary

---

[97]Ibid., 129–68.
[98]Ibid., 158–59.

cause, natural or secondary causes were taken to be sufficient to account for ordinary observable events. But this schema was unable to account for certain extraordinary events—for example, the creation of life, the inspiration of the prophets, and the incarnation in Jesus—which were typically attributed to supernatural divine intervention.[100] As a consequence, the emergence of scientific naturalism and the demise of supernaturalism in the modern period also meant the demise of theism in any intelligible and meaningful sense. A deistic conception of God as the divine "clockmaker" who fashioned the world and got it going might be credible, but there was no room for a theistic God who continues to exercise influence in natural events or even in human affairs.

Process philosophy provides the needed conceptuality for a theistic conception of God without resort to supernaturalism:

> The key to this solution is a fundamentally different way of understanding the relation between divine and worldly causation. Every actual entity prehends all the actual entities in its environment, which includes God (as the term *panentheism* emphasizes). An actual occasion is, therefore, partially constituted by its (physical) prehension of God. Because physical prehension and efficient causation are simply two ends of the same relationship, there is divine causation on, thereby divine influence in, every event.[101]

On the one hand, this view of divine influence reaffirms "the traditional view that the world's continued existence in each moment depends upon the sustaining influence of God."[102] On the other hand, although the divine influence is formally the same for all occasions, it is variable in content and effectiveness with respect to every occasion. It is variable in content because what God contributes to each occasion is its "initial subjective aim," and "different initial aims are appropriate for different actual entities," depending on what constitutes the ideal possibility for an occasion "given its location and complexity."[103]

---

[99]Ibid., 159. My aim in this brief and very partial explication of Whiteheadian process thought is to avoid specialized language as much as possible with the hope that the meaning of what little specialized language is employed will be relatively clear from the context. Concrescence, for example, refers to the subjective, prehensive process of self-determination through which an occasion realizes its subjective aim and attains an objective status with respect to subsequent events; to "reach satisfaction" is to complete this process; cf. 161–62 above. Observing that "Whitehead's dipolar theism is deeply problematic" in part because he identified what he called the "primordial nature of God" not only with the unchanging pole of one dipolarity but also with the influencing pole of the other, Griffin argues that the "primordial nature" of God belongs specifically to God's "abstract essence"; cf. *Reenchantment without Supernaturalism*, 150ff.

[100]Ibid., 144.

Recall that every occasion first exists as a subject of experience, and in this mode prehends prior experiences, to which it makes a self-determining response.[104] The subjective aim of an occasion is the overall aim or purpose of this response. The claim of process philosophy is that "an occasion of experience's subjective aim is partially created out of an *initial* subjective aim derivative from the occasion's prehension of God."[105] This is not to say that God determines the subjective aim of any occasion, but only that this is the process by which God contributes some measure of influence, extremely trivial in lower-level (e.g., subatomic) events but potentially significant in high-grade occasions of experience (such as those of human beings), to all occasions.

The divine influence is variable in effectiveness due to differing degrees of complexity of organization and of freedom. The greater the degree of complexity or freedom, the greater the possibilities that are open to an occasion, and the greater the power to go against the initial aim received from God. For human beings, "[t]he possibility that they choose to make their subjective aim may be greatly different from the initial aim received from God."[106] One crucial implication of this is that God is not the only source of power and creativity in the universe. Power is inherent in the world, both for good and for ill.[107] Human beings, for example, can choose subjective aims in keeping with the initial divine subjective aim, thus joining their creative powers with the divine creativity. Or they may choose subjective aims that resist and oppose the initial divine subjective aim, thus causing conflict, destruction, and genuine evil. Although all things are not possible, in the sense that anything can happen, the future truly is indeterminate for process thought, both for individual entities and for the world. Traditional views of divine omnipotence are rejected. God is not simply one influence among many others, however. God is "the only causal power that is eternal and universal, being involved in *every* event in the universe."[108] But God must exercise influence persuasively rather than coercively, in terms of the "lure" of the initial subjective aim rather than in terms of any irresistible force.

Another crucial implication of variable divine influence is precisely the ability to give an account of the possibilities for those crucial events in the

---

[101] Ibid., 146.
[102] Ibid.
[103] Ibid., 146, 147.
[104] See 161 above.
[105] *Reenchantment without Supernaturalism*, 146.
[106] Ibid., 147.
[107] *Religion and Scientific Naturalism*, 93.

storied histories of religious communities that seem to lie beyond the ordinary:

> Process philosophy's idea that the divine aims for occasions differ in both content and effectiveness allows theologians of the theistic religions to accept and conceptualize the assumption, central to these religions, that some events, such as certain crucial events reported in the scriptures of these traditions, are far more important than others for revealing the divine nature and purpose. Christian theologians, for example, can develop a Christology that supports the conviction that Jesus' life especially incarnated God in a way that makes it appropriate to receive Jesus as especially revelatory of God.[109]

One should note that the claim here is not that Jesus was an ontologically unique individual, as held by traditional Christian theology. Nor is the claim that any of the crucial events reported in the scriptures are to be accepted as miraculous, in the sense that they can only be explained as manifestations of the supernatural. The claim is simply that in Jesus, and in certain events recounted in scripture, the divine is especially revealed. This is to say that there appears to have been an extraordinary congruence between the initial divine aims and the actual subjective aims of the person or persons and events in these situations, such that they became transparent of the divine nature or purpose.

We have, then, in process philosophy a naturalistic worldview that rejects both epistemic and ontological supernaturalism, yet is very unlike the scientific materialism, or naturalism$_{sam}$, that has made theistic belief unintelligible in the modern period. Griffin's version of naturalism, naturalism$_{ppp}$, is characterized by an epistemology of prehension in place of sensationism, a panexperientialist ontology in place of materialism, and a panentheistic understanding of God and the God–world relation instead of atheism. This naturalistic theism addresses the primary problem that we have encountered in the theological construals of the God–world relation provided by James Gustafson and Sallie McFague, namely, that of providing a conceptuality of how God—not simply the idea of God—can make a real difference in what transpires in the world.

---

[108]Ibid., 95. Although Griffin attributes to God an eternal abstract essence, which Whitehead called the "primordial nature of God," in this context it might have been better to refer to God as everlasting, rather than eternal. The latter term tends to reflect a different cosmology and view of time with regard to the God–world relation.
[109]*Reenchantment without Supernaturalism*, 148.

Addressing Some Objections

Before we explore this version of naturalistic theism in broader perspective, there are three objections to be acknowledged. One of these, as Griffin notes, is the charge leveled by some critics that process theism does not really have a doctrine of *God*.[110] In other words, the notion of God developed by process thinkers does not merit or measure up to traditional definitions of God. To be sure, a panentheistic conception of God differs in some significant ways from traditional theistic conceptions. But, as we will see shortly, it is actually a very robust conception of God when compared to many other current theological options.

A second objection is that the conception of God developed by Griffin and other process thinkers relies upon a remarkably strange metaphysical worldview, one whose epistemological and ontological claims may strain credulity. Despite Griffin's defense, this is a worldview that many find far too speculative and abstract. Apart from the cumulative effect of the arguments Griffin makes on behalf of his version of process theism, which I can only begin to lay out in this chapter, there are two other arguments for the reader to consider. One, which I have already intimated, might be called the argument from elimination. Most traditional theological worldviews fail the test of naturalism, and must be rejected by anyone who accepts the modern commitment to reason and experience. Those theological approaches that accept the modern commitment tend to be non-realist, and thus are unable to warrant any claim to knowledge about the way things ultimately are, which is to say they are non-metaphysical and hardly qualify as worldviews. Those theological approaches that accept the modern commitment and also claim to be realist (e.g., those of Gustafson and McFague) tend to lack any account of how God might actually exercise influence in the world. Process theism appears to be the only naturalistic, critically realistic, theistic worldview that takes both science and logic seriously, thus meeting the two truth criteria of adequacy and coherence, while also providing a conceptuality of the God–world relation that accounts for divine agency.

A second argument on behalf of Griffin's process theism might be called the argument from complementarity. Consider what science is telling us about our world today. As strange as process theism's worldview may seem, it is hardly stranger than the view of the world that science continues to unveil. From Einstein's theories of relativity to quantum mechanics to Bell's theorem,[111] string theory,[112] and the "Big Bang," we are coming to recognize the incomprehensibly weird, wonderful, and mysterious nature of our universe.

---

[110]Ibid., 163.

If process theism is recognized as a serious attempt to provide a complementary theological worldview, one that does justice to what we know from the natural sciences in particular, then why would we expect this theological worldview to be conventional and familiar? If the world itself is a strange place, then the God who in some sense is thought to be the creator of this world, its soul and constant companion, sustaining it from moment to moment, constantly influenced by it while also ceaselessly exercising influence within and upon it, can hardly be conceived in pedestrian terms. This is not to say that process theism has "got it right," only that strangeness as such should not count against the worldview of Griffin or any other process philosopher or theologian.

To be sure, Griffin hardly sounds tentative when critiquing views he discredits, or when describing the world as he regards it to be. He insists that "we have sufficient warrant to say that we know sensationism, dualism, and materialism all to be false." Moreover, he says, "one can claim to know that the truth involves some form of non-sensationist doctrine of perception and some form of panexperientialist ontology." Nonetheless, by his own verdict, claims to knowledge or certainty regarding his particular metaphysics would be presumptuous:

> Having placed the bar very high for using the term knowledge, we certainly should not claim knowledge for any highly ramified doctrine, such as that of process theism . . . I speak not of knowledge but only of "over-whelming probability," and this in comparison with atheism and supernaturalism . . . I would say that some form of naturalism$_{ppp}$ is overwhelmingly more probable than either some form of supernaturalistic dualism or some form of naturalism$_{sam}$.[113]

The real question, therefore, is whether Griffin has provided a conception of the God–world relation that is intelligible and coherent, adequate to reality as best we can know it, and better able than any alternative to show how it can be true to speak in terms that are meaningful, in light of tradition-

---

[111] Named after physicist John Bell, the theorem has been successfully tested by experiments demonstrating that once two photons have been "entangled" by being in close proximity, a correlation continues to exists between them such that, even when separated by macroscopic distances, a change in the polarization of one photon results in a corresponding instantaneous (i.e., faster than light) change in the other. The tests are taken to confirm the intrinsic nonlocality of quantum mechanics, or what Einstein called "spooky actions at a distance." This and other quantum phenomena suggest that the universe may be constituted of more than four dimensions.

[112] A theory of quantum gravity, holding promise for a unified description of the fundamental particles and forces in nature. In simplest terms, the view that the elementary units of the universe may be thought of as vibrating strings, the average length of which is thought to be about 10^{-33} cm.

al definitions of God, regarding an ultimate, purposeful, and agential reality called God that (or, who) makes a difference in our lives and world.

This brings us to a third, and potentially more problematic, objection. Is Griffin's conception of God and the God–world relation really intelligible and coherent? Griffin, along with Whitehead and other process philosophers and theologians, has sought to overcome the metaphysical dualism of nature and supernature, matter and deity, with a form of nondualistic monotheism called panentheism. In Griffin's conception, God is not to be identified simply with the world, but remains "distinct from the totality of finite causes."[114] By virtue of God's "abstract essence," God is the only absolute and eternal individual, possessing a primordial nature that is home to the ideals that give form to the initial aims that God contributes to all occasions of experience. By virtue of God's "concrete states," on the other hand, God as the supremely relational individual, in whom the world is fully immanent, is always changing. We have seen how Hartshorne invokes the analogy of the relationship between a person's character and the actualities of that person's existence to help us understand the relationship between God's abstract essence and concrete states.[115] As with any explanatory scientific theory, metaphysical explanations must resort to claims about reality that lie beyond explanation, those claims being themselves the general patterns, processes, principles, or features of reality that are taken to explain everything else. So, claims about God's abstract essence and concrete states, or God's absolute nature and God's relatedness, are integral to Griffin's explanation of divine action in the world, as well as a number of other phenomena such as the experience of moral values or ideals and the hard-core commonsense notions, *but these claims about God are not themselves to be explained.* If one insists on asking, How can God be both abstract and concrete, or both changing and unchanging? the most meaningful response is a rhetorical rejoinder, Given the world as we know it, how can God *not* be thus and so?

Nonetheless, accepting Griffin's (and Hartshorne's) dipolar theism, there does seem to be a lack of clarity, if not incoherence, regarding the sorts of distinctions that Griffin wants to make between God and the world. Two of these distinctions are at least confusing. On the one hand,

Griffin distinguishes between God and "a world of finite actualities."[116] God, in contrast to the world so understood, is infinite and may be characterized in terms of abstract essence. On the other hand, Griffin also distinguishes

---

[113] *Reenchantment without Supernaturalism*, 392.
[114] "Religious Experience, Naturalism, and the Social Scientific Study of Religion," 103. Cf. above, 166, n. 84; 167, n. 95.
[115] Cf. above, 168.

between two ultimate realities, God and "creativity," or as he prefers (following Hartshorne), "creative experience."[117] "Creativity" was Whitehead's rendering of Aristotelian "matter." It is the "stuff" or "primary substance" of the universe, that of which all actualities are composed. It is primordial and uncreated, equally ultimate with God. We are not to think of creativity in substantialist or materialist terms, however. Nor are we to think of it as passive. Hence, Griffin prefers Hartshorne's term, "creative experience." Creativity, or creative experience, is not self-existent, any more than God is self-existent. "Creativity and God mutually presuppose each other."[118] Creativity must always be embodied, in God and in the world of finite actualities:

> It is the very nature of God to be the experiential unification of the multiplicity constituting the parts of the universe. Creativity, therefore, is *necessarily* instantiated in a multiplicity of finite actualities as well as in the supreme actuality. Although God is the "aboriginal instance" of creativity, creativity is also aboriginally instantiated in some multiplicity or other of finite actual entities.[119]

In a recent and as yet unpublished work, Griffin contrasts creaturely creativity, or the creaturely embodiment of creativity, with divine creativity, or creativity as embodied in God.[120] The distinction between God and "the world of finite actualities" clearly does not parallel Griffin's distinction between God and creative experience. Yet "creative experience" is another word Griffin uses to denote that which is distinct from God. Griffin calls it the "*formless ultimate*," clearly distinguishing it from the concrete, finite, *formed* actualities in which it becomes instantiated. He also calls it the "impersonal ultimate" to distinguish it from God as "personal ultimate," and suggests that it may also be denoted as "being itself" in contradistinction to God as a personal being.[121]

Despite the brevity of this exposition of Griffin's conceptualization of God in contradistinction to the world, there are three questions to be raised. First, is it possible to achieve greater clarity on the relationships among God, the world of finite actualities, and creative experience, as Griffin understands

---

[116] *Reenchantment without Supernaturalism*, 260.
[117] Ibid., 260–71.
[118] Ibid., 267.
[119] Ibid., 261.
[120] The 2003 Brennan Lectures, Lecture II: "The Divine, the Demonic, and the Parable of the Tribes," delivered at Christ Church Cathedral, Louisville, Kentucky, June 2, 2003, p. 14. The lecture was presented as a draft of the second chapter of a book with the proposed title *Thy Kingdom Come*. I am grateful and indebted to David Griffin for permission to cite from this work in progress.

these? It strikes me that "the world of finite actualities" can be thought of as the body of God. Thus, while distinguishable from God as a whole, it is not to be regarded as other than God—just as the human body is distinguishable from the human person, yet never regarded as something other than an integral part of the person. In much the same sense that there are bodily processes that transpire without any conscious direction or control from the individual whose body is in question, so the world as God's "body" may have a kind of life of its own, in which the various differentiable parts may be thought to function in differentiable ways, yet never entirely independently of the whole, including the mind or soul (i.e., God) to whose body they belong. If the distinction between God and the world of finite actualities can be dealt with in this way, then the primary distinction remaining to be addressed is that between God and creative experience.

A second question, therefore, has to do with the metaphysical significance of Griffin's claim that there are two ultimates, one personal, the other impersonal, each equally primordial and neither subordinate to the other. The question is whether this re-introduces a metaphysical dualism of precisely the sort that Griffin has sought to overcome. Griffin has good reasons for rejecting the idea of God without a world, or a world without God. But must the only alternative to "God *or* world" be "God *and* world" (where "world" is the "stuff" of existence, i.e., creative experience)? If God may be thought of as the soul or mind of the world, and hence if the world may be thought of as God's body, can we not think of the totality of existence as a single living being, let us say, "God–world"? In this case, either "God" or "world" could be taken to refer to the whole of existence, but each in a different respect, the former being personal and the latter impersonal. In this case we could say that there is only one ultimate reality without, I think, adopting a purely monistic or pantheistic worldview.

If it is objected that there can be no self-existent individual or reality, and that we must necessarily affirm two ultimate realities, then I think we must also accept a kind of metaphysical dualism. Perhaps Griffin would allow that there is nothing inherently problematic about metaphysical dualism so long as it does not entail any actual existential independence, and so long as the other (impersonal) ultimate is not understood to be an inherently opposing power or source of evil. In fact, Griffin writes of creativity in itself as "neutral with regard to values, therefore 'beyond good and evil,'" although "creativity has never existed neutrally, without being shaped by God's primordial aim toward value realization."[122]

---

[121] *Reenchantment without Supernaturalism*, 269.

At the end of the day, however, a third question persists. Does Griffin overreach by attempting to say too much about God? If God exists, and is anything like what philosophers and theologians have claimed, it would seem that human minds could hardly begin to fathom God. We certainly cannot purport to know God in God's aseity, as Gustafson and McFague rightly contend. How much of God can we know even in God's relation to the world? On the one hand, Griffin's serious and thorough effort to give an account of the God–world relation is to be affirmed. It is intellectually and religiously dishonest, I believe, for philosophers and theologians to make any claims about God as creator of the universe, or as One who exercises influence and makes a difference in the world, without providing some kind of warrant for such claims. Moreover, if one hopes to warrant such claims to those who share the modern commitment to reason and experience, the claims must be congruent with the best of our scientific knowledge and understanding of how things in the world really are.

On the other hand, there are also intellectual and religious reasons for modesty and reticence in our theological and metaphysical claims. Some kind of balance must be struck between the need to give a coherent and truthful account that would warrant any claims about God and the God–world relation, and the need to acknowledge the opacity of that which surely lies beyond the limits of our experience and reason. I do not find Griffin's account of God to be *completely* coherent, partly because some of his concepts require further refinement and integration, but also because he has tried to make rationally clear and distinct what may be epistemologically inaccessible and/or intractably obscure. That is to say, I doubt that a completely coherent account of God is possible. But then, neither have natural scientists been able to provide a completely coherent account of the "natural" world. We may be dealing with realities that lie beyond human ken.

Despite Griffin's speculative excesses, nonetheless, I believe he has provided a *sufficiently* coherent and experientially warranted account of the God–world relation to merit our further consideration. I come to this judgment

---

[122]Ibid., 267. In his essay, "John Cobb's Whiteheadian Complementary Pluralism" (*Deep Religious Pluralism*, 39–66), Griffin says that Cobb affirms not just two ultimates but three—God, creativity, and the cosmos, or the totality of finite things—each distinct, and none separable, from the others. These three ultimates do not exist on the same level, however, and so do not imply some sort of polytheism. "They differ as the one Supreme Being, the many finite beings, and Being Itself, which is embodied by both God and finite beings" (49–50). Griffin does not explicitly identify himself with Cobb's view, though he seems implicitly to accept it. This formulation may actually resolve some of the confusion in Griffin's position, and incidentally even provide a basis for a sort of process trinitarianism, though I wonder if the language of "being" is not problematic for a process conceptuality.

because Griffin's account comprehends the greater part of human experience in terms that meet the criteria of empirical adequacy and logical consistency without making any significant claims that are clearly refutable.

Evil and the Problem of Goodness

For traditional monotheisms, the presence and reality of evil is a major theological problem. Christian theologians have struggled mightily to explain why an all-powerful God, who is also benevolent and just, would permit evil to exist. I make no attempt to rehearse those arguments here. Recognizing the seriousness of this question, Griffin has written two books on the problem of evil, the first of which consists primarily of critiques of various "solutions" that other theologians and philosophers have attempted, the second of which expands and refines his own argument in the first book while also responding to its critics.[123]

Evil is a problem for traditional monotheistic theology precisely because of its presuppositions about God. Griffin notes that major theologians of the West, including Augustine, Thomas, Calvin, Luther, and Barth, have all finally understood the omnipotence of God to mean that God ultimately determines every event, including all human actions, and including all events that are regarded as evil.[124] When the presupposition of God's perfect goodness is added to the presupposition of God's all-determining power, the tendency is to find some way finally to deny the existence of evil, whether understood as an ontological reality or as a deficiency of actuality with respect to possibility. We can find this tendency even in someone like Sallie McFague, whose theology would hardly seem to require a commitment to a traditional view of divine omnipotence.[125] James Gustafson, more willing to countenance the ineradicability of evil from a human perspective, but also committed to a radically monotheistic faith, underscores the tragic character of much of human existence. Divine goodness is not denied, but the theocentric critique of anthropocentrism means that human fortunes must not be the measure of God's benevolence.

Evil is simply not a problem for Griffin and other process thinkers in quite the same way that it is for traditional monotheism, precisely because process theology does not presuppose that God is an all-determining power. However, Griffin notes that in addition to traditional all-determining theism

---

[123] *God, Power, and Evil: A Process Theodicy* and *Evil Revisited: Responses and Reconsiderations*.
[124] *Evil Revisited*, 13. Cf. *God, Power, and Evil*, chapters 6, 7, 9, 10, and 12. James Gustafson also provides an account of how several of these theologians view the divine determination, coming to essentially the same conclusion, namely, that in their theology God ultimately determines all events.

there is also traditional free-will theism.[126] Free-will theism argues to the effect that God has optimally constituted and ordered the world "to encourage the formation of beings who freely develop moral-spiritual character," and that the occurrence of natural and moral evil under such circumstances does not contradict God's goodness and power.[127] Griffin raises ten objections to this view, none of which count against a process perspective.[128]

For Griffin and other process thinkers, there is no need to try to justify the existence of evil or explain it away. Quite the contrary:

> One of the hard-core commonsense notions, I claim, is the reality of genuine evil, by which I mean evil that would retain its evilness when viewed from an all-inclusive perspective. To believe in genuine evil is to believe that some things happen that, all things considered, should not have happened; the world would have been better if some alternative possibility had happened instead.[129]

Instead of being problematized, due to incompatible presuppositions about God, evil is defined as a less than optimally possible circumstance, whether attributable to human or nonhuman interactions. The point, of course, is that we do not live in the best of all possible worlds, and that all that appears to be evil cannot be rationalized as instrumental to some greater good.

For many people evil may seem to be too strong a word simply to denote non-optimal outcomes, and its use should be reserved to refer to positively destructive forces or demonic powers. But Griffin also develops the idea of evil as demonic, which he defines as "evil that diametrically opposes divine power and does so with such strength as to destroy divine creations in a way

---

[125]In fact, McFague does not have a consistently articulated view of evil. On the one hand she can write, "Evil is not a power over against God; in a sense, it is God's 'responsibility,' part of God's being, if you will"; "Imaging a Theology of Nature," 215. On the other hand, she can lay the bulk of responsibility for evil at the feet of humanity, as we saw in Chapter 3; cf. esp. 115–16, 131 above. But in one of her most recent statements she declares, "Evil does not 'exist.' It does not have ontological status; rather, it is a perversion of good. All that lives depends on God or comes from God; evil does not depend on God or come from God"; "Intimate Creation," 45 (see also "Sallie McFague," in Placher, 114). Though McFague clearly recognizes the existence of suffering and tragedy in the world, it is hard not to read this last statement as a denial of the reality of evil. The thrust of her argument, in any case, is to reaffirm the two traditional claims about God, namely that God is perfectly good, and therefore cannot be the source of evil, and that God is all-powerful, or at least sufficiently so, that all so-called evil will ultimately be overcome by good.
[126]*Evil Revisited*, 14ff.
[127]Ibid., 15.
[128]Ibid., 16–22.
[129]Ibid., 3.

that threatens divine purposes."¹³⁰ It is crucial to recognize that Griffin has more than a merely formal sense of the reality of evil. Not only is this *not* the best of all possible worlds, and therefore a world of unnecessary limitations and suffering, but, because of the "unprecedented power of self-determination" of human beings,¹³¹ this world is one in which evil can now manifest itself in truly demonic ways.

The existence of evil, in any event, does not pose the problem of theodicy for process theology that it has for traditional theism. For Griffin and other process thinkers, God is not the only source or locus of power in the universe. Every entity is understood to possess some element of creativity and self-determination.¹³² And even though God is said to exercise influence upon each actual occasion by providing an initial aim, this influence is always of a persuasive nature. That is, the divine influence is not manifest as external coercive force, but always exerts itself internally and is never sufficient alone to determine the actual subjective aim or the outcome of the occasion. In other words, "God cannot unilaterally determine what happens in the world."¹³³ Consequently, God can hardly be held accountable for all that happens in the world. If there is evil in the world, as there surely is, this evil does not implicate the divine goodness.

On the other hand, there is a sense in which divine goodness is a problem for process thought. In a world filled with real evils, with enormous tragedy and suffering, what basis do we have for affirming that God is good? There seems to be plenty of evidence to the contrary. Moreover, there would appear to be no logical reason why God must be assumed to be good or just. In an important essay titled "The Holy, Necessary Goodness, and Morality,"¹³⁴ Griffin notes the widespread view that there is no necessary connection between the metaphysical attributes of God, at least as traditionally understood, and the moral attributes we would prefer God to possess. He cites philosopher Henry David Aiken, who observed, "'there is no reason why an almighty and omniscient being might not be a perfect stinker.'"¹³⁵ Of course, when

---

¹³⁰"Divine Goodness and Demonic Evil," William Cenkner, editor, *Evil and the Response of World Religion* (St. Paul, Minn.: Paragon, 1997), 26; cf. *Evil Revisited*, esp. 31–34.
¹³¹Ibid., 232. Griffin mentions the Nazi holocaust, the rapes and murders of little children, the slaughter of war, and the building and proliferation of nuclear weapons as examples of demonic evil; 225, 227.
¹³²Griffin writes: "From the point of view of a theology of universal creativity, the existence of chaos and evil is no surprise. They are to be expected, given a multiplicity of centers of creative power. The surprise is the existence of order and goodness. They beg for explanation in terms of an all-inclusive creative influence. Whereas starting with the concentration of all creativity in one divine being finally led to the denial of God, starting with many centers of creativity leads to the affirmation of God"; *God and Religion in the Postmodern World*, 43.
¹³³"Whitehead's Deeply Ecological Worldview," 200.

one also takes into consideration the traditional view of God as creator, it becomes more difficult to imagine that God would be anything but favorably disposed toward the creation. Nonetheless, traditional conceptions of God necessarily require certain presumptions about God's goodness that are not strictly entailed by their metaphysical conceptions. The situation is quite different for process theology.

Griffin first addresses the question of how we are to define or identify what it means to say that something is morally good or right by introducing the notion of an ideal observer:

> My first point is that there is a widespread consensus, among those who consider moral judgments to be objective and therefore capable of being true or false, that right and wrong must finally coincide with what a fully informed, impartial, sympathetic observer would approve and disapprove. The attempt to achieve this perspective is quite often referred to as adopting the "moral point of view." . . . [T]he spectator must be both *impartial* and *sympathetic to the interests of all* as well as *fully informed*.[136]

It will be obvious from the foregoing account of process metaphysics that God is a prime candidate for ideal observer status in Griffin's thought.[137] After all, God is the only "fully informed" entity in the universe, always knowing everything that it is possible at any given moment to know.[138]

But how do we know that a universal and impartial sympathy is also an attribute of God? The key to answering this question lies in the Whiteheadian understanding of perception as prehension, and the claim that God prehends all other actual entities or occasions of experience. Griffin asks, rhetorically:

> What if *to know* other sentient beings *immediately* with *perfect knowledge* is *necessarily to share their enjoyments, their sufferings, and their desires*? Then an *omniscient* being would *necessarily* be *sympathetic*, and *impartially* so, since this being would *equally* share the feelings of all other sentient beings.[139]

It is precisely God's direct and immediate knowledge or prehension, that is, perception in the mode of causal efficacy, that insures the divine feeling, or sympathy, for every occasion. That sympathy may be said to be equal or

---

[134]*Journal of Religious Ethics* 8 (1980) 330–49.
[135]Ibid., 338.
[136]Ibid., 337.
[137]Although, as Griffin notes in *Reenchantment without Supernaturalism*, in a Whiteheadian perspective, *ideal feeler* would be a better term than *ideal observer*, 316.
[138]Above, 168 and n. 98.

impartial, not in the sense that it is the same for every occasion, but in the sense that it corresponds fully to the self-experience or degree of subjectivity of every occasion.[140]

Drawing on Hartshorne, Griffin observes the positive relation between knowledge and sympathy, a relation that cannot be assumed in other metaphysical conceptions but is necessary in a process perspective. He invokes the analogy of the mind-body relation as a model for the God–world relation to provide a more concrete image for thinking about God's unmediated, sympathetic knowledge of the world. This "leads to the view that God, as omniscient, naturally and necessarily is motivated by the interests of others, since they become God's own interests."[141] Divine omniscience, therefore, results in a complete coincidence of God's interest and the interest of the world as a whole. In any given situation, therefore, God may—indeed, must—be understood as willing the good or the right, as such good or right would be judged from the perspective of a fully informed, impartial and sympathetic ideal observer. The term "observer" may be misleading, however, for God does not observe as one who looks out upon a world external to God, but as one whose knowledge is constituted by the prehension of all actual entities, that is, the direct, immediate experience of and feeling for all occasions of experience in their concrete actuality. God is "fully informed" inasmuch as the world is fully immanent in God.

It bears repeating that this way of understanding God's sympathetic care for the world is basically a metaphysically conceptualized version of the relation between God and world that Sallie McFague has sought to express by her metaphor of the world as God's body.[142] In McFague's view, God can be counted on to exercise compassion and care precisely because the world is (metaphorically) God's body. McFague's metaphorical image of the God–world relation, like Griffin's metaphysical conception of that relation, clearly provides the warrant for affirming the divine goodness with respect to all that exists.

On the other hand, James Gustafson's affirmation of divine goodness is essentially a matter of piety. It cannot be substantiated by the empirical evidence of natural and historical events, nor is it warranted by Gustafson's

---

[139]"The Holy, Necessary Goodness, and Morality," 340.
[140]I am extrapolating a bit in this sentence from what Griffin actually says in order to clarify what I think his argument implies. He is not clear about the meaning of "equally" and "impartially" in the immediate context of the statement quoted. Later in the article he addresses the question of equality in terms of equal regard for all persons, making an argument that I do not think coheres well with a thoroughly process perspective; cf. 344ff. See also his discussion in *Reenchantment without Supernaturalism*, 314ff.
[141]Ibid., 341.

understanding of the God–world relation. God is deemed to be good, but the divine dispensation toward humanity is not the final measure of that goodness. God has purposes that do not necessarily serve specifically human ends, and therefore cannot be adequately judged from any human perspective. Consequently, as we saw in Chapter 1, Gustafson resists the traditional way of framing the question about God's goodness: Are God's ends good because God wills them, or does God will them because they are good?[143] He sees this way of framing the question as one that has conspired to confirm the assumption that the divine ends serve what is taken to be right and good from a human perspective. What we find in Griffin (and McFague), however, is a way of addressing the question that does not arbitrarily, and unacceptably, define the good in terms of God's will, nor does it succumb to an anthropocentric view of divine goodness. Griffin's metaphysical conception of the God–world relation thus takes evil with utmost seriousness while making the affirmation of God's goodness not only possible but necessary without resort to an anthropocentric perspective.

A major objection is often leveled against process theology at this point, however. Given this view of the divine power and goodness, there seems to be no way to assure that goodness will ultimately prevail. The objection always carries with it the implicit assumption that goodness must prevail with respect to the human venture. It is an essentially anthropocentric objection. And it is true that Griffin has no basis to assure that there will be a favorable or just outcome to the human venture. We human beings may irrevocably destroy all life on this planet, and God may not be able to stop us. Or our planet may be struck by an asteroid of such magnitude that the earth becomes uninhabitable. That would not mean the defeat of God's goodness, however. In process thought, there will always be God and there will always be some world—this one or another—in relation to which God's goodness will continue to be embodied. To demand more of God's goodness is to attempt to put God at our disposal.

Nonetheless, it is clear that Griffin has felt the weight of the objection. Moreover, all process thought entails the claim of objective immortality. Death, whether with respect to an individual human being, the human species, or all of life as we know it, clearly raises the question of meaning. As Griffin points out, "[p]rocess theologians have usually dealt with the question of ultimate meaning solely by further appeal to . . . God's 'consequent nature.' If God appreciatively preserves all that we have been, there is a ground for the ultimate meaning of our lives that nothing, not even nuclear holocaust—let alone moth, rust, and thieves—can take away."[144] God's "conse-

[142]Cf. 136–37 above.
[143]Cf. 14.

quent nature" refers to the Whiteheadian notion that all worldly occasions are said to be prehended by, and thereby included in, the divine experience.[145] Metaphorically speaking, God never forgets. Moreover, God immortally preserves all that which can be comprehended and appropriated from the past in keeping with God's subjective aims and enduring purpose. This is the meaning of objective immortality. All that any entity or individual contributes to the divine experience is everlastingly preserved.

In his more recent writings Griffin has come to the conclusion that objective immortality, along with such assurances as process theology may provide regarding the divine possibilities for unexpected transformation in our world of increasingly ominous threats of ecological, nuclear, and other forms of destruction, "are not sufficient to allow many of the most sensitive souls to give an unambiguous yes to the process that has brought us forth."[146] In most people, says Griffin, the desire for immortality is not satisfied by the idea that they will be objectively immortal in God.[147] This desire has to do not simply with a longing for more of life, but with the felt need for the realization of unfulfilled potentials. Death typically precludes satisfaction of the need for ultimate meaning, which is contingent on having made a contribution to the universe with which one can rest content.[148]

However, the idea of subjective immortality is clearly at odds with process theology's claim, especially as articulated by Hartshorne, that God is the only source of ultimate meaning.[149] Only God is immortal. This leads Griffin to argue for the possibility of temporally finite subjective (human) experience after bodily death. Process metaphysics, he insists, at least allows for this possibility, so long as such "life after death" is not understood to be immortal. Presumably, at some point for every individual, such life after death would reach its culmination and then cease. Although strictly an optional element in his theodicy, belief in a continuing life is regarded by Griffin as strengthening process theology's claim on behalf of God as the source of ultimate meaning and hope in the face of the genuine evils of this world.[150] Griffin goes so far as to say that "belief in life as a journey that continues beyond bodily death is probably an essential ingredient if there are to be religious communities combining a vital spirituality with a liberal approach to religious belief."[151]

---

[144] *Evil Revisited*, 34–35.
[145] Cf. above, 165ff.
[146] *Evil Revisited*, 35.
[147] Ibid., 36.
[148] Ibid., 36–37.
[149] Process theologian Marjorie Suchocki argues, however, that Hartshorne's position can be construed to imply subjective immortality. In fact, she claims that on the occasion of meeting him at a conference in 1974 he expressed agreement with her view in a paper she wrote arguing

While insufficient evidence exists to deny the possibility of life after death, the case that Griffin makes—even if intended in part to strengthen convictions regarding God as source of ultimate meaning and hope—seems much too closely tied to an anthropocentric view of what is required to affirm the existence of a source of ultimate meaning and hope. It would be wonderful to think that every individual human life is ultimately accorded justice and blessed with fulfillment. For some people, especially those whose lives are marked by great inequities and suffering, it may even be emotionally and psychologically necessary to believe in life after death in order to secure the conviction and maintain the hope that this life remains worth living and that God is worthy of worship and service. Even so, in a truly theocentric theological perspective, this kind of instrumental consideration does not warrant making any claims for life after bodily death. For theocentric reasons, if not for naturalistic ones, we may assert a conviction of objective immortality but must demur on the question of continued subjective existence after death. Not only is there genuine evil in the world, but it may not be remediable so far as those who suffer it are concerned.

Griffin's Generic Conception of God

The metaphysics of Griffin's naturalism$_{ppp}$ entails a panentheistic conception of God that is intellectually coherent, insofar as it coheres with Griffin's epistemology of prehension and his panexperientialist ontology. But does that make it a religiously adequate conception, capable of evoking piety and gaining acceptance among religious adherents? Is it a conception of God that is continuous at least with the major monotheistic religious traditions, a conception of God not only as agential and purposeful but also as worthy of worship? As we have just seen, process theism's understanding of divine power gives rise to reservations regarding the capacity of a panentheistic God to overcome evil in the world. I do not consider these reservations to be decisive, however, certainly not from a theocentric rather than anthropocentric perspective. But there are other features or attributes besides omnipotence that are widely regarded as constitutive of any adequate conception of God within the monotheistic traditions. Griffin identifies these features as part of

---

to that effect. While statements he later made regarding objective immortality do not affirm subjective immortality, she notes, neither do they absolutely rule it out; "Charles Hartshorne and Subjective Immortality," unpublished paper, Center for Process Studies.

[150] Ibid., 40. For more extended discussions by Griffin regarding life after death, see "Postmodern Animism and Life after Death," in *God and Religion in the Postmodern World* (Albany: SUNY Press, 1989) 83–108; *Reenchantment without Supernaturalism*, 230–46.

[151] *Reenchantment without Supernaturalism*, 240.

the "generic idea of God." In *Reenchantment without Supernaturalism*, he lists thirteen such features.

According to Griffin, the generic idea of God refers to: 1) a personal, purposive being who is 2) perfect in love, goodness, and beauty, as well as 3) perfect in wisdom and knowledge. This God is 4) supreme, perhaps even perfect, in power; 5) Creator of our universe; 6) holy; and 7) omnipresent. This God is also 8) necessarily and everlastingly existent; 9) providentially active in nature and history; and 10) experienced by human beings. Finally, this God must be 11) the ultimate source of moral norms; 12) the ultimate guarantee of the meaning of life; and 13) the ground of hope for the victory of good over evil. Griffin observes:

> Whether all these features are necessary for a concept of God could be argued, but that these features are sufficient is beyond reasonable debate. No one believing in a being thus characterized could plausibly be said not to believe in God. All these features are affirmed by traditional theism. They are also all affirmed by process theism.[152]

It is beyond the scope of this chapter to provide a complete explication of Griffin's conception of God in terms of these attributes. Surely a God describable in these terms would be deemed worthy of worship and service. But what reason is there to believe that such a God really exists? In most general terms, the answer to this question is fairly obvious. The existence of such a God is coherent with, and in fact seems to be indicated by, process metaphysics itself. If the world is such as process philosophy describes it, then God must be such as process theism affirms. Or as Griffin puts the matter, *"insofar as process philosophy's construal of the world is otherwise convincing, seeming more adequate and self-consistent than other known options, the reality of a divine being, as portrayed by process philosophy, is implied."*[153]

However, Griffin does not simply rest his case on the convincingness of his argument for naturalism$_{PPP}$. He devotes an entire chapter in *Reenchantment without Supernaturalism* to making a cumulative case for naturalistic theism.[154] The case is made on the basis of a number of arguments, none of which is taken to be decisive, but all of which together are taken to be compelling. There are five arguments from fundamental aspects of the world in general, the metaphysical, cosmological, and teleological arguments and the arguments from novelty and from excessive beauty. There are also four arguments from fundamental aspects of human experience. These include argu-

---

[152]166. Griffin has a shorter list of seven slightly differently worded attributes in *Evil Revisited*, 11–12. In *Religion and Scientific Naturalism* nine attributes are listed, including that God "alone is worthy of worship," 90.

ments from ideals, from truth, from importance, and from religious experience. As noted by reviewer Kevin Schilbrack, "though Griffin has claimed in the past that natural theology is not essential to process theism, he now holds that a process philosophy of religion not only presents a credible idea of God but also provides strong reasons for believing in God's existence."[155] My own view is that Griffin's natural theology arguments are not entirely persuasive as arguments for the existence of God. However, they point to realities, the experience of which may well serve to engender such conviction. That is to say, they identify and articulate possible bases for religious conviction, and thereby help corroborate continuing belief in God.

In any event, if we accept as credible Griffin's account of God's relation to the world, including the existence of variable divine influence in nature and history, his process theism would seem to promise both an intellectually and a religiously adequate—though hardly distinctively and exclusively Christian—conception of God. But we must explore further whether Griffin's understandings of God and the world are sufficiently congruent with those of Gustafson and McFague so that his conception of the God–world relation can be appropriated in the articulation of the theocentric, naturalistic worldview that we are seeking as a basis for an intellectually and religiously adequate theological ethics.

Griffin's Theological Perspective in Profile

In the preceding chapter I compared and related various features of Sallie McFague's theological ethics to those of James Gustafson in order to identify a substantial congruence between the two. I now wish to explore the extent to which David Griffin's theological perspective exhibits a similar congruence with the perspectives of both Gustafson and McFague.

Naturalism

Little more needs to be said about Griffin's naturalism. I have taken his position to be normative for my project, and have attempted to measure the adequacy of Gustafson's and McFague's naturalistic perspectives largely in terms of their coherence and adherence to Griffin's formulation. Key features of Griffin's position are his rejection of epistemic and ontological supernaturalism, his endorsement of domain uniformitarianism (the explanation of religion in terms of the same causal categories used in other cultural domains),

---

[153] *Reenchantment without Supernaturalism*, 170–71.
[154] "Natural Theology Based on Naturalistic Theism," 169–203.
[155] Op. cit., 640.

and his acceptance of empirical groundedness (no radical differentiation of religious from scientific claims in terms of susceptibility to empirical testing). To these we must now add his naturalism$_{ppp}$, with its tenets of prehension, panexperientialism, and panentheism as radical alternatives to sensationism, materialism, and atheism. The incorporation of naturalism$_{ppp}$ into a naturalistic theological ethics that draws substantially on Gustafson and McFague will require some modifications to the thought of each of these. In particular, Gustafson's view of God must be amended by Griffin's panentheism, with its purposive, agential view of God. And Gustafson's notion of piety may be accorded status as a mode of knowledge in light of Griffin's notion of prehension. On the other hand, McFague's view of God is already panentheistic, at least at the metaphorical level. Her worldview is often otherwise implicitly materialistic, however, and her epistemology rules out any direct, unmediated experience of God or anything else.[156] Griffin's epistemology of prehension and his panexperientialism imply significant changes in the underlying assumptions of her theology of nature, with consequential implications regarding the warrants for metaphorical theological language. These are all matters to be taken up again in the chapter to follow.

Theocentrism

Just as Griffin's naturalistic perspective is normative for this book, so Gustafson provides the normative theocentric perspective. In that light we have already seen how McFague's cosmocentric perspective does not fully capture the radically monotheistic vision and critique of instrumentalist ethics that distinguish Gustafson's theocentrism. In the introduction to this chapter we have also seen that one of Griffin's aims for his process theism is a kind of instrumentalist aim, namely the reenchantment of the world, to provide adequate "cosmological support for the ideals needed by contemporary civilization."[157] This practical aim is balanced, however with the theoretical one of integrating science and religion into a single worldview.[158] The goal is to provide a coherent account of reality that corresponds adequately to actual human experience and empirical knowledge of the world.

Thus, Griffin's work is not explicitly theocentric. It is, however, clearly nonanthropocentric:

> [P]rocess theology, being evolutionary, nondualistic, and nonanthropocentric, specifically rejects the idea that the world was designed for human beings in particular. To regard the world as reflecting a divine

---

[156]This applies to her major works, as interpreted in Chapter 3. In her most recent book, *Life Abundant*, written after her "fourth conversion" (8), a different epistemology appears.

teleology is not to say that everything is supposed to work together for *human* good. The divine purpose promotes harmonious intensity of experience in general. We humans generally benefit from this promotion, both directly and indirectly, but this promotion has necessarily had the possibility of resulting in forms of order and types of events, such as viruses, cancerous growths, earthquakes, and meteorites, that sometimes conflict with our welfare.[159]

One can also say that Griffin's perspective is not geocentric. That is, the world is not limited to planet Earth, and he does not identify our planet as the locus of all value in the universe. One may even say that Griffin does not regard the universe as the ultimate repository of all value. Only God, as the only personal ultimate, the mind and soul of the universe, can be said to be the preserver of all value. There is nothing else of ultimate meaning, significance, or value.

A careful distinction needs to be made here. Griffin would never say that nothing matters but God, or that all value is for God's sake alone. For Griffin, as for Whitehead, the world is the locus of value realization. Every actuality, being an occasion of experience, "as such has value for itself and for others."[160] But because God prehends all actualities, which is to say that the world is immanent in God, all realized value becomes part of the consequent nature of God. There would be no value for God to enjoy were it not for the value of every occasion of experience, yet there is nothing of *ultimate* value or significance apart from God. Just as all pain and evil are felt and suffered by God, all value that is realized redounds to the enjoyment of God. In this important respect nothing (except God) can be said to be an end in itself. Griffin often speaks of God as the "Holy Reality." In this context he uses the term holy to refer to "*that which is of ultimate intrinsic worth, in relation to which everything else finally has its worth.*"[161] Griffin's theology is necessarily theocentric in this regard.

Nonetheless, it is hard to avoid the sense that Griffin sometimes claims justification for his metaphysical worldview because it serves, instrumentally, as a basis for addressing his moral concerns. He urges the need for reenchantment, in large part because he wants to re-establish a basis for ideals, possibilities, norms, and values, without which he sees contemporary civilization to be in jeopardy.[162] Yet this sense is mitigated by the fact that his philosophical method hardly seems to be dictated by instrumental values. He persistently

---

[157] 149.
[158] Ibid.
[159] *Evil Revisited*, 203.
[160] *Reenchantment without Supernaturalism*, 301.

argues for his worldview as the one that best fits the facts of human experience, or most closely corresponds to what we know empirically about the world. In fact, he seldom draws out the concrete moral or ethical implications of his process theism to any great extent. To be sure, he seeks a theory that can make sense of many of our moral, religious, and aesthetic intuitions, no doubt in part to validate those intuitions, but also to render an intelligible account of how they come to be. Few of his critics are likely to complain that his philosophy is but a pretext for some moral or political agenda. In fact, process thought has often been criticized for lacking an incisive moral vision. In my judgment, while Griffin clearly has a moral vision, I think he intends for his work to adhere to the same strictures against ideology that he identifies with proper science.[163]

On the whole, therefore, I find Griffin's work to be much more consistently nonanthropocentric, and more theocentric, than McFague's. Yet they both face a similar challenge, for they both see our planet in peril. They both recognize the real possibilities that we human beings may destroy ourselves and all other planetary life. And they both hope to help provide a remedy, in the form of a fresh understanding of the God–world relation and its significance for the human venture. Thus Griffin, who sees the need for spiritually vital religious communities, argues for life after death, not because his process perspective requires it, nor simply because human yearnings and intuitions suggest it as a possibility, but specifically because belief in life after death seems necessary to evoke the requisite spiritual vitality.[164] Granted, Griffin is not saying, "Be religious so that you can live after death." Rather, he is saying, "Affirm life after death in order to evoke spirituality." But the need to evoke spirituality is to provide support for those ideals and actions necessary for the survival of human civilization. The theocentric focus is blurred, to say the least, for the sake of anthropocentric preoccupations. Fortunately, this is not an irremediable defect of Griffin's thought, which in its most complete expression exhibits a theocentric character. Process theology emphatically recognizes the vast difference between what God knows and purposes and what human beings, even at their highest and best, are capable of knowing and purposing. Perhaps what process theology needs at this point is an infusion of metaphorical theological language that accents that difference.

---

[161] Ibid., 252.
[162] Cf. 149 above.
[163] Cf. above, 151–52 and n. 28.
[164] Cf. above, 184–85.

Conversion

To my knowledge, Griffin never employs the language of conversion in his writings. Unlike Gustafson and McFague, there is no concentrated focus in his published work on the need to turn from anthropocentrism to theocentrism or cosmocentrism as such. On the other hand, there has surely been no one with greater zeal for promoting the gospel of process philosophy and theology. At its core Griffin's work is a call for the reconciliation of science and religion through the replacement of modern epistemological and ontological paradigms with Whiteheadian process formulations and the consequent metaphysical re-conceptualization of the God–world relation. His epistemology of prehension constitutes a trenchant critique of the sensationist epistemology of Hume and most of scientific naturalism in the modern period. His adoption of panexperientialism means the rejection of "the basic ontological premise of modern thought in all its forms . . . , that is, that the fundamental units of nature are devoid of experience and aim."[165] Griffin's aim is clearly to establish his "cosmological postmodernism"[166] as a live and preferable option to prevailing thought forms in science, philosophy, and religion in the modern period, as his general editorship of the multi-volume "SUNY Series in Constructive Postmodern Thought" also attests.[167]

Of course, Griffin's postmodern cosmology also constitutes a profound critique of various modern social anthropologies. Generally this critique is implicit, but occasionally Griffin makes it explicit, as when he identifies the following themes as "characteristic of postmodern spirituality and social thinking":

> a nondualistic relation of humans to nature and of the divine reality to the world; the immanence of both the past and the future (albeit in different ways) in the present; the universality and centrality of creativity; postpatriarchy; communitarianism (versus individualism and nationalism); the "deprivatization" of religion, meaning the rejection of the autonomy of morality, politics, and economics from religious values; and (specifically) the rejection of materialism, in the sense of economism, meaning the subordination of social, religious, moral, aesthetic, and ecological interests to (short-term) economic interests.[168]

We cannot examine here the ways in which all these themes are implicated by Griffin's worldview but should note that, like Gustafson and McFague,

---

[165]Griffin, "On Ian Barbour's *Issues in Science and Religion*," *Zygon* 23 (1988) 66.
[166]In contrast to poststructuralist postmodernisms; Catherine Keller and Anne Daniell compare and contrast these two forms of postmodernism as editors of *Process and Difference*.
[167]Over thirty volumes in the series have been published to date.

Griffin sees the need to overcome a number of dualisms (e.g., human/nonhuman; nature/spirit; male/female; individual/society) that continue to plague Western thought and culture. Griffin's work may also be seen, therefore, as a call for a new anthropology and social vision.

There is yet a third sense in which Griffin's work may be understood as a call to conversion, and it has the greatest resonance with traditional religious understandings of conversion. We have observed that the category of the demonic has come to play a significant part in Griffin's understanding of evil. In some of his most recent and as yet unpublished writings, Griffin has come to associate the demonic with the political, military, and economic hegemony of American empire. In *Reenchantment without Supernaturalism* he mentions only in passing his view that Whiteheadian thought "implies the movement to a democratic world order."[169] Now his call for a global democracy is being presented as an urgently needed antidote to American imperial ambitions. He writes, "Christians in America need to consider whether the situation created by American imperialism creates a *status confessionis*," that is, a confessional situation not unlike that in Nazi Germany in the 1930s and in South Africa under apartheid, in which the church must publicly and unequivocally express its opposition to the prevailing political order and work for change as a matter of faithful Christian witness. "The primary change I have in mind," he says, "is the *transformation* of the present world order, which allows for war and imperialism, into a global democracy."[170] Griffin seems poised to be one of the first Christian thinkers to make a significant contribution to the emerging public debate about American empire. Whether or not Gustafson and McFague publicly enter this debate, it is reasonable to assume that they would render similar, though probably less radical, critiques of current American imperialism. In any event, in light of Griffin's critique of America's exercise of power, the nature and significance of his view of human sin can now be seen in bolder relief.

Sin

Though Griffin says very little explicitly about sin as such, he has a way of conceptualizing sin that is highly significant in its implications for theo-

---

[168] *Sacred Interconnections*, 3. In *The Reenchantment of Science* Griffin calls for "the emergence of a society in which individualism, nationalism, militarism, anthropocentrism, and androcentrism have been transcended" by a "relational, ecological, planetary, postpatriarchal spirituality"; xiii.

[169] 311.

[170] The 2003 Brennan Lectures, Lecture I: "Empire Now and Then, Jesus, and the Reign of God," delivered at Christ Church Cathedral, Louisville, Kentucky, June 1, 2003, 1–2 (my

logical ethics. In simplest terms, sin means going against the divine will.[171] Alternatively, "morally evil acts are ones in which selfishness or egoism prevails over unselfishness in agents who have the capacity for acting unselfishly."[172] Obviously, Griffin does not understand sin in terms of violation of some external standard, rule, law, or command of God. Sin is basically understood as acting in accordance with *perceived* self-interest.[173] As Griffin observes,

> self-centeredness does not need explanation but is given with sentience. What does require explanation is the development of a negligible concern for other beings into a significant degree of altruism. Whitehead accordingly speaks of God as "that element in virtue of which our purposes extend beyond values for ourselves to values for others."[174]

I identify sin with acts of *perceived* self-interest because it is possible, indeed more than likely given Griffin's understanding of the interrelatedness of all human beings and all things, that a self-centered act will be contrary to self-interest as well as the interest of others. Griffin does not distinguish between the motive and the objective nature of an act. That is to say, he does not distinguish between an act that is self-centered, and therefore motivated by perceived self-interest, and an act that is actually contrary to the divine will, and therefore presumably contrary to the best interests of others and possibly one's own interest as well. With such an understanding of sin, the question regarding any particular act is not whether it is sinful, but to what degree does it manifest a responsiveness to the divine will given in the initial aim. Because every individual has the freedom and the power of self-determination, given the range of possibilities in a particular situation, every individual subjective aim may conform to greater or lesser degree to the divine initial aim.

In a discussion of creativity, understood as the expression of the freedom and power of self-determination, Griffin explains why individuals can never hope to act with the same degree of sympathy, or responsive love, and goodwill, or creative love, as God:

> In one sense, to be sure, creativity as embodied in God is the same as that embodied in creatures—it involves the twofold power to exert both self-determination and then causal influence on others. But in

---

emphasis). The lecture is a draft of the first chapter of a book with the proposed title, *Thy Kingdom Come*. I am grateful and indebted to David Griffin for permission to quote from this work in progress.

[171] *Evil Revisited*, 13.
[172] Ibid., 223.
[173] This is my interpretation of Griffin. Griffin never puts it quite this way.
[174] Ibid., 224.

other respects it is radically different. For one thing, every creaturely embodiment of creativity is a local embodiment, which is significantly influenced by only a small portion of the universe and has significant influence back upon only a small portion. Creativity as embodied in God, by contrast, is universal, because the divine experience encompasses the whole universe. Likewise, creaturely creativity is always directed by limited knowledge, even in the most informed human beings, whereas divine creativity is always directed by omniscience, the knowledge of everything knowable at the time. Because of these metaphysical differences, furthermore, divine creativity is also—and this is the main point here—*morally* different from creaturely creativity.[175]

In other words, even with the best of intentions human beings are simply incapable of feeling and thereby knowing and acting in accord with the needs and interests of others in the way that God can feel and know and act. With less than the best of intentions, human beings become insensitive to the divine will as well as the feelings of others, and can act not only with indifference but with malice and hate.[176] The same freedom and power of self-determination that makes possible compassion, self-sacrifice, and creative love, also makes it possible for human beings to act in selfish and malevolent ways.[177]

The ethical implications here are obviously in keeping with important themes in Gustafson and McFague. Against our natural tendencies toward self-centeredness, we must endeavor to see things in larger perspective, in their interrelatedness and interdependence, and in the contexts of their larger wholes. And against our predisposition toward narrow and limited sympathies, there is need for the cultivation of wider sympathies, of the capacity to recognize and to share the feelings of others who may not exist in close proximity or be much like ourselves. Griffin does not develop such themes, but they suggest the need for an approach to theological ethics that is largely congruent with the perspectives of Gustafson and McFague.

There is a larger issue that begs attention here, however. As becomes evident from the contrast Griffin draws above between divine creativity and

---

[175]"The Divine, the Demonic, and the Parable of the Tribes," 14.

[176]Cf. *Reenchantment without Supernaturalism*, 392. Given human finitude, human beings are necessarily incapable of embodying the fullness of divine goodness. Given Griffin's view that genuine evil arises wherever something happens that is less good than some other alternative possibility that could have happened (cf. 43 above), one wishes he would explore the meaning of human sin in light of the human condition. It appears that we human beings are necessarily complicit in natural evil, inasmuch as we are incapable of embodying optimal goodness. Can one distinguish this inevitable participation in natural evil from moral evil, or sin—and if so, how?

[177]In *Reenchantment without Supernaturalism*, Griffin identifies five variables of power and value that are necessarily correlative in a process perspective: "1. The capacity to experience intrinsic good. 2. The capacity to experience intrinsic evil. 3. The power to be extrinsically good—that

creaturely creativity, and the moral difference between the two, human beings must always "fall short of the glory of God."[178] Human beings are never capable of actions of perfect goodness because, unlike God, we can never be fully informed—we can never know all there is to know. Even selfless acts fall short. Sin, as conventionally understood, may not be a very helpful category for process thought. This is because sin is generally understood in terms of a failure to conform to the will of God. But in this process perspective, no human actions succeed in conforming in more than a partial way to the divine will. Some actions may be more selfish or self-centered than others, but all actions are deficient insofar as the conditions of finitude preclude any individual from knowing all that would be necessary to know in order to act in accord with perfect goodness. Inasmuch as all human actions fail to conform fully to the will of God, it appears that process thought can meaningfully distinguish between sinful acts and those not considered sinful only by means of the conceptual distinction between acts that are willful, or self-centered, and those that are not. Of course, one may argue that, in its most profound expressions, Christian thought has always understood sin to be precisely of this nature—a selfishness or turning away from the divine will— and never simply a matter of violating the rules, laws, or commandments presumed to be given by God.

In a process perspective, every human action partakes of more or less importance, more or less beauty, more or less value, more or less goodness. A major implication of this conceptuality is that the sphere of the moral is not to be equated with the sphere of morality, if one means by morality that for which the measure must be rules, principles, codes, norms, laws, or other criteria that are held to distinguish right from wrong, good from evil. The sphere of the moral, in contradistinction to that of morality, must be understood in terms of the whole of life. The moral is to be understood in terms of the ideal form of human action. As will be discussed further in the next chapter, there are various dimensions of the moral. These dimensions include morality, but also the intellectual, the spiritual, and the sensible. All of life is infused with value, and all human actions have significance in terms of value, but human actions are not to be measured strictly in terms of morality.

A second important implication of this perspective is that there is no clear method for the specification of moral ideals, norms, principles, or rules.

---

is, to contribute positively to the experience of others. 4. The power to be extrinsically evil—that is, to contribute negatively to, or even be destructive of, the experience of others. 5. The power of self-determination—which in its higher forms we call 'freedom,'" 225. Cf. "Values, Evil, and Liberation Theology," 194.

[178]Cf. Romans 3:23.

There are no requisite criteria by which process thought can identify and establish the meaning of particular moral notions or ideas. Nor is it possible to define just how the sphere or domain of morality is to be distinguished from the rest of life. To my knowledge, Griffin does not give serious attention to this problem of the identification and specification of moral norms and values. Clearly, he assumes that certain values follow from his metaphysics. These include interdependence and interrelatedness, the intrinsic worth of every individual, a concern not only for individuals but for wholes, persuasion rather than coercion, and a critique of hierarchical relations and various dualisms that have become reified in our social structures, for example. What is not clear is how one moves from such general values to more specific moral claims.

It is not clear, for example, how one might argue whether an action is just or unjust. Even if human beings possess an elemental intuition, or hardcore commonsense notion, of fairness, it is not clear how such an intuition or notion could be translated into a social ethic. The idea of justice is not simple but complex, and can be defined in a number of ways. Important questions arise in human society regarding what sorts of political processes, or social arrangements, or legal requirements and restrictions, or judicial proceedings, or distributions of wealth and power, are just. Clearly, Griffin would argue against unnecessarily coercive processes and practices, socially divisive arrangements, and hierarchical structures that stultify and oppress. The question is whether this is sufficient to provide a social critique or prescription.

My own view is that, from a process perspective, and indeed from a radically theocentric perspective as well, one can only undertake the tasks of moral discernment and ethical reflection in a kind of empirical, inductive, and intuitive fashion. Moreover, the identification and specification of relevant moral norms, rules, and principles, while strongly guided by one's general value perspective or worldview, requires a process of selective attention to precisely those kinds of claims, assertions, ideals, issues, and values that exist in a particular context and that are constitutive of moral argument as generally conceived. The assessment of moral claims must be made in light of their logical coherence as well as whatever knowledge of the facts and/or empirical realities are deemed relevant to the situation. To deem any action right or wrong, good or bad, responsible or not, in this process perspective, often requires a rather thin abstraction from the thick, concrete complexity and multiplicity of values that are at stake in every situation. The more complex the situation or the more contested the significance of the behavior in question, the less adequate to reality such abstractions are likely to be.[179] Precisely for this reason, morality must be regarded as only one dimension of value with respect to the pursuit of goodness in human action. I will return to this argument in chapter 5.

Critical Realism

Griffin's epistemology is *realistic* in that he regards the language of his worldview to be referential and he endorses what he calls "the notion of truth as correspondence."[180] It is *critical* in that he recognizes that his metaphysics is underdetermined, and that its adequacy must be judged not only by the internal criterion of coherence but also by the verifications of human experience and empirical testing. He also rejects the notion that truth as correspondence implies naive realism.[181] It is important to keep in mind here that most epistemologies that reject correspondence notions of truth assume that no direct knowledge of other actualities is possible. The epistemology of prehension, to the contrary, holds that direct knowledge of other actualities is not only possible, but more basic than the knowledge obtained through stimulation of the sensory organs. Moreover, given the understanding of the God–world relation expressed by naturalism$_{ppp}$, direct experiential knowledge of God is also affirmed.

It must also be stressed that Griffin considers his general Whiteheadian perspective to provide the basis for a philosophy of science as well as a philosophy of religion. Thus it is important that his metaphysics be capable of rendering an account of "natural" or scientifically studied phenomena. We have already seen that Griffin judges scientific materialism to be incapable of explaining the emergence of mind.[182] Griffin sees the emergence of conscious

---

[179] This is not to say that adequacy to reality correlates directly with adequacy of moral discernment. Moral judgments based on abstractions that are less adequate to reality—as judged by their greater degree of simplification—may be preferable to judgments based on abstractions that are more adequate to reality, for example, if the former contribute to a greater realization of future possibilities than the latter. The simplification of complexity is not only a necessity of human perception and action, but may under certain conditions be understood as intrinsically and instrumentally good. See the discussion in Chapter 5, 237ff.

[180] *Reenchantment without Supernaturalism*, 322. Griffin says it is misleading to speak of correspondence as a *theory* of truth. After all, he maintains, the correspondence of our language to reality is one of our hard-core, common sense notions. He begins chapter 9, on "Religious Language and Truth," with the observation: "In process philosophy . . . there is little if any departure from customary usages. Most religious language that appears to be referential, such as 'God is loving,' is understood to be *really* referential. Religious beliefs are considered *cognitive*—that is, capable of being true or false—and truth is understood straightforwardly as *correspondence* between a proposition and that to which it refers. Religious knowledge is understood, like knowledge in general, as *justified true belief*, and the kind of justification needed is held to be similar to that needed for other beliefs," 320.

[181] Ibid., 331–32.

experience itself, the efficacy of the mind for bodily behavior, and the existence of freedom (choice or free will) as also problematic for materialism. So is influence or causation at a distance, as are quantum leaps or saltations in evolutionary history. Even parapsychological events, many of which Griffin takes to be scientifically well-documented, conflict with materialist assumptions. Griffin argues that each of these phenomena can be better explained given the metaphysical assumptions of process philosophy. Moreover, the empirical evidence of parapsychological phenomena—in particular, extrasensory or nonsensory perception—is such, he says, that it provides support for the major features of his metaphysical worldview.[183]

While his critique of materialism is highly convincing, Griffin's arguments regarding the explicability of these various phenomena in process metaphysical terms are not all equally persuasive. I find him most convincing with respect to the phenomena of immediate human experience—consciousness, freedom, and the efficacy of the mind. These phenomena represent long-standing issues in philosophy, and continue to be perplexing to cognitive scientists, neurobiologists, and other scientists of human behavior. Solutions do not seem to lie either in philosophical idealism or scientific materialism. Griffin's case against neo-Darwinian gradualism on behalf of a strong version of punctuated equilibria and evolutionary saltations is part of a much more extended and nuanced critique of dominant neo-Darwinian evolutionary theories that cannot be recounted here. The issues he identifies and the proposals he makes, however, seem to me to merit serious attention. His citations and argument regarding the evidence for parapsychological events persuade at least that such events deserve closer study than they have yet received from the larger scientific as well as academic religious communities. His treatment of non-local influence is least satisfactory, first, because it encompasses sufficiently dissimilar phenomena (e.g., gravity, magnetism, entanglement, telepathy, the cohesiveness of the atom) that one can imagine they require different sorts of explanations and, second, because it leaves unanswered questions regarding the compatibility of apparently instantaneous causality with the understanding of all entities as spatio-temporal events.[184] Even so, unless and until more convincing explanations are found for some of the most puzzling phenomena of the natural world, none of Griffin's arguments should be dismissed without serious engagement and critique. In any event, the larger point to be made here is that Griffin regards the validity of his process metaphysics to be based on its explanatory power and empirical testability and confirmability with respect to all real-world phenomena,

---

[182] Above, 159 and n. 54.
[183] *Religion and Scientific Naturalism*, 230ff.

whether such phenomena are considered to be of a religious or scientific nature.[185]

Resources for a Theological Ethics

As stressed throughout this chapter, Griffin sees his own work, like that of Whitehead, as intended to provide support for the moral life. Can an adequate moral theory be developed on the basis of the worldview that Griffin has set forth? Griffin begins the attempt to show that it can in a chapter of *Reenchantment without Supernaturalism* titled "Religion, Morality, and Civilization."[186] He identifies a number of elements as central, each of which merits some attention.

Human Freedom

Process theism, with its anti-materialist, anti-determinist understanding of events as expressions of final as well as efficient causation, attributes a kind of freedom to all entities or occasions of experience, not just the human. Clearly, that freedom is highly conditioned by antecedent events and future possibilities. Obviously, however, that freedom is greatest, and of particular moral significance, with respect to human occasions of experience. Consider the following account of an individual act or occasion of experience:

> In any particular moment, my conscious experience arises out of the efficient causation of past actualities, most impressively the immediately antecedent occasions of my own experience and the immediately antecedent occasions of experience constituting my body at that moment. (This is the physical pole of the occasion of experience.) Then, being initially constituted by these influences from the past (including an "initial aim" from God . . .), I freely decide exactly how to respond to them, which involves deciding upon my "subjective aim," meaning the complex aim to be realized in that occasion of experience. This aim is twofold, being directed both at my immediate "satisfaction" and at

---

[184]In a footnote Griffin refers to "the possibility of virtually instantaneous influence between spatially remote events," but does not, to my knowledge, ever provide an account of what such a possibility would imply with respect to his view of the role of time in all events; *God and Religion in the Postmodern World*, 148, n. 7.
[185]Griffin's *Religion and Scientific Naturalism* is the single best statement of his critique of scientific materialism and of his claims regarding the explanatory power of process metaphysics with respect to scientifically studied phenomena. Chapters 5–8, 107–310, are most relevant to matters touched on here. The "Introduction" to *The Reenchantment of Science* provides a briefer, helpful statement of Griffin's critique. See also *Reenchantment without Naturalism*, 205–16, on neo-Darwinian evolutionism.
[186]*Reenchantment without Supernaturalism*, 284–319.

my intended influence upon subsequent events, including most directly my immediately following occasions of experience and the state of my body in the next moment. Deciding upon and realizing this twofold aim constitutes the final causation, or self-determination of that occasion of experience (which is its mental or conceptual pole). When satisfaction is reached, the occasion of experience then exerts efficient causation upon subsequent occasions, most immediately my next occasion of experience and the living occasions of experience in my brain cells, which prehend that previous occasion of experience in terms of its aims for them.[187]

Griffin describes this view of human action as a *nondualistic interactionism*, one that does justice to our presuppositions about freedom and rational activity.[188] It entails a rejection of compatibilist views of determinism and human freedom, and also assumes that freedom is constitutive of rational activity itself. Especially relevant to the task of this book, there appear to be important convergences between this interactionism and the interactional model advocated by James Gustafson, though Gustafson might well find Griffin's interactionism too organic, tending to favor the interests of the group over the individual.[189] In any event, Griffin's interactionism is explicitly set within an ontology, or worldview, of interdependence and interrelatedness with respect to all existence. In this regard his outlook seems highly congruent with that of both Gustafson and McFague.

The Interdependence of All Actualities

Griffin's Whiteheadian process theism entails a "deeply ecological worldview," as the title to one of his previously cited essays puts it.[190] Actual entities are not atomistic "things" or independent substances, but prehending occasions of experience whose subjectivity is defined in terms of their multiple relations with antecedent occasions. Actualities that endure, including electrons, molecules, and minds, are thought of as enduring individuals or "temporally

---

[187]Ibid., 116.
[188]"Morality and Scientific Naturalism: Overcoming the Conflicts," in *Philosophy of Religion for a New Century: Essays in Honor of Eugene Thomas Long*, edited by Jeremiah Hackett and Jerald Wallulis (Dordrecht: Kluwer Academic Publishers, 2004) 98.
[189]Compare Chapter 2, 72–73. This is a judgment I cannot adequately warrant here. Griffin is certainly aware of the moral problem created by the tension between individual and group interests. He writes, "We typically seek our own satisfactions, even if by so doing we detract from rather than contribute to, the common good"; *Reenchantment without Supernaturalism*, 307. In the surrounding discussion, however, he seems more confident than Gustafson would be that individual self-interest can and should be transcended for the sake of a larger harmony of interests; cf. 306–10.

ordered societies." "Any given occasion of experience," says Griffin, "belongs to that temporal society that consists of all those members that came before it and all those that will come after it." He continues:

> This doctrine makes social relations fundamental, while making "enduring substances" derivative. What appears to be an independent substance, such as a proton, is in reality a pattern of social relations, with perhaps a billion such relations occurring in each second. Each actual occasion, however, does not simply arise out of its predecessor in the temporally ordered society to which it belongs. Each occasion is also influenced, even if less significantly, by other past occasions. In fact, each occasion is influenced, to some slight degree, by the whole past universe.[191]

It is particularly noteworthy with regard to occasions of human experience that, although they are like other occasions of experience in that generally the most significant of their antecedent occasions lie in close spatial and temporal proximity, they may also prehend occasions distantly removed in time and/or space.[192] Thus, all "things" are constituted by their relations, but this is especially the case for human beings, whose capacities for significant relationships are greatly enlarged by their expansive capacities for prehending antecedent events.[193]

The Objectivity of Moral Experience

According to Griffin, "the moral life presupposes that the moral dimension of experience involves apprehensions of truth about the nature of reality, especially the idea that some aims are really better than others." He invokes Whitehead, who pointed out that "'our moral and aesthetic judgments involve the ultimate notions of "better" and "worse."'" The very fact of moral disagreement argues for an element of objectivity. The argument assumes some common referent in experience. In Whitehead's words, "'The discordance over moral codes witnesses to the fact of moral experience. You cannot quarrel about unknown elements. The basis of every discord is some common experience, discordantly realized.'"[194] "This inescapability of moral notions means that they belong to our hard-core commonsense notions," says

---

[190]Cf. 159ff. above.
[191]"Whitehead's Deeply Ecological Worldview," 197.
[192]The human capacity for memory, or past-self-perception, as we have seen, is perhaps the most vivid example of a potentially significant prehension that may be distantly removed in time.
[193]Cf. the preceding discussion, 161–62.

Griffin.[195] As noted earlier, however, this does not seem to mean that there are any specific moral rules or principles that are necessarily derivative of our moral notions.[196]

The Primordial Nature of God as Home and Source of Moral Ideals

The primordial nature of God belongs to the eternal abstract essence of God, which Griffin encourages us to think of in terms of the unchanging divine character. The ideal attributes of God comprise God's primordial nature. These attributes include all possible values. They are conceptualized as eternal Platonic objects or forms. Griffin says of Whitehead, "His doctrine of the primordial nature of God allows him to affirm both the reality of such ideal entities and their efficacy in the world."[197] The primordial nature of God is understood to be the source of the ideals that God contributes to the initial aim of every occasion. These ideals have influence in the world "by virtue of being envisaged by God with appetition for their actualization in the world, which provides them with the prescriptivity, or 'to-be-pursuedness,' with which we experience them. . . . Whitehead says that we experience ideals by virtue of their presence in the divine, nonlocal agent."[198]

The Reality of Nonsensory Perception

The notion of prehension, or nonsensory perception, means that moral ideals can be experienced without a special faculty of moral intuition. Our moral intuitions are rather to be accounted for precisely in terms of the epistemology of prehension. Griffin agrees with Whitehead in rejecting a strong view of moral intuitionism, "according to which morality can be justified in terms of moral intuitions alone, without any cosmological support." Our intuitions regarding the ontological existence of moral ideals must be corroborated by empirical warrants for claiming that we can directly experience such ideals. We have direct intuitions of moral ideals, just as we have direct experience of God, but there is nothing exceptional about our capacity to prehend these ideals. "Because God is the home of the moral ideals," says Griffin, "our moral experience and our religious experience are closely intertwined."[199]

---

[194] *Reenchantment without Supernaturalism*, 298.
[195] Ibid., 299.
[196] Cf. 156–57 above.
[197] *Reenchantment without Supernaturalism*, 299.
[198] "Morality and Scientific Naturalism," 99.

The World as a Locus of Value Realization

As we saw earlier, every actuality is an occasion of experience that as such has value for itself, for others, and for the whole.[200] Interpreting Whitehead, Griffin writes:

> The idea that every actual entity enjoys value-experience is contained in the idea that each concrescence concludes with a "satisfaction." This satisfaction is discussed in terms of the aesthetic criteria of beauty: harmony and intensity. Experience that is "aesthetic" in this sense is said to be the whole point of existence: "The teleology of the Universe is directed to the production of Beauty". The evolution of the universe, with its increasingly complex societies supportive of higher modes of value-experience, is reflective of this divinely rooted teleology toward experiences with greater intrinsic value. "The actual world is the outcome of the aesthetic order, and the aesthetic order is derived from the immanence of God". Whitehead explicitly connects this idea with morality: "By reason of this character, constituting reality, the conception of morals arises. We have no right to deface the value experience which is the very essence of the universe."[201]

Griffin comments by way of pointing out the obvious moral implications, "if there were nothing deemed valuable in itself, the idea that we have moral duties—duties to do certain kinds of things, duties to refrain from doing other kinds of things—would be meaningless."[202]

Additional Morality-supporting Elements in a Whiteheadian Cosmology

Griffin lists four other elements in Whitehead's cosmological support for the moral life that can be briefly summarized. First, human beings are especially persuadable by divine ideals. The degree of freedom, and thus the range of choices, available to human beings is directly correlated with our susceptibility to moral suasion, as previously noted. More than any other known creature, we are capable of prehending the divine ideals and appropriating them into our subjective aims. Thus, a respect for human beings as human beings

---

[199] *Reenchantment without Supernaturalism*, 300; moral intuitions alone cannot justify morality, if only because these intuitions are usually vague; ibid., 318.

[200] Griffin also makes a distinction between intrinsic value, which is the value an occasion of experience has in and for itself in its subjectivity, and extrinsic value, which is the value individual experiences, a temporally ordered society of occasions, or an aggregation of societies, can have in their objectivity with respect to other occasions; cf. "Whitehead's Deeply Ecological Worldview," 192, 198.

[201] *Reenchantment without Supernaturalism*, 301.

may be engendered by our direct prehension of (humanitarian) moral ideals, which, says Griffin, "we prehend whether we 'believe in God' or not." [203] Second, respect for human beings as human beings (and, presumably, for life as life), is also supported "by explicit *reverence for a Holy Power*, understood as the power that is the source of all ideal possibilities and also, through persuasion, creates beings who can consciously choose among these possibilities."[204] Third, as we have seen, God, or the Holy Reality, is wholly good and, with an all-embracing sympathy, seeks to persuade every individual to act toward the highest realization of value for the whole. Given this understanding, "the natural desire to imitate the Holy Reality supports the moral life."[205] Finally, the Holy Reality, "as the ultimate recipient of our experiences and of the experiences that we influence," is enriched by our actions.[206] The notion of the consequent nature of God means, among other things, that the finite and immediate participate in the infinite and ultimate. Our actions, therefore, are not merely of passing value. The moral life is undergirded by a vision of its potentially enduring significance.

Although Griffin does not develop a theological ethics, we can now see that his process theism provides many of the ingredients for doing so. Foremost is his construal of the God–world relation, including his account of divine influence and the human capacity for direct prehension or experience of God. More needs to be said about his vision of the divine aim, which is understood in terms of the maximization, alternatively, of value, importance, and beauty. In the concluding chapter we will need to explore the contours of this vision in the context of a comparison with Gustafson's and McFague's understandings of the divine purposes.

Griffin also has a strong view of individual moral agency, and of the human freedom requisite for speaking meaningfully of human responsibility, though it is not clear how he would describe moral agency and action on the part of groups or collectivities. He has a social and interactionist view of self, and of other entities, that shares Gustafson's and McFague's emphasis on the interrelatedness and interdependence of all existence. His critique of anthropocentrism calls for an enlargement of vision and the cultivation of wider sympathies far beyond the narrow particularities of self-interest. The aesthetic character of his metaphysical worldview entails a regard for larger wholes, and ultimately for the God who alone embodies a universal sympathy and care for

---

[202] Ibid.
[203] Ibid., 302. It could also be said that a respect for non-human life is similarly engendered by our direct prehension of other moral ideals.
[204] Ibid., 302–3.
[205] Ibid., 303.
[206] Ibid.

the world. The nonanthropocentric character of his vision is strongly underscored by the panexperientialist ontology, which affirms the value of all life, indeed of all individual existence, as having intrinsic worth in and for itself, extrinsic worth for others, and ultimate worth in relation to God. We have also noted the theocentric implications of this vision.

Griffin's doctrine of God is in fact the linchpin in his effort to accomplish the reenchantment of the world. That *God is immanent in the world* means that the world is infused with the presence of God. All entities, actualities, occasions, or events can be thought of as bearers of the divine presence. Nothing that transpires is aimless, or of no significance. That *God is transcendent with respect to the world* means that the world is not simply identical to God. The world is transient and changing, but one may speak of a divine essence that is absolute and unchanging, a constant source of norms, ideals, and values, and thus of enduring and ultimate meaning. Experiences can thus be judged in terms of greater or lesser value, importance, or significance, while actions are of greater or lesser goodness or morality. That *the world is immanent in God* means that the finite participates in the infinite, the immediate in the ultimate. Whatever value is realized in actuality, or whatever goodness is attained, endures forever.

This vision of God, or Holy Actuality, is not simply a counter to moral relativism. It is also, in Griffin's view, an answer to the problem of motivation for the moral life. Many moral theories purport to tell us what we ought to do, or point us toward the good, but they often fail to provide any convincing reason why one should care to do the right or the good. Like many moral theorists, Griffin recognizes the important role that sympathy can play in moral motivation. The problem is that our sympathies are typically rather narrow and need to be greatly widened. The key to an adequate theory of moral motivation, therefore, lies in the basic religious motive, which is the "desire to be in harmony with that which is *ultimate in the nature of things*."[207] Moreover, Griffin believes that this religious motive is not limited to the overtly religious:

> Religious theists . . . do care about *God's* reactions. Although this fact has surely been partly due to the theologies that have portrayed God as holding out the promise of heaven and the threat of hell, theists who no longer share these beliefs still care about the divine "point of view." This is because . . . we are inherently religious beings and thereby want to be in harmony with the Holy Reality as we understand it.[208]

If we are inherently religious beings, and thereby desire to be in harmony with the ultimate nature of things, then the vision of the ultimate Holy Reality has profoundly moral and ethical implications. In Griffin's understanding, the reenchantment of the world is an undertaking that must necessarily enlarge our vision of the community of interests in the world around us, expand our sympathies, and inspire our response, participation, and action in pursuit of the best in each occasion and the greatest common good.

It remains now to consider which of those features in the thought of Gustafson, McFague, and Griffin can be most creatively and productively appropriated toward the construction of a theological ethics that may prove intellectually coherent and religious compelling for our time.

---

[207]Ibid., 250.

[208]Ibid., 319. Griffin's statement that "we are inherently religious beings" seems to derive not only from the claim that we want to be in harmony with ultimate, or holy, reality, which is the source of meaning in human existence, but also from the twofold claim that "(1) all people at all times feel, albeit usually only at an unconscious level, the existence of a Holy Actuality, which accounts for what is sometimes called 'the religious dimension of experience,' and (2) in some people this direct prehension sometimes rises to the level of conscious awareness, producing what is called an 'experience of the Holy' or a 'mystical experience.' Because all people (by hypothesis) have religious experience in the first sense, a responsive chord may be evoked in them by verbal reports of religious experiences in the second sense"; ibid., 85.

5
A Synthesis for the Making

Introduction

IN this book I have argued that James Gustafson, Sallie McFague, and David Griffin each contributes elements necessary to the articulation of an intellectually and religiously adequate theological ethics within the Protestant Christian tradition as it confronts the religious and intellectual challenges of today's world.

An *intellectually* adequate theological ethics, in my view, must accept the modern commitment to experience and reason. Negatively, this means that such an ethics must not make *a priori* appeals to the authority of religious tradition. Positively, it means that such an ethics must be naturalistic, at least in the sense that it rejects ontological and epistemic supernaturalism.

It is also necessary for an intellectually adequate theological ethics to articulate an intelligible theistic construal of the relation between God and the world. It is hardly enough to assert that God, being God, must be capable of influencing what happens in the world. Nor is it sufficient to view God only as the primary cause of world events, the originating, underlying, and sustaining force or presence that makes all things possible, but not as One whose "hand" can ever be felt in everyday events. Christian theism holds that God remains an active, creative, directive presence or power within the world. Christian theism also views God as responsive to the creation, including human beings who relate to God in worship and prayer. Without some conception of how God may exercise influence within the causal nexus of world events, however, any notion of God as active, guiding, creative, responsive presence or power within the natural world remains largely unintelligible. Assertions of supernatural divine intervention or communication are to be rejected, not because they falsely claim to be based on actual experiences of God, but because they unintelligibly claim to be supernatural. What are intelligible are the empirically observable patterns and processes that manifest the causal relations of the natural world.

One must be careful to understand, however, that a naturalistic perspective does not imply that all natural phenomena are to be understood as manifestations of strictly natural laws. Of the eight kinds of naturalism outlined by David Griffin, the form that asserts the existence of strictly natural laws by which all things are governed is one of those to be rejected.[1] As Griffin observes, following James, Peirce, and Whitehead, the patterns and processes of the natural world are better understood in terms of "habits" than of "laws." Laws, from Griffin's perspective, suggest external, absolute, strictly deterministic and therefore naturally inviolable relations between and among actual entities. The regularities discovered by physics are, rather, the most widespread, long-standing "habits of nature" and, as such, "describe *the average behavior of the entities in inorganic environments.*"[2] In this process perspective, no violation of the natural order of things is implied by the behavior of entities that fail to conform to strictly deterministic laws, because such laws are false abstractions from real world phenomena. Nor is any violation of the natural order of things necessarily implied by claims of divine action in the world. The main point here is that efficient causation is not sufficient to account for natural phenomena, both because there is a dimension of indetermination, or freedom, in every occasion of experience and because there is final causation, which becomes more evident with increasing organic complexity, and is most evident in human beings. In effect, there is room for God to contribute to the initial aim of every occasion of experience, and thus to exercise influence in the world without any supposedly supernatural intervention.

On the whole, I find process metaphysics' construal of the God–world relation to be intellectually compelling. In the previous chapter I have maintained that it is, in any event, the most intellectually adequate metaphysics currently available. I have also argued that there can be no intellectually adequate theology, or theological ethics, without a metaphysical conception of the God–world relation. Griffin's argument for his process metaphysics, as we have seen, is based largely on criteria of adequacy and coherence. However, Griffin never claims that this worldview can be empirically proven. Nor does

---

[1] Cf. Chapter 1, 10.
[2] *Reenchantment without Supernaturalism*, 125.

he rely on his metaphysics to persuade us of those convictions that he calls hard-core, commonsense notions. Rather, he sets forth what he believes must be the case, metaphysically speaking, for these hard-core commonsense notions to be true. In so doing he makes it clear that acceptance of process metaphysics does not depend on some sort of inherent or self-evident credibility. As with many scientific theories, some of which seem quite incredible and counterintuitive, process metaphysics simply provides the best available account or explanation of all the dimensions and empirical data of human knowledge and experience.

Another claim is largely implicit in my case for an *intellectually* adequate theological ethics, the claim that assertions about the way things are, theologically or metaphysically speaking, lack intellectual responsibility and integrity if they are made without any metaphysical conceptualization and explanation of how things can be as they are asserted to be. General assertions about God, for example, insofar as they are intended to refer to and describe, define, or characterize an ultimate reality or supreme being, and thus are *not* meant simply to express an individual's subjective state of belief, require explanatory metaphysical conceptualization in order to be taken with intellectual seriousness. General assertions about God's creativity, influence, or action in the world require a metaphysical conceptualization of the God–world relation that can provide an intelligible account of divine agency.

Why impose such a requirement regarding what may properly be claimed about God? Why go so far as to say that this is a matter of intellectual responsibility and integrity? Precisely because claims about God and God's relation to the world are seldom made for frivolous reasons. Those who make such claims may do so in order to justify themselves, but they also do so in order to persuade, exhort, commend, condone, or condemn. People generally make assertions about God, not simply to express their own perspective on reality, nor only to legitimate a particular orientation in their own lives, but to help shape the ultimate orientation of other people's lives. They hope to point others toward what they regard to be the ultimate source of meaning and purpose in human existence. I simply assert, without further argument, that the making of theological claims demands the highest intellectual as well as moral scruples.

Additional criteria come into play when we consider what is required for a *religiously* adequate theological ethics. The religious life involves the affective as well as the cognitive dimensions of human apprehension. Specifically, a language is needed in order to speak of God in terms that are expressive of the human apprehension of God and that evoke affective response. For religious adherents within the major Western religious traditions, including Christianity, God is not an idea to be conceptualized but a Being or Person to be worshipped and served. Therefore, language is needed that speaks of God in personal terms, as One who possesses not only power but also character and purpose and agency. Language is also needed that speaks of God's responsiveness toward the creation, as One with whom human beings—indeed, all creatures—may be in a mutually affecting relation.

At the same time it is important to understand that no language about God even begins to capture the essence or fullness of the divine. Nor is such language to be taken literally regarding what little it can express. As Sallie McFague has impressed upon us, all our language about God is metaphorical. It possesses the character of "is" and "is not." It is referential language—more so, I believe, than McFague is willing to claim—but it is language that always falls short of the realities of which it speaks. Indeed, it is language that falls short even of our experience of those realities.

William James once used the figure of a dog to express the disparity between the ultimate realities we partially apprehend and the capacities with which we comprehend. Consider a dog lying at the feet of its master as the man engages in conversation with friends. The dog hears the conversation, that is, the sound and rhythm of the voices. The dog feels the warmth of the fire and the conviviality of the occasion. But the dog knows nothing of the structure of the meaning conveyed in the conversation itself. It is a level of relationship that transcends the canine structure of consciousness, though the dog participates in it in ways consonant with its kind.[3]

With respect to what we can know and understand of God, it seems to me, human beings are much like this dog, though much more greatly disadvantaged. God would seem to be far more elusive to us than a man is to his dog. On the other hand, as the analogy suggests, even without knowing the structure of meaning conveyed in the conversation between the man and his friends, the dog surely can sense something of the disposition of its master. The dog knows by whose hand it is fed and cared for, and has probably learned to discern and interpret a variety of clues regarding its master's intentions. Particularly at an affective level, the dog will be able to sense how to respond to the entreaties, commands, and exclamations of the master. It does not seem unreasonable to suppose that human beings may also know something, however partial, of the divine disposition.

We need theological language in order to think and talk about God and God's relation to the world, in order to image for ourselves what we sense and feel and apprehend to be the case regarding God's nature and purpose, God's presence and activity in the world, and God's disposition toward us and the

---

[3] As cited by Bernard E. Meland, *The Realities of Faith: The Revolution in Cultural Forms* (New York: Oxford University Press, 1962) 183.

rest of creation. We need theological language that appropriately orients us toward God, others, and the world, given the apprehension we have of the divine reality. But we also need to understand the inescapably metaphorical nature of such language. Religiously adequate metaphorical language about God will be referential but not literal, indicative but not descriptive. It will be primarily imagistic and personal, rather than conceptually abstract. And always, regarding such language, we need to recognize what theologian Bernard Meland identified as "the disparity between the concepts and language in our minds or on our lips, and the reality which intermittently reaches, but mostly eludes us."[4]

An adequate theological ethics, in my view, must also emphasize a theocentric perspective. *Intellectual* adequacy requires that the idea of God and the construal of the God–world relation be intelligible. *Religious* adequacy requires that the God so conceived be worthy of worship. Together, I am convinced, these two criteria of intellectual and religious adequacy move us toward a monotheistic, and indeed a theocentric, perspective.

Now, it may be conceded that it is not intellectually necessary to claim that there is one supreme God. It is at least conceivable that we live in a pluralistic universe, in which there are various loci of "ultimate" value, or various gods. Or there may be no gods at all. With atheism, however, we hardly have a religiously adequate conception of god as worthy of worship! With polytheism, on the other hand, we may have gods who seem worthy of human allegiance and devotion. But unless we can provide an account of their divine agency, any claim that there are such gods and that they make a difference in human existence is intellectually insupportable. The intellectual difficulties of accounting for the respective influences of a multiplicity of deities seem insurmountable. Monotheism appears to be the only religiously adequate option for theological ethics for which intellectual adequacy can also be claimed.

But is monotheism possible without theocentrism? In Chapter 2 we saw how James Gustafson argues for a theocentric perspective as a critique of the prevailing instrumentalism and anthropocentrism in Christian thought. If most Christian thought is actually instrumental and anthropocentric, then what grounds are there for claiming that only a theocentric perspective is religiously and intellectually adequate? I propose two major rejoinders to this question. In the first place, a *prima facie* case can be made for theocentrism as normative Christian theology. Christian theologians and ethicists may resort to instrumental and anthropocentric theological arguments, but they rarely if ever defend their positions by overt appeals to anthropocentrism or

---

[4]Ibid., 159.

instrumentalism. They can hardly deny that God belongs at the center of Christian scripture and teaching. The very nature of God is understood to be such that only God can claim our utmost loyalty. The first and greatest commandment, reportedly taught by Jesus, is the love of God with heart and soul and mind and strength.[5] The greatest sin is idolatry, the worship of, or devotion to, someone or some thing other than God.[6] God alone is worthy of ultimate allegiance, and God alone endures. The heavens and the earth may—indeed, will—pass away, but God will remain forever.[7] Any theological ethics that is situated in and responsive to the Christian tradition must aim to be theocentric.

In other words, the strong theocentric emphasis that Gustafson attributes to the Reformed tradition within Protestant Christianity, though a distinctive emphasis of that tradition, is hardly unique to Christianity as a whole. Insofar as Gustafson is correct in identifying widespread tendencies toward instrumentalism and anthropocentrism within Christian theology, his emphasis may be seen as a rightful insistence upon restoring a theocentric perspective to its proper place in Christian thinking. Therefore, I maintain that a theocentric perspective is essential as a matter of faithfulness to what is most central and fundamental to a Christian interpretation of life and the world.

On the other hand, there are also theological warrants for a theocentric perspective that are not specifically tied to Christianity or any other major faith tradition.[8] These warrants derive from reflection on matters of ultimate religious concern. The question is whether there is any way to address matters of ultimate concern except from within a theocentric perspective.

As I see it, the theocentric perspective relates, implicitly if not explicitly, to the question of what is ultimate and what endures. James Gustafson asserts that human beings exist for the service of God,[9] and I agree. But it needs to be asked, Why should this be the case? Why should there be this claim on us and our lives? Gustafson appears to take the Christian view that God has

---

[5] Mark 12:29-30; cf. Matthew 22:37-38; Luke 10:27.
[6] Exodus 20:2-6; cf. Deuteronomy 5:6-10.
[7] Psalms 102:25-26; cf. Matthew 5:18; Luke 16:17; 2 Peter 3:7, 12-13; Revelation 21:1.
[8] It is important also to recognize that theocentrism does not need to be warranted by its critique of anthropocentrism. The critique of anthropocentrism can be sustained by an ecological perspective, for example, without any resort to theology. An empirical assessment of the human prospect, and of the relationship between human beings and the supporting biosphere, may be sufficient to disabuse one of anthropocentric tendencies. Thus, theocentrism is not an ethically and ecologically motivated theological antidote to anthropocentrism. Rather, it is a perspective or orientation that is rooted in a theological conviction about God—one that I wish to claim need not be specifically Christian.
[9] Cf. Gustafson, "Afterword," in Beckley and Swezey, 250.

made us for God's self for granted, perhaps even *a priori*. In so doing, he comes too close to saying, in piety, "Ours is not to reason why, ours is but to do and die."[10] This is not to suggest that he regards the human calling to be one of self-abnegation. Indeed, he acknowledges the real possibilities for joy in human existence. But it is not clear how such joy relates to the service of God, or to any moral endeavor.[11] Gustafson seems to rely on piety alone to provide a sufficient basis for the service of God. In my judgment, the senses of gratitude, obligation, and possibility, as well as the other senses Gustafson associates with religious affectivity, are not sufficient to sustain human striving.

What is it that makes life worth living—even when life is filled with great suffering, or no longer blessed with pleasures and delights? What is it that gives life ultimate meaning and purpose, when we know that everything we accomplish, and all the good that we may hope to do, will someday perish? What is there of significance, if anything, that endures beyond our deaths? These are fundamentally religious questions. They are not questions Gustafson is given to asking, or answering. From his perspective they probably smack too much of human self-interest and self-concern. Or they may simply be questions that we have no basis in knowledge or experience to answer. For Gustafson, the emergence of piety does not appear to count on answers to such questions of ultimate and enduring goodness and meaning. But piety can hardly pre-empt, nor is piety exempt from, such questions. These are religious questions that, I submit, no religiously adequate theological ethics can ignore.

Charles Hartshorne invites us to reflect on such questions in terms of the literary character, Robinson Crusoe. Shipwrecked on an island, cut off from all human contact (save his servant, Friday), what is to be said about the life prospects that lie before him? "Is Robinson Crusoe's sole inspiration to be the hope that he may be rescued or his story become known?" Hartshorne asks. "Suppose the island should sink into the sea, as sometimes happens. Is there no hidden meaning of life that such an outcome could not obliterate?"[12] The process philosopher answers that there is something permanent about "the quality of the moment of life," that "the universe contains our entire past histories, our every moment, and it forevermore *will have* contained them."[13] "Our abiding value is indeed what we give to posterity, to the life that survives us." Crusoe's case is ultimately no different from our own in this

---

[10] A gloss on lines from Tennyson's "Charge of the Light Brigade."
[11] "Afterword," 250.
[12] "Science, Insecurity, and the Abiding Treasure," *Journal of Religion* 39 (1958) 172.
[13] Ibid., 172, 173.

regard. Ultimately, the only life that will survive us—and not only survive us, but endure—is that of God, "who is our final posterity."[14] As Hartshorne concludes:

> The question we have been discussing is, How can the passing moment have value, once for all, and, in this sense, security? Our answer has been that the passing moment is cherished forevermore by One who knows how to do justice to all its beauty and value. . . Our faith then is as follows: we live not ultimately for self alone, nor yet even for mankind, or "all sentient creatures," but for that hidden reality which enfolds us all, with all that we can rightly claim to be, the book of truth which some envisage as a divine life. That this life is holy means that it gives to every moment of every life its full due—not in subsequent reward . . . but rather in absolute appreciation for the world of each moment. . . . [T]he future of every moment, its essential destiny, is to present itself as a gift to the One from whose possession it can nevermore be cast out.[15]

What I mean to be suggesting here is that Gustafson's theocentric perspective needs to be framed within a process metaphysics or theology that addresses some of the fundamental religious questions he largely ignores. David Griffin, following Hartshorne in such matters, provides the needed framework. I invoke his metaphysical conception of God, not to replace or even significantly modify Gustafson's radically monotheistic theocentrism, but to supplement and undergird it.

Gustafson eschews metaphysics for epistemological reasons. Writing about the limits of our knowledge of God as Other, he parenthetically comments, "I continue to be amazed at how much some theologians know about God."[16] I share this amazement. But I am also persuaded that if talk about God is going to continue to be meaningful, and if God is to be regarded as worthy of our worship, we must have more to say than Gustafson does, particularly with regard to the significance of God as the ultimate reality with whom we have to do. Griffin's conception of God, far from being a fabrication, is an account of what must be true about God if it is to continue to make sense for human beings to commit themselves to the service of God. By his entire life and work, Gustafson implicitly and explicitly affirms—no less than Griffin—that such commitment does make sense. Later in this chapter I will argue, further, that it is not mere wishful thinking that has us believing in the meaningfulness of life. This hard-core commonsense notion, in Griffin's terms, derives from the human apprehension of the divine.

---

[14]Ibid., 173.
[15]Ibid., 174.
[16]"Afterword," 247.

A Synthesis for the Making   215

A *religiously* adequate theological ethics, then, must in every case possess a language for speaking about God that is capable of evoking both worship and service. For those who share the modern commitment, and thereby require an intellectually adequate conception of God, a religiously adequate theological ethics will also be one that understands God in theocentric perspective.

The Theocentric Perspective Revisited

Having just made my case that an intellectually and religiously adequate theological ethics requires a theocentric emphasis, let me turn to some difficulties that continue to be identified with Gustafson's theocentrism. In a critique of Gustafson's *Ethics*, philosopher Robert Audi observes:

> Gustafson seems to face a serious dilemma here: if he adheres to his strong rejection of anthropomorphism in the conception of God, he is hard pressed to make the connection between science and ethics required by this theocentric view; if he allows the apparently necessary anthropomorphism, he is hard pressed to sustain his view about the ultimate power.[17]

Gustafson notes that Audi has properly located his dilemma.[18] On the one hand, in rejecting anthropomorphism, Gustafson also seems to reject any notion of a personal God. How, then, can he speak of what God is "enabling" or "requiring" us to do? How, then, can he claim that God has purposes, even if purposes can be distinguished from intentions? Science describes for us a world of patterns and processes in which some kind of ordering occurs. But where is the connection with ethics, unless it be allowed that the divine governance discerned to be manifest in this ordering bears some analogy to such human qualities as will and agency? On the other hand, if this kind of anthropomorphism is allowed, then it seems we risk a kind of *assimilationism*: "a tendency to regard God as essentially like us, only infinitely greater in the degree of his (sic) possession of the same virtues."[19]

Audi argues that it is possible to reject anthropocentrism and assimilationism without "wholly giving up the conception of God as a personal being."[20] One need not assume that God is essentially like us in order to assert substantive similarities between God and us. God may possess a kind of intel-

---

[17]"Theology, Science, and Ethics in Gustafson's Theocentric Vision," in Beckley and Swezey, 173.
[18]"Response," in Beckley and Swezey, 213.
[19]Audi, op. cit.
[20]Ibid., 174.

ligence or a kind of agency without assuming that these qualities are similar to our own. Audi counsels resort to metaphor, implying that such attributes as intelligence and agency are metaphors when applied to God, for we really cannot say precisely how God's intelligence or agency is like or different from our own.[21] Gustafson expresses appreciation for Audi's attempts to interpret him in a more orthodox vein, but he remains uneasy about the results.[22]

Audi's attempt to rehabilitate personal, anthropomorphic language about God within Gustafson's theocentric framework is not entirely satisfying for three reasons. First, Audi does not supply any evidential warrants for assuming that God is personal, only arguments why this need not be denied. His aim seems to be to maintain continuity with Christian tradition, and to provide at least some basis for the move that Gustafson makes from the empirical to the ethical, or from science to ethics. In Chapter 3 we saw that Sallie McFague also finds it necessary to assert that God is personal and agential as a matter of Christian orthodoxy, and as a basis for constructing metaphors of God and the God–world relation that provide a proper ethical orientation. These instrumental arguments for theological claims are inherently problematic from Gustafson's and my perspective. The way God is conceived as personal in Griffin's process theology, on the other hand, is integral to his general process metaphysics. His conception of God is congruent with most of Christian tradition (except for the rejection of a certain kind of omnipotence), and his conception of the God–world relation provides a basis for the moral life. Above all, these features of his conception are not constructed simply to warrant his argument for a personal, agential God.

A second weakness in Audi's argument relates to his claim that to avoid assimilating the divine to the human we must not assume that God is essentially like human beings in any specific way. Audi takes seriously Gustafson's worry that anthropomorphic language about God leads to anthropocentrism. If the problem is as serious as Gustafson seems to think, however, Audi's proposal for a minimalist use of anthropomorphic language, carefully distinguishing an acceptable substantive similarity from an unacceptable essential similarity between God and human beings, hardly seems adequate. Gustafson certainly seems unpersuaded by Audi's modest attempt to retrieve anthropomorphic language. Gustafson's position begs for a more fundamental critique.

If we share the non-anthropocentric commitment, and if anthropomorphic language invariably tends to anthropocentrism, then it becomes unclear how we can talk about God at all. Of course there are familiar non-anthro-

---

[21] Ibid., 173.
[22] "Response," in Beckley and Swezey, 213ff.

pomorphic metaphors for God within the Christian tradition, such as rock, tower, fortress, water, and light. But each of these receives its metaphorical meaning in reference to human needs and desires—for security, shelter, protection, sustenance or cleansing, clarity and truth. These metaphors image God for human's sake. Ironically, non-anthropomorphic metaphors for God may be more conducive than anthropomorphic ones to instrumental anthropocentrism.

Are we left, then, with only the *via negativa* in theology? Ironically, even the *via negativa* depends on concrete language about creaturely existence for its negations: God is *not* mortal, *not* finite, *not* visible, *not* changing, *not* corruptible. In the absence of any positive language about God, however, is it really possible to have a meaningful conception of God? How is something immortal, infinite, invisible, unchanging, or incorruptible to be distinguished from an elementary particle, for example? And what difference would it make? Whatever the risks of anthropocentrism in employing anthropomorphic language about God, these are surely outweighed by the inherent difficulties of employing primarily non-anthropomorphic language about God. In fact, the use of anthropomorphic metaphorical language about God, to the extent that it effectively images a being who is in some ways substantively if not essentially like us, would seem to suggest that there is someone in the universe with whom to be preoccupied besides ourselves. A morally effective theological critique of anthropocentrism may well require a fairly robust anthropomorphic conception of God as One, for example, who loves and cares deeply about all of the creation.

A third failing in Audi's reinterpretation of Gustafson's theocentrism is that Audi does not go far enough. Surely he is right that we need not abandon personal, anthropomorphic language for God altogether in order to avoid assimilating the divine to the human. However, we may actually need to embrace such language, and to argue the truth of the biblical view of the human being as created in the divine image, as *imago Dei*. Granted, Christians have inveterately constructed God in their own image, but so have the adherents of other major theistic traditions, as anyone familiar with Greek or Egyptian mythology or the *Bhagavad Gita* well knows. The *imago Dei* doctrine is not to blame for the human tendency to assimilate the divine to the human. Critically appropriated, the *imago Dei* doctrine may serve just as well to challenge and transform our human self-understanding.

As Sallie McFague's work attests, highly imagistic and personal metaphorical language for God has always played a very important part in shaping Christian moral and ethical sensibilities. To re-shape those sensibilities along more inclusive, life-affirming, non-patriarchal, and non-anthropocentric lines will require rich, evocative, alternative images and metaphors that reflect new and emerging insights and understandings regarding the human as well as the divine.[23] Furthermore, to reiterate an argument I have made before, personal and imagistic language for God would also seem to be necessary for Christian worship, for the evocation of religious piety of the sort that Gustafson finds essential to generate the religious affections or virtues. Ironically, even Gustafson seems to concede as much.[24]

On this interpretation, Gustafson's theocentric perspective is not nearly so problematic with respect to the use of anthropomorphic language as he himself has made it out to be. More still needs to be said about what kind of anthropomorphic language is theologically appropriate, or justified, and what is not. So far I have suggested only that we need language that is more evocative and personalistic than Gustafson's language of creating, ordering, governing, sustaining, requiring, and bearing down. I have also indicated, following McFague, that there are significant moral implications to the language that we use. In keeping with Gustafson's theocentric emphasis, however, I affirm that the moral or ethical warrants for our language about God must be subordinate to the theological warrants. So the first question becomes, What sort of personal, imagistic, metaphorical language about God is warranted by our construal of God and God's relation to the world? What metaphors can we use to talk about God while remaining faithful to our conceptual understanding of God and the God–world relation? Before we address that question, there is another dimension of Gustafson's theocentric perspective that remains problematic, and that deserves prior attention, because it bears on Gustafson's construal of God in what appears to be an unfortunate way. I am referring to the way in which Gustafson's radical monotheism unduly accents the remoteness of God.

Rethinking the Otherness of God

In Chapter 2 I dismissed Gordon Kaufman's view that Gustafson has a Calvinistic conception of God that rests on "radically dualistic metaphysi-

---

[23]In *Metaphorical Theology*, McFague writes, "as we were made in the image of God (Gen. 3:27), so we now, with the model of Jesus, have further support for imagining God in our image, the image of persons. This means that personal, relational images are central in a metaphorical theology—images of God as father, mother, lover, friend, savior, ruler, governor, servant, companion, comrade, liberator, and so on. The Judeo-Christian tradition has always been personalistic and relational in its religious languages. This need not be seen as crude anthropomorphism, but as foundational language, the dominant model, of God-talk," 20. In *Life Abundant*, she says, "Made in God's image, we are to grow into that reality by doing what God does: love the world," 13.

[24]Recall my discussion of the tensions in Gustafson's position in Chapter 2, 89ff. Cf. Gustafson, *Ethics I*, 322.

cal assumptions."²⁵ Nor do I think Gustafson's view of the otherness of God implies that, from a human perspective, God stands over against us as the Wholly Other (and Holy Other), as is stressed in some neo-orthodox theologies. However, Gustafson's radically monotheistic conception of God as "powerful Other" does lend itself to the impression that God is rather unlike us and largely inaccessible to us. Unfortunately, Gustafson appears to have an emotionally distant view of God.

There can be no question that Gustafson wishes to avoid some of the biblical language about God's severity and punishment. He wants to disabuse us of the idea that sin has turned us into such miserable creatures that God's wrath can only be averted by the vicarious sacrificial atonement of Jesus Christ. Our natural impulses and desires are not to be understood as standing over against the moral, but rather as needing to be guided and directed by moral thinking and action. But Gustafson does not want to give up the language of God's wrath altogether.²⁶ He argues that we may speak of the judgment and wrath of God in reference to those adverse consequences of human actions that "signal a serious disordering of relationships between persons, in society, in relation to nature."²⁷ I think this is right. Gustafson is also right in wanting to deliver us from pious and sentimental self-righteousness. We are responsible for much that afflicts us. God's wrath is not a punishment imposed on us for sin, but a way of understanding how the working out of adverse reactions to events in history and nature follows from disordered relations for which we are accountable. Gustafson want to disabuse us of too comfortable and comforting views of God as One who rescues us from all our follies and sin.²⁸

There are a couple of problems here, nonetheless. First, how can it be meaningful to speak of adverse consequences as signs of God's wrath without any conception of divine agency? For Gustafson, this is done "in piety," in affirmation of God's ordering, governing power. Even so, then what are we to make of those adverse circumstances that seem to bear no relation to human disorder or sin? In Gustafson's thought, on the one hand, it seems that God must be responsible for so-called natural evils, including what many insurance policies euphemistically call "acts of God." On the other hand, Gustafson does not identify God's wrath with punishment, or acts of special divine agency, in response to particular human failings. Thus, certain adverse circumstances—those for which human beings are responsible—are seen as

---

[25] 77.
[26] *Ethics I*, 242–47.
[27] Ibid., 246.
[28] Cf. *An Examined Faith*, 107.

signs of God's wrath. Other circumstances—those for which God must be responsible—are not seen as signs of God's wrath. Is "the wrath of God" really anything more than a specification of human culpability?

Gustafson's conception of divine judgment might work if he understood God's wrath in terms of the absence of divine solicitude. The wrath of God would then refer to God leaving us to our own devices, letting us suffer the consequences of our disorder and sin. It could be understood in terms of divine withdrawal, disengagement, or even abandonment. This would constitute a very powerful and meaningful notion of divine wrath, and one with biblical precedent: God abandoning us to our own fate, having no more to do with us, letting us reap what we have sown. But this way of thinking about divine wrath presumes that God is otherwise present and engaged in our lives and in our world, actively exercising solicitude for us and the creation.

So we come to the other and more problematic failing of Gustafson's language about, and conception of, God: he has so little to say about divine love. As noted previously,[29] Gustafson's construal of God does not allow for any discriminate, individual, divine response to particular human circumstance and need. There is no allowance or provision for what Griffin calls "variable divine influence."[30] There is no way to think about God at work in the world responding to particular events, actions, circumstances, and predicaments as they arise. There is only the very general sense of God's governance in terms of the patterns and processes of our physical and social worlds as manifestations of God's ordering, sustaining, and bearing down upon us. In the teaching of Jesus, God is not indifferent even to the fate of a single sparrow.[31] But in Gustafson's construal of God and God's relation to the world there is no way for God to manifest a particular love for human beings, yet alone for sparrows.

To be clear, my argument is not that Gustafson is altogether silent regarding divine love. He does attribute love to God, and says that this attribution "arises out of the human experiences of loving forgiveness."[32] The experience of human love and forgiveness is taken by Gustafson as indicative of one aspect of the ultimate ordering power of the world. Thus he can say, "In piety one aspect of the ultimate power is construed to be mercy, forgiving love."[33] Therefore, individual human beings can relate to God as a loving power. But how is it that God relates to individual human beings?

---

[29]Chapter 2, 84–85.
[30]Cf. Chapter 4, 169ff.
[31]Matthew 10:29; Luke 12:6
[32]*Ethics I*, 250.
[33]Ibid.

Gustafson lacks a compelling notion of the divine compassion. We may experience particular expressions of *human* love, but it does not appear we can experience particular expressions of *divine* love. Suppose we never experienced particular expressions of human love. Could we even be persuaded of the existence of such love? We certainly could not know what it means to be loved by another human being. Apparently we can make general *attributions* of divine love. But what does it mean to be loved by God if we cannot *experience* particular expressions of that love? Or would Gustafson say that we do actually experience divine love in the love of a parent, neighbor, spouse, colleague, or friend? Is so, how is this divine love to be distinguished from (merely) human love?

Part of the difficulty here may be that we are again confronted with the inadequacy of anthropomorphic language for speaking of God. But if speaking of love as an attribute of God is to mean anything, surely such love must be thought of as surpassing what we know of human love. And one thing we know about human love is that impersonal and indiscriminate love is a poor cousin to love that is directly and immediately responsive to the particular individual in his or her particular situation. Parents seek to love their children equally and magnanimously, but in order to do so they must *not* love each of them in exactly the same way, without regard to their particularities. Simply to treat their children all alike, irrespective of their differences, might in some sense be considered fair or just, but it is hardly loving. Loving parents must take into account their children's particular needs, temperaments, aspirations, circumstances, and so on. There is no indication in Gustafson's construal that God is able to exercise this kind of discriminating (not discriminatory!) love. Indeed, to reiterate once more, in the absence of any conception of divine agency, there is no reason to believe that God is able to exercise any influence or manifest any compassion at all.

In this light, the emotional valence—or affectivity quotient—of God as "powerful Other" tends to be rather negative. God may not be hostile or punitive toward humankind, but God appears to be supremely distant from our daily lives and indifferent to our human lot. Indeed, it is often said that indifference, rather than hate, is the opposite of love. An indifferent God may actually be unloving. At the least, in Gustafson's construal, and possibly despite his conscious intentions, God is simply too aloof and austere.

There is a way to articulate the otherness of God, however, when combined with a conception of God's discriminating love, that seems to me to address Gustafson's concern not to assimilate the divine to the human. As I argued in Chapter 4, Griffin's process conception of God provides for variable divine influence, and thus for the possibility of a divine love that is responsive to every particular individual and situation. Moreover, based on his argument regarding the disposition of an ideal observer, Griffin's conception of God provides assurance of the fullness of God's love for the world both in all its particularities and as a whole. Undeniably, this conception of God presses us well beyond the limits of our human understanding. And this brings us precisely to what is most at stake for Gustafson in his insistence on the otherness of God. We should not think of the divine Other as alien, distant, or indifferent, but rather as far-surpassing all our attempts at assimilation and domestication by means of language that is anthropomorphic and conceptions that are comprehensible.

In his latest book, Gustafson complains:

> Preachers assure congregations that God really loves each individual, indeed that God is love *as if love is God*, and God is not all the other things God is in the prayers of St. Francis and Karl Rahner—wisdom, power, wrath, and ultimately with the Cappadocians and all great mystics since, the ineffable, the unspeakable, the unknowable.[34]

This is a valid criticism regarding a fairly large and eviscerated segment of American Christianity, but even with respect to those he criticizes, it is not entirely fair. Gustafson does not seem willing to acknowledge that the preachers in question may be right regarding what they affirm, however much they may be faulted for what they neglect (and probably never would deny). A theocentric ethics rightly underscores the otherness of God, when God is understood as ineffable, unspeakable, and unknowable. It misses the mark, however, if it fails to offer a compelling portrait of the divine love and compassion as a profoundly transformative reality in the human experience of God. Gustafson largely fails here, while Griffin has provided the conceptual basis for the kind of articulation that is needed.

What Language Shall We Borrow?

In the footnote to the passage just cited, Gustafson excerpts language from the prayers of St. Francis and Karl Rahner to illustrate how we may, and presumably should, speak of God. Among the excerpted phrases from St. Francis we find "almighty," "King of heaven and earth," "Great and wonderful Lord." Among the phrases from Rahner we find "Near One" and "Distant One."[35] Are these suitable metaphors for God? How are we to decide? Our first criterion must be our understanding and construal of God and God's relation to the world. On that score the language of St. Francis seems more problematic than that of Rahner.

---

[34]*An Examined Faith*, 107. In note 5, pp. 118–19, he cites language from the prayers of St. Francis and Rahner.
[35]Ibid.

Is God "almighty"? Not if we mean omnipotent. As argued in Chapter 4, God may be understood to be supreme in power, but not as possessing either all power, unlimited power, or arbitrary power. God's power is to be understood as primarily persuasive, as contributive to the initial subjective aim of every occasion of experience. It is surpassing power, but it is not the power traditionally attributed to an "almighty" God.

Is God "King of heaven and earth"? The personal, anthropomorphic metaphor, "King," is problematic, but not because it is personal and anthropomorphic. "King" is problematic for other reasons, especially its monarchical connotations. As both McFague and Griffin would agree, God's relationship to the world does not resemble a monarch's relation to his subjects or kingdom. Kings tend to exercise power in rather arbitrary and unilateral ways. They preside over hierarchical social orders that constitute impositions on, and distortions of, the truly interrelated and interdependent character of all relations in the natural and social world. Monarchical and other forms of coercive and authoritarian order may be preferable to various forms of disorder, but they fail to optimize the possibilities for the flourishing of human and other life. The metaphor of God as king provides us a seriously distorted image of the relation of God to the world. McFague would also argue that kings, being male, reflect the legacy of patriarchy and male domination, an argument that invokes ethical as well as theological criteria. A God in whose image and likeness both male and female have been created should not be imaged as one but not the other.

What about "heaven and earth"? Is this an adequate metaphor to refer to the cosmos? At least two reservations should be registered. The word "heaven" continues to carry the connotation of an afterlife, even though, when conjoined with "earth," it may be taken to denote the whole of existence. Moreover, the juxtaposition of "heaven" and "earth" has connotations of two distinct places or realms, the realm of this life and the realm of the life to come, or the realm of physical existence and the realm of spiritual existence, or the realm of human and other habitation and the eternal realm of God. There are implied dualisms here that all three thinkers whose works we have been examining would find objectionable. If the language of "heaven and earth" is to be retained in theological discourse, including use in worship, it should be set in a context where it can be seen as a poetic way of speaking about the whole of existence, the cosmos, which consists of "earth," our planetary home, and "heaven," which is all the rest of creation. In this light, it would be better to speak of "the heavens and the earth."

Gustafson also cites St. Francis' metaphor, "Great and wonderful Lord." To call God "great and wonderful" would seem to pose no problem. However, the historical, political, and cultural meanings of the term "Lord" are similar to those of the term "King," making it similarly problematic. "Lord" is also clearly a male, patriarchal term. Just how much so becomes more evident when we contemplate what it would be like to address God as "Great and wonderful Lady"!

Karl Rahner speaks of God as "Near One" and "Distant One." If we were to speak only of God as "Distant One," and not as "Near One," we would not escape the difficulties I have identified regarding Gustafson's construal of God as Other. But to speak of God as both "Near One" and "Distant One" is suggestive of both the immanence and the transcendence of God. Such language connotes an affectively accessible God as well as a God of majesty and ineffability. In one of his published prayers, the noted preacher Harry Emerson Fosdick addressed God as "high above yet deep within us all."[36] This language also suggests a God with whom we can be intimately connected as well as a God who remains so much more than we can know or comprehend.

The language we need for God, to be congruent with the construal of God and the God–world relation that I have been developing throughout this book, needs to be a language of immanence and transcendence. It also needs to be personal, and thus in some ways anthropomorphic, language. God must be imaged in ways that express God's experience of, and feeling for, the world. We also need language that communicates that God is experienceable by human beings.

Shortly after Sallie McFague's *Models of God* was published, Gordon Kaufman offered the following appreciative assessment.

> Her analysis shows that many of the difficulties that modern theology has faced are dependent not so much on the *personalistic* character of the root metaphors of the tradition, as I had been inclined to believe; they are, rather, largely a function of the *patriarchal* and *monarchical* character of those metaphors—that is, it is the vision of the human (and God) as essentially dominating *will*, the powerful individual *ego*, the great "I AM," that is at the root of many of our theological problems.

Theologians have not been sufficiently aware how much their thinking has been governed by a vision of the human grounded in these unquestioned notions. McFague's method of metaphorical analysis enables her to show what a difference it makes for the understanding of the human and of God if we conceive of God as, for example, mother and lover rather than father and king.[37]

---

[36] *A Book of Public Prayers* (New York: Harper & Brothers, 1959), 142. Most of Fosdick's prayers, in fact, are exemplary in expressing both the immanence and transcendence of God without resort to monarchical language.

[37] "*Models of God*: Is Metaphor Enough?" *Religion and Intellectual Life* 5 (1988) 12.

Kaufman's observations are very much in accord with the argument I have been pursuing in this chapter. My argument on behalf of personalistic metaphors for God has been primarily theological thus far. I have indicated that not all personalistic metaphors will suffice, however. In particular, I have noted that monarchical and patriarchal language for God is theologically as well as ethically problematic. There are surely many non-monarchical and non-patriarchal personalistic metaphors that would be equally or even more unacceptable. One has only to think of the host of terms we use to express our opprobrium regarding other people we dislike or of whom we disapprove. The point is, having made a case for personalistic language for God, it still remains to comment on what kinds of personal metaphors and images are most appropriate and justifiable, first, given our theological construal, and, second, given our concern for the ways in which metaphors can shape perceptions, orient our thinking, and influence our actions.

Theologically, the most appropriate personal and imagistic metaphors for God are those that personify God in terms of the qualities and the actions that we attribute to God. Among the attributes that I judge to be most essential are those that derive from what Griffin has characterized as the generic conception of God[38] and those that have been emphasized by Gustafson, as well as some that are prominent in Christian scripture and tradition. I will not attempt any systematic or thorough account of the divine attributes, but simply wish to point to the thematic richness of images potentially suitable for critical engagement in McFague's task of metaphorical theology.

The metaphors that we need will be suggestive of God's perfection in goodness, love, justice, compassion, wisdom, knowledge, and persuasive power. Just as traditional notions of omnipotence are not to be attributed to God, however, neither should traditional notions of omniscience be imputed to God. God's knowledge must be understood to encompass all that has been and is, but not all that will be. We need metaphors of God as everlasting and omnipresent Creator, providentially active in nature and history, caring for the world as a whole and in all its particularities. As the One in whom all things have their being, God must be imaged as the One to whom all things owe their existence and in whom all things have their destiny and hope. We need metaphors that are intrinsically relational, metaphors that intimate our interrelatedness and interdependence, with one another and with all that exists. We need metaphors that can communicate God's encouragement and guidance, watchfulness and solicitude. We need metaphors that evoke a sense of God's inspiring, comforting, abiding, and intimate presence, as well as

---

[38]Cf. Chapter 4, 186, regarding Griffin's generic idea of God. I seek to encompass but not be confined to his list of divine attributes in my construal of God.

those that enliven us to God's awesomeness and majesty and transcending beauty. We need metaphors that can be elaborated in terms of God's governance, God's ordering, sustaining, and bearing down, God's requiring and enabling us to be and to do. We need metaphors that confront us with the reality of a goodness that is not our own, an embodied holiness that beckons us to place our lives in the context of ever-larger wholes. God must be portrayed as One to whom all human beings are in some sense accountable, for their lives, their intentions, and their actions, and as One toward whose perfection we are to aspire. We need metaphors that speak to us of a certain constancy of character, of One whom we can trust and on whom we can rely, come what may. We need metaphors that invite our consent to the One who is the final measure of the meaning of our days.[39]

---

[39] There is plenty of language within Christian scripture and tradition that can be appropriated to speak of God in these terms. Particular biblical texts that especially commend themselves include a passage from the book of Acts where God is referred to as the One in whom "we live and move and have our being" (Acts 17:28). The Pauline doxology in Romans declares, "For from [God] and through [God] and to [God] are all things. To [God] be glory forever. Amen" (Romans 11:36; the masculine pronoun, "him," appears where I have inserted "God" in brackets). In the book of Revelation, God is identified as "the Alpha and the Omega, the first and the last, the beginning and the end" (Revelation 22:12; cf. also 1:8; 21:6; Alpha and Omega are the first and last letters of the Greek alphabet). In each of these cases we have metaphors that are highly expressive of the conception of God and God's relation to the world developed in Chapter 4. There is no shortage of texts that are expressive of God's power and might. Care needs to be taken only to avoid those that picture divine power as arbitrary, extrinsic, or unconditioned. The language of God as Creator is found in the major Christian creeds as well as in many biblical texts. There are many other texts that speak of God's goodness and kindness, God's mercy and steadfast love, God's compassion and providential care. In the book of Proverbs, God is personified as wisdom, or Sophia. Psalm 139 is an eloquent meditation on the omnipresence of God. Other psalms speak of God's beauty or the "holy splendor" of divine worship (Psalms 27:4; 29:2; 96:9). A number of the psalms proclaim the everlastingness of God (Psalms 41:13; 90:2; 103:17; 106:48; 119:142; 145:13; cf. 93:2; 100:5). Throughout the biblical texts one finds references to God's will or commands, affirmations of God's justice and righteousness, and portrayals of God's judgments.

It lies beyond the scope of this chapter to identify all of the traditional language about God that might continue to be appropriate for speaking of God today. Some of the passages I have identified speak about God, or in reference to God, without employing metaphors that speak of God. However, much language *about* God can readily be employed in metaphorical ways as language *for* God. If God is wise, then we can speak of God as Wisdom. If God is loving, we can speak of God as Love. If God is everlasting, we can speak of God as Everlasting. Descriptive or denotative language, including language that is part of our conceptualization of God, can often be employed more directly as metaphorical language. We can also turn prepositional language into direct metaphor. If God is a God of hope, or of comfort, or of help, we may speak of God as our Hope, our Comfort, or our Help. The fact that monarchical and patriarchal language for God has become theologically and ethically problematic hardly means that an entirely new vocabulary must be invented to speak of God and to God in religiously meaningful ways that are congruent with our conceptions of God.

There are many images and personal metaphors, or personifications, of God that are expressive of one or more of these themes. We have seen reference in McFague and Gustafson to such metaphors for God as Creator, Liberator, Sustainer, Governor, Judge, and Redeemer. Other metaphors that have common currency include Maker, Protector, Giver, Helper, Guardian, Guide, Counselor, Teacher, Potter, Author, Architect, Shepherd, Healer, Savior, Physician, Comforter, Spirit, Advocate, Companion, Lover, and Friend. In a somewhat more contemporary vein, and in keeping with the sensibilities that inform the critique of patriarchal images of God, are such metaphors for God as Weaver, Gardener, and Poet, as well as Sophia, the feminine personification of wisdom.[40]

Of the three personal metaphors proposed and elaborated on by McFague in *Models of God*, I find that of God as mother to be the most satisfactory overall. Its meaning is funded by the most commonly experienced, and one of the most profound, of all human relationships. It can be elaborated in ways that are suggestive of many if not most of the attributes of being and action that seem central to our understanding and construal of God. Because it is a gendered metaphor, however, God as mother remains problematic on three accounts. One is simply that it seems desirable to avoid gendered language for God if we do not conceive God to be gendered. Another problem is that use of the metaphor of God as mother creates so much cognitive dissonance among those who have grown accustomed to hearing God spoken of as father, and perhaps even among those who have adopted non-gendered language for God, that its use in worship tends to evoke something other than authentic religious piety. Third, while mothers tend to exhibit many human qualities, including parental qualities, that may be taken as true reflections of the *imago Dei*, fathers tend to exhibit other complementary parental qualities that also may be taken as true reflections of the *imago Dei*. As McFague herself has proposed, the metaphor of God as mother should not altogether replace the metaphor of God as father, but is needed as a corrective and complement in order to move toward a more adequate view of God, whose parental qualities may be best expressed with both maternal and paternal imagery.[41] Attempts have been made simply to substitute the metaphor, "Parent," for the language of God as father. The term, "Parent," however, fails to convey the level of intimacy and directness of either "Mother" or "Father." It is too impersonal. What child ever uses "Parent" as a form of address, or a term of affection? As

---

[40]Most of these metaphors can be found in the hymns in current hymnal collections. Others are familiar to me from my professional reading and from participation in worship in various settings.
[41]Cf. 133 above.

in the case of Rahner's language of "Near One" and "Distant One," I think we have an instance here of the need to use two metaphors in tandem and in tension, that of God as father and as mother.

We must also recognize that efforts to employ appropriate metaphors for God that take seriously the critiques of patriarchy and monarchy, and that strive to be congruent with our conceptualization of God and the God–world relation, need to be undertaken on a tentative and experimental basis. It is premature to suppose that any suitable new *models* of God can be identified and agreed upon until they have been lived with for some time, tried and tested, and found to possess staying power. Recall McFague's own distinction between models and metaphors. Models are metaphors that have stood the test of use and time. Recall as well McFague's stipulation throughout *Models of God*, namely, that her metaphorical theology requires a necessarily experimental approach. Determining what models of God will actually prove religiously adequate is not simply a rational exercise, nor a matter of theological fiat, but a matter of experimentation, the outcome of which must be assessed over time. In the meantime, it is important to be able to identify a range of theologically appropriate personal and imagistic metaphors, many quite traditional and familiar, others relatively new but apparently resonant with contemporary worldviews, that hold promise of contributing to a language of worship and prayer that is emotionally and spiritually evocative and affecting, and thus capable of engendering authentic piety.

Although Gustafson, McFague, and Griffin each recognizes that our primary metaphors for God tend to imply some view of the God–world relation, most of the metaphors we have been reviewing to this point focus on God as related especially to humankind. There are important exceptions: God as Creator, Maker, Architect, and Gardener are ready examples of metaphors that speak of God's relation to the natural world. Moreover, there is no inherent reason why such metaphors of God as Sustainer, Governor, Weaver, Poet, Lover, and Friend cannot also be understood as expressive of God's creative love and care for all that comprises the natural order. In any event, it is important that our metaphorical language help us to keep in view all of the world in relation to God if we are to maintain a vital theocentric perspective and critique of anthropocentrism.

In this regard, it is well to underscore the obvious. There is no metaphor for God more indispensable for Christianity, or for this book, than that of Creator. It is precisely because Christianity understands God as Creator that scientific and theological understandings must be brought into dialogue and, if possible, congruence. It is also precisely because God is understood to be Creator that science and theology must not be regarded as "nonoverlapping magisteria."[42] Both science and theology make claims about the same reality.

---

[42]Cf. Chapter 1, 7.

Science tends to call it nature, while theology tends to call it creation, but both make claims about "the way things really are" in the world. Moreover, because God is understood to be Creator, a distinction must be maintained within Christian thought between God and the world. That distinction need not be radical, or absolute, in the sense that God is understood to be entirely unrelated to, and therefore unaffected by, the world. In fact, when God is so understood, there does not seem to be any intelligible way to account for divine influence in the world.[43] What is required, if God is to be understood as Creator in a meaningful fashion, is some notion of divine agency or influence that is not reducible to merely materialistic processes. Divine influence must be somehow constitutive of the causal nexus of events. The most adequate construal of the God–world relation of which I am aware is that provided by process theology, not incidentally because of its conception of divine agency. Within Christian thought, Griffin's process theology commends itself in large part because it rescues affirmations of God as Creator from intellectual obscurity.

Our understanding and construal of the God–world relation is such that we cannot dispense with the metaphor of God as Creator. But likewise, we can hardly dispense with the less personalistic, more conceptual metaphor of the world as God's body, as McFague puts it, or God as the mind or soul of the world, as Hartshorne and Griffin might add. This should not be problematic for Christian theology.[44] Body language is deeply rooted in Christianity, with its incarnational theology and its familiar metaphor of the church as the body of Christ. The challenge is to employ body language for the world in new ways that are vivid and evocative, ways that enliven Christian worshippers to the creative and sustaining presence of the divine throughout the non-human world, in every dimension of existence.

Metaphor and the Moral Life

It has been one of my basic contentions in this book that the way things are is indicative, in terms of available future possibilities, of the way things

---

[43]To be sure, an Aristotelian view of God as "unmoved mover" implies divine influence without any contingency or relatedness on God's part. However, in Aristotle's conception, God is the object of thought and desire and, as such, final cause only, not efficient cause, and not creator of the world.

[44]Of course, it is highly problematic for Christian theologians whose thinking remains indebted to certain notions that reflect the influence of Greek philosophy, especially divine impassibility. It is also problematic for those who continue to insist on the radical distinction between Creator and creation, a distinction that appears to reflect early Christian attempts to counter heretical tendencies to implicate the Creator God in the corruptions of the creation, and continues to reflect a very "high" (i.e., monarchical) view of divine sovereignty and freedom.

should be. That is why, from the standpoint of theological ethics, adequacy to reality is so crucial to our construal of God and the God–world relation. It is also why our metaphorical language for God must be congruent with this construal. Our metaphorical language must be truthful, in the sense of being adequate to reality.

Another basic claim is that our language for God, if it is to be religiously adequate, must be capable of evoking affective response, of engendering authentic religious piety. That is why abstract, conceptual language about God is not religiously adequate. Rich, imagistic, and personal metaphorical language is indispensable.

A third claim, about which I have been somewhat less explicit, is that the moral life is contingent on certain attitudes and dispositions that are sustained by religious piety, as we have seen Gustafson define it. Gustafson does not insist that religious belief is essential for such piety, nor does he claim that such piety necessarily entails belief in God.[45] It seems clear, nonetheless, that for him and for most Christians, authentic religious piety exists symbiotically with engaging, meaningful worship, and that the latter requires rich, imagistic, and even anthropomorphic metaphorical language for God.

In consequence of these claims, theological congruence and religious adequacy are the first and second criteria for an appropriate metaphorical language for God and the God–world relation. For theological ethics, however, there must also be a third major criterion. Our religious language must also be relevant to the lives we live, to the conditions on which we reflect, the circumstances in which we decide, and the contexts in which we act. Language shapes our self-understanding, our perceptions of importance, our moral valuations, and our dispositions. Our religious language must serve to shape, orient, and enlarge our perceptions in critical, illuminating, and life-enhancing ways. The feminist critique of monarchical and patriarchal religious language has been so compelling precisely because it has shown how such language is implicated in the legitimation of social, economic, and political structures, cultural attitudes, and human valuations that diminish the role, status, and prospects for flourishing of women in particular, and of non-valorized persons and groups in general. All our theological language has moral significance, and must be examined and critiqued for its evident real-world implications and effects.

---

[45]Cf. my discussion in Chapter 2, 56ff. Gustafson seems to view religious belief and piety as existing in a kind of mutually supporting relationship, but he also seems to find the equivalent of his kind of piety in non-believers. I have not attempted to provide a complete account of how Gustafson views the genesis of piety. Both the natural world and religious tradition and worship seem to play a part.

It would take another book to explore fully the possible significance of various theological metaphors we have been considering from the distinctive perspective of a theocentric theological ethics. My main concern has been to identify a range of appropriate metaphors, theologically congruent, religiously adequate, and responsive to a non-anthropocentric ecological worldview. But there is one other concern that warrants attention. In response to feminist critique of traditional theological language, I have endorsed McFague's proposal to substitute maternal and paternal images and metaphorical language for the language of patriarchy. But theological language is not limited to images and metaphors that intimate the nature of our relation to God as individuals for whom personal relationships are paramount. We are also related to God as—and in the context of our lives as members of—groups, communities, and societies for whom the most appropriate language of relationship is that of governance.

Monarchical language no longer speaks to our situation, nor does it fittingly express our conception of any facet of the God–world relation. God is not, nor should be imaged to be, our King, Sovereign, or Lord. God's sphere of governance in the world is not a kingdom, empire, or realm. To some extent, these metaphors once served to claim the supremacy of divine governance over that of earthly rulers. The early Christian affirmation, "Jesus Christ is Lord," for example, implicitly contested the imperial cult. It intentionally expressed the conviction that, despite all his pretensions, Caesar is *not* Lord. In our current context, however, such language is more simply suggestive of the possession of unbridled authority and the capacity to exercise unchecked and arbitrary power. But we live in a world where few such manifestations of authority and power are to be found, and none are to be commended. What is to take the place of such archaic language?

One of the most explicit efforts to address this question has been made by William Everett. Everett has argued, regarding our framework for thinking about Christian ethics, that we need to move from the symbolism of kingship to that of democracy, republics, and federalism.[46] More recently he has turned his attention specifically to the language of worship. Worship, he notes, "shapes the religious affections, indeed our entire emotional and motivational structure."[47] Worship is "the bridge between theology and ethics."[48] Everett's view of worship is partly descriptive, partly normative. "In the central traditions of Judaism and Christianity," he maintains, "worship rehearses the

---

[46] William Johnson Everett, *God's Federal Republic: Reconstructing Our Governing Symbol* (New York: Paulist, 1988).
[47] *The Politics of Worship: Reforming the Language and Symbols of Liturgy* (Cleveland: United Church Press, 1999) 11.
[48] Ibid., 36.

governance of God."⁴⁹ Worship within these traditions ought to be regarded primarily as "the symbolic and dramatic rehearsal of the ultimate structure of just relationships that God—the author and source of justice—intends for all creatures of the cosmos."⁵⁰ It should shape the worshippers' vision of their place and role within the larger social and public order.⁵¹

In actual practice, however, Everett says the public character of worship has been largely lost and the symbolism of worship has become highly privatized. In the process, the view of God as person has been reduced from that of "a public actor in history," "present and active in the drama of salvation," to that of a merely intimate God.⁵² How is this claim to be reconciled with the obviously still pervasive use of monarchical language in worship? According to Everett, "the church has preserved a monarchical paradigm of governance in its worship by translating it into a psychological model of self-control over our passions."⁵³ Not only does language about God come to function as a symbolic representation of conscience or the superego, but the public dimensions of divine engagement in the world virtually drop out of view. "The retrieval of God as person in its original sense"—that is, as public actor—"means a recovery of worship and theology as articulations of the ultimate order of governance—a long and arduous process indeed."⁵⁴

A full assessment of Everett's argument cannot be undertaken here. Nor will I attempt to discuss and evaluate his proposals for the needed retrieval. If there is an obvious weakness in his treatment, it is the relative inattention he gives to considerations of language that would speak of God's governance with respect to the natural world as well as the social and historical world. I am persuaded, nonetheless, that Everett's argument deserves careful attention not only from students and practitioners of Christian worship but also from theological ethicists seeking a morally and ethically adequate metaphorical language for speaking about God and the God–world relation. In many respects, Gustafson, in his *Ethics from a Theocentric Perspective*, has provided just the sort of articulation "of the ultimate order of divine governance" that Everett is urging. Gustafson also gives adequate attention to the natural order. What Gustafson lacks, in addition to a conception of divine agency that would warrant claims of divine action in nature and history, is a richly serviceable vocabulary of appropriate theological metaphors for use

---

[49] Ibid., 53.
[50] Ibid., 7; cf. 30ff., 72.
[51] Note the clear affinities with Gustafson in the way Everett describes the relations among worship, the religious affections, theology, and ethics in the context of divine governance.
[52] Ibid., 65.
[53] Ibid., 81; cf. 48ff.
[54] Ibid., 65.

in Christian worship. Everett's project accents the need to experiment with new metaphors for God and the God–world relation that are expressive of an understanding of divine governance within both history and nature. Such metaphors will need to convey both an immanent and a transcendent sense of God's relation to history and to nature, including a tension between the "is" of realized actualities and the "ought" of unfulfilled possibilities. Such metaphors must also evoke genuine affective response within the contemporary cultural context.

It will be a major challenge to find appropriate metaphors of the sort needed, especially with respect to divine governance in history. We inhabit a world currently lacking in exemplary models of governance in the corporate life of our communities, organizations, nations, and international bodies. One possible metaphor that could serve well, if adequately contextualized, might be that of Head. God as Head would seem to be congruent with the metaphor of the world as God's body. The term is also resonant with the traditional Christian metaphor of Christ as head of the Church. Furthermore, in much of our corporate life the term can be used to designate the person whose governance is supreme. For example, we speak of heads of staff, heads of organizations, and heads of state. If God as Head seems overly hierarchical or transcendent, perhaps we could also speak of God as Lifeblood, a metaphor that is also often used with respect to organizational life, and that conveys a vital sense of immanence. Used in tandem and in tension, the two metaphors of God as Head and Lifeblood could be strongly suggestive of the conviction that, apart from the divine presence and governance in the corporate structures of our existence, there is disorder and misdirection, and life does not flourish. I do not think this conviction would be controverted by any of the three theologians whose work we have been considering.

The Moral Question

As we have previously seen, for Gustafson the practical moral question is: *What is God enabling and requiring us, as participants in (and through) the patterns and processes of interdependence of life in the world, to be and to do?*[55] For McFague, the question is never so precisely formulated, in part because she is more engaged in prophetic discourse than practical moral reasoning. Perhaps we could state her primary concern in this way: How are we to embody the Christian gospel's destabilizing, inclusive, nonhierarchical vision of fulfillment for all of creation, thus averting nuclear and ecological disaster and promoting the flourishing of all life? For Griffin the general moral principle

---

[55]Chapter 2, 79.

can be stated as follows: In any concrete situation we human beings should act to maximize importance insofar as it is attainable by us in that situation.[56] For all three thinkers, the moral question may also be understood in terms of the question, What serves the purposes of God? Or, as Griffin would phrase it, What does it mean to adopt the divine aim as our own?

In his *Ethics*, Gustafson presents a fairly comprehensive account of how his theocentric perspective frames and informs the way one goes about the process of moral decision-making. In the latter half of the second volume he provides concrete examples of his own engagement in that process. I have noted that his method may be characterized as descriptive and prescriptive, experiential and evaluative, inductive and pragmatic, empirical and practically reasoned. It is a process of discernment, deeply informed by human experience, strongly oriented by theocentric piety, and highly dependent on the knowledge we can gain about our world from the natural and social sciences. As practiced by Gustafson, and as illustrated by the examples in volume 2, discernment is not a free-form activity. There are certain patterns or features that give shape to the discernment process: "points to be considered," boundary conditions, presumptions in favor of certain values and principles, and general rules.[57] The end result of discernment, however, is not the culmination of a logical argument or process of deduction, but an informed intuition. The theocentric perspective counts for a lot in this approach, in some quite specific ways that are part of the profile I reviewed in Chapter 2.[58] Nonetheless, moral discernment never reaches a foregone conclusion, but is always an exploratory undertaking, as one seeks to relate oneself and all things in a manner appropriate to our and their relations to God.

A major difficulty in Gustafson's approach, which he acknowledges, is how to specify and circumscribe the larger wholes that are to be considered relevant and taken into account as the contexts for interpretation of their constituent parts. Although Gustafson does not invoke the notion of the impartial, sympathetic, and fully informed "ideal observer," as does Griffin, he seems to hold to a similar conception of what would constitute the ideal "informed intuition." The problem is that under the conditions of human finitude, one cannot be fully informed. One cannot attain a God's-eye view. One cannot take into account the whole of existence.

In addition to this somewhat practical problem, in which decision and action must wait upon the practicing ethicist's consent to finitude, there is the fundamentally conceptual problem of how to distinguish between what

---

[56] Chapter 1, 35.
[57] *Ethics II*, 302ff. These are not identifiable in the abstract, but are context-dependent.
[58] 68ff.

God is requiring and enabling us to be and to do, and the naturalistic patterns and processes of interdependence of life in the world, in and through which God's governance is said to occur. In other words, it remains problematic how God is to be distinguished from what Gustafson regards as nature. Clearly, the limiting conditions and the possibilities for human *being* and *doing* are to be discerned in light of the "isness" of our existence. But among the possibilities available for future human interaction, how is the "oughtness" to be discerned? Gustafson says, "Moral action involves the ordering and directing of existing powers in accordance with moral principles, values, ends, and ideals."[59] What still seems lacking in his account is greater specification and identification of the source of the requisite principles, values, ends, and ideals. What is it that constitutes the good—for the natural world, for other individuals, groups, and societies, and for ourselves?

McFague answers this question with little hesitation: the good, that which God seeks, is the flourishing of all life. Gustafson also identifies the good with the flourishing of life, but he declines to elaborate on what this means in general. What he does say is that there is no natural harmony or coincidence of interests among all living things, including human beings. Therefore, what might be judged good for human life may not be good for life as a whole. But there are no *a priori* rules for deciding when and where this will be so. McFague, on the other hand, envisions an ultimate harmony of interests as an ideal toward which to strive. As we saw in Chapter 3, her prophetic discourse leads her away from a descriptively realistic account of the disharmonies of the natural world in favor of an eschatological vision of the peaceable kingdom. In this vision, the disorders that human beings have introduced into world are abolished and creation is restored. McFague admits that there can be no return to an Edenic state, but seems to say that should not keep us from trying.[60] Human beings are largely to blame for the mess the world is in, and largely capable of making it right.

In any event, she sees God as "on the side of life, seeking the enhancement and fulfillment of *all* living beings."[61] But, in a world of evolutionary process, *all* that this might mean in concrete terms is hard to fathom. Surely it entails the protection of species, the reclamation of habitat, the purification of water, soil, and air, and other steps toward a healthier environment and greater ecological balance for all life as we know it. The flourishing of life demands what McFague terms "an ethic of care," care for the Earth, and care for those who inhabit it.[62] It also means a new way of living abundantly on Earth,

---

[59]*Ethics II*, 8-9; cf. 70–71 above.
[60]*Super, Natural Christians*, 158ff.
[61]Davaney, "*Models of God: Theology for an Ecological, Nuclear Age*," 40.
[62]*Super, Natural Christians*; cf. 150–75.

trading in our high-consumer lifestyle for one that is not exploitative of the planet's natural resources and its other inhabitants.[63] McFague invites us to engage in a form of Christian praxis that she calls Christian nature spirituality. Specifically, she suggests that we need to exercise care toward some particular places, and in general to treat the natural world as we do, or should, treat God and other people. An ethic of care must give preference to "the least of these," as in Jesus' story of the last judgment.[64] The "least of these" includes the vulnerable and endangered plant and animal inhabitants of the natural world, but also "the oppressed, the poor, the despised, the forgotten."[65]

McFague's work can be viewed as a prophetic critique of prevailing cultural attitudes and economic practices that serve the perceived advantage of the planet's economically and politically most powerful citizens at the great expense of the lives and life prospects of most of the planet's human and non-human inhabitants. She does not lay out a constructive program for social rehabilitation, cultural transformation, or environmental reclamation. However, her proposed new models of God clearly bear moral significance, and constitute a constructive moral theology of sorts. She advocates the adoption of such metaphorical language to shape how we think and what we perceive about ourselves and our relations to the world, and thus to shape our actions, presumably in life-enhancing ways. Her emphasis on praxis in her two most recent books provides further indication of what she judges to be required in order to embody the Christian Gospel's vision of fulfillment for all creation.

From the perspective of theological ethics, there are at least two major and related deficiencies in McFague's approach. The first, to which I have just alluded, is that she does not provide us anything like a comprehensive ethics of flourishing. It is a simple ecological fact that some life flourishes at the expense of other life. One need only think of bacteria and termites, vultures and cancer cells. McFague is not unaware of the issue. In a brief discussion of care and justice, she implies that some life has a greater right to survive than other life.[66] Nonetheless, on the whole she seems to think that all values worth preserving in creation (and human society) are commensurable, that all can be reduced to the measure of life-enhancement and fulfillment. In her view, even an ethics of rights and justice can be readily included within an ethics of care.[67]

---

[63] *Life Abundant*; cf. xi–xiv.
[64] Matthew 25:31-46.
[65] *Super, Natural Christians*, 169.
[66] Ibid., 157.
[67] Ibid.; cf. 155–58.

The second weakness in McFague's approach is that she focuses primarily on the natural world. What would a political or social ethics of fulfillment look like, apart from being environmentally friendly, nonhierarchical, and inclusive of diversity? What might moral, intellectual, or aesthetic fulfillment require? To a large extent, the course of human civilization can be correlated with the development of new levels of mastery over the elements, contagions, co-habiting species, and resources of the natural world. By what criteria might we judge whether the flourishing of human civilization—measured by such capacities as the provision of food, protection from the elements, and greater time for leisure pursuits, or by increasing longevity and declining death rates—is a good thing? McFague does not articulate her vision of fulfillment for all creation in ways that provide the critical intellectual resources for addressing questions such as these. In partial acknowledgment of the fact that not all life has equal claim upon us, and in light of an overriding concern for our (human) survival, which depends on the development of "a social, sustainable planet," she simply acknowledges that "the well-being of the whole is the final goal."[68]

For David Griffin, the well-being of the whole is precisely what God has in heart and mind. God not only desires, but perfectly pursues, the good of the whole of existence. Griffin is very explicit that the moral life has its source and end in God. God is the ultimate source of our moral norms. But what is the good? How is the divine aim to be understood? I noted in Chapter 4 that Griffin interprets the divine aim in terms of the maximization, alternatively, of value, importance, and beauty. In stating his one general moral principle, he writes only of maximizing importance. It is not always clear how these terms are to be understood. The one thing that is clear is that one cannot derive from process philosophy a single concrete moral code applicable to human beings at all times and places.[69]

Following Whitehead, Griffin identifies importance with greatness of experience. It "points to an extremely general notion, not to be reduced to any one of its specific forms."[70] Those forms, or species, include morality, logic, religion, and art, none of which, says Whitehead, exhausts the whole meaning of the term. Whitehead understood the teleology of the universe to be directed to the production of beauty, such beauty being "'the one aim which by its very nature is self-justifying.'"[71] Insofar as there is a Whiteheadian or process ethics, it is often mistakenly judged to be merely an aesthetics. Griffin

---

[68] Ibid., 157, 158.
[69] *Reenchantment without Supernaturalism*, 304.
[70] Ibid., 305.
[71] Ibid.

is quick to point out that the teleology of the universe, or divine aim, and hence moral goodness, is not to be equated with the aim to maximize aesthetic enjoyment. Rather, this is an aesthetic ethics in the sense that it seeks to unite or encompass various forms or species of beauty, or importance—the moral, intellectual, and spiritual as well as the sensible. In other words, the moral, understood as an ideal form of human action, is not to be reduced to morality, understood as conformity to rules, principles, and other directives for how to live. For Griffin, then, the quest for the moral may be described as a creative pursuit. Moral action involves a creative bringing together of various dimensions or expressions of value.

As with Gustafson, Griffin's ethics cannot be described as either teleological or deontological, though it resembles the former more than the latter. Nor can it be described as instrumental. In the previous chapter we saw that Griffin attributes intrinsic value to every occasion of experience. Intrinsic value appears to be another way of denoting beauty (which Whitehead says is the one self-justifying aim), or importance (which Griffin says we are to seek to maximize in every concrete situation), or intrinsic good. Griffin defines the intrinsically good as "that which is good in and for itself, apart from considerations as to its usefulness for other things."[72] Drawing again from Whitehead, he says that the criteria of intrinsic good are aesthetic criteria, and can be summed up under harmony and intensity. "That is, experience is good to the degree that it is both harmonious and intense."[73] Stating that the opposite of harmony is disharmony, or discord, and the opposite of intensity can be called triviality, Griffin observes:

> The fact that intensity is at least as important as harmony is evidenced by the fact that we often risk great pain, both physical and psychic, for the sake of excitement. Of course, people differ in regard to the relative value that they place on each of these criteria, with some risking present harmony for increased intensity, while others forgo the possibility of greater intensity for the sake of preserving the harmony which has been achieved. But everyone wants both factors to some degree. A person may even prefer death to the continuation of experience in which either harmony or intensity is outweighed by its opposite.
>
> Why is it that intensity and harmony are somewhat in tension, so that efforts to achieve one may endanger the other? It is because increased intensity requires increased complexity which can bring together a greater variety of detail into contrast. Bringing more details into experience may upset the harmony which had been achieved

---

[72] *God, Power, and Evil*, 282.
[73] Ibid.

among the elements that had previously been combined. If harmony is to be achieved, it will have to be a more complex harmony.[74]

Griffin says that there are two senses in which an experience can be complex, both of which contribute to intensity. "First, there is complexity in the sheer amount and variety of elements which are integrated in an occasion of experience."[75] The more contrasting elements that are effectively integrated, the greater the intensity. But there is also complexity that is, paradoxically, the ability to simplify the data of a previously complex occasion and thereby achieve a greater intensity of experience. "Conscious sense experience, in which myriads of feelings are transmuted into the appearance of a relatively few objects, is the most obvious example."[76] How, then, does one assess experiences in terms of their intrinsic goodness?

> The recognition that there are two criteria of evil, discord and unnecessary triviality, complicates the attempt to rate experiences in terms of intrinsic goodness. One cannot simply say that an experience which is harmonious is *ipso facto* "better" than one which is more discordant. It is true that "the more discordant the feeling, the further the retreat from perfection." But it is also true that "Perfection at a low level ranks below Imperfection with higher aim." Accordingly, encouraging the emergence of forms of experience which will be more intense but also more discordant than present ones is not necessarily inconsistent with moral goodness.[77]

In this aesthetic conception of moral goodness, the aim is to maximize both harmony and intensity, consistent with a minimization of discord and triviality. This demands a complexity of integration, a capacity to comprehend a diversity of disparate elements in a kind of creative fusion that creates and preserves effective contrast and intensity, thus avoiding unnecessary triviality.

Although Griffin owes his terminology to Whitehead, this aesthetics of complexity (and simplicity) bears significant resemblance to Gustafson's own aesthetics of moral discernment, in which there is also accent on complexity. In fact, there are striking parallels between Gustafson and Griffin when it comes to their fundamental moral outlook. Gustafson speaks of serving God

---

[74] Ibid., 282–83.
[75] Ibid., 283.
[76] Ibid., 284. Oliver Wendell Holmes is reported to have said, "I would not give a fig for the simplicity this side of complexity, but would give my life for the simplicity on the other side of complexity"; Margaret J. Wheatley, *Turning to One Another: Simple Conversations to Restore Hope to the Future* (San Francisco: Berrett-Koehler, 2002) 20.
[77] Ibid., 284–85. The quoted phrases are from Whitehead's *Adventures of Ideas*.

by acting in accord with the divine purposes, Griffin speaks of making the divine aim one's own. Inasmuch as Gustafson distinguishes purposes from intentions, his perspective is less teleological than Griffin's, but both have a theocentric perspective that requires them to think of moral goodness, in non-instrumental terms, as that which accords with the divine governance, as each understands that governance. Both thinkers also argue the need to view the elements or parts of any situation in terms of the whole of which they are a part, and to interpret these elements in the context of that whole.[78] While both would admit that human finitude precludes a God's-eye view of the world, for any circumstance in which human beings must interact and exercise moral responsibility, both tend to want to view the particulars of any circumstance in terms of the largest possible whole. And for both of them, this introduces a highly significant element of complexity.

I have noted that McFague also ultimately acknowledges the need to consider the well-being of the whole, not simply of the individual or aggregated parts, in her ethics of care. Even so, with respect to their holistic viewpoints and the complexity that entails, both Gustafson and Griffin can be clearly distinguished from McFague in their approach to moral decision-making. Gustafson and Griffin have a more fundamental sense of the existence of discordant elements in all existence. In the passages I have cited from Griffin's *God, Power, and Evil*, he associates discord (as well as unnecessary triviality) with evil, thus implying a somewhat different view of evil from what we have seen in his more recent work.[79] That issue aside, the fact is that both Gustafson and Griffin have a more definite sense of evil as a constitutive dimension of existence than does McFague. Evil is not an independent metaphysical principle or force for either Gustafson or Griffin, but it denotes the existence of essentially ineradicable conditions that compromise or limit the potential for good. That is to say, there is not a simple and natural harmony of interests among all that exists. Reality is complex because it is comprised of disparate elements, whose goods are never entirely commensurable. The good of some can only be had at some expense to the good of others.

---

[78] As noted throughout this book, neither Gustafson, McFague, nor Griffin provides criteria for delineating, in the abstract, or *a priori*, what constitutes "the whole" of a situation; cf. 73ff.; 108–9; 195; 234; 237; 247–48. Clearly, "the whole" is never simply an aggregation, but a totality characterized by relatedness and interdependence of constituent parts, and some degree of integration. For these thinkers it may perhaps be said that the idea of "the whole" is as much an ontological or metaphysical category as it is an empirical one. It denotes a view of the world as ordered and processive, in which all parts, entities, or individuals are understood to be constituted by their temporal and spatial relationships to other parts, entities, or individuals within the contexts of their spatio-temporal wholes.

[79] Cf. 178ff. above.

McFague does not give the same weight to evil as do Gustafson and Griffin. Correlatively, she does not accent the disharmonies and complexities of existence in the same way. She worries about what human beings are doing to threaten existence, but is rather sanguine about the threats to existence that appear to be endemic to the constitution of the cosmos. Consequently, although she advocates a holistic perspective in her critique of various conceptual, cultural, and social dualisms, and in her ethic of care, she never seriously confronts the problematic of moral discernment that arises in the attempt to specify and circumscribe the relevant larger wholes that are to be taken into account as the contexts for interpretation of their constituent parts. She claims "the necessity of thinking responsibly and deeply about *everything that is*,"[80] but never attempts to do so in a critical, discriminating, comprehensive, holistic fashion. Griffin, on the other hand, shares with Gustafson the persisting problem of specifying how to identify the relevant wholes or contexts for interpretation for moral reasoning and decision-making.

The following assessment of Whitehead's ethics by John Spencer would also be applicable to Griffin:

> [W]e have seen that Whitehead does have an ethical system. That it is not a typical philosophical one, but more nearly like a theological ethic. That the ultimate category is an aesthetic one within which morality functions to determine right action as service to objective Goodness. That Goodness is ultimately to be understood as the Beauty which God himself (sic) aims at in the universe in various forms. That Beauty is the balanced intensity which characterizes strong individuals in communal harmony, i.e., the reconciliation of unique individualities under a harmony which enables them to be mutually enhancing.[81]

In sum, what Griffin derives from Whitehead is a kind of theocentric perspective with certain broadly characteristic features. This perspective is not unlike that of Gustafson, but with fewer indications of how one might go about identifying the middle principles, axioms, norms, codes, or rules that are necessary for practical moral reasoning.

---

[80] "Imaging a Theology of Nature," 203; cf. 108 above. McFague's ethic of care is largely dispositional, calling for respect and a "loving eye" toward the world of nature, regarding and treating all others—human and non-human—as subjects rather than objects. She clearly assumes that certain kinds of activity will follow (e.g., creating and maintaining wilderness areas and parks), emphasizing the need to exercise care toward some particular part of the natural world, but does not engage in the particular tasks of ethical decision-making; cf. *Super, Natural Christians*, passim.

[81] John B. Spencer, "Whitehead as a Basis for a Social Ethic," in Cobb and Schroeder, op. cit., 179.

It is important to underscore that Griffin's perspective does not preclude moral principles or rules as such, though he views them, and appropriates them, in ways that differ from what one would find in a deontological or teleological ethics. Griffin explicitly identifies the following implications of his one general moral principle of maximizing importance:

> First, because we all have different backgrounds and capacities, what it is most important for one person or society to do at a given time and place is not necessarily the same thing that it is most important for others to do. Second, because there are so many things that are important, even for a given individual, there is not necessarily only one course of action in a given situation that would exemplify the general ideal of seeking to maximize importance. Third, the central objection typically raised against utilitarianism does not apply to Whitehead's principle. That is, utilitarianism is usually taken to involve the following notions: that we have equal obligations to all human beings . . . ; that only the future, not the past, is morally relevant; and that moral rules, such as rules against lying and breaking promises, are to be violated if so doing will fulfill the utilitarian formula . . . Against these notions, it is rightly urged that we have a greater obligation to some people (such as family members and benefactors) than to most; that the past is often morally relevant (as when one has made a promise or accepted a favor); and that certain "deontological" prohibitions, such as those against lying, stealing, cheating, killing, and promise-breaking, are objectively (even if not absolutely) valid . . . Whitehead's principle . . . can incorporate all these dimensions of moral importance.[82]

The main point to be made here is that an aesthetic ethics, such as Griffin's but also Gustafson's, does not imply the rejection of other forms of moral reasoning. Rather, an aesthetic ethics seeks to incorporate various forms of moral reasoning within a spatially and temporally larger perspective in which other kinds of value, or species of beauty, or dimensions of importance, besides morality must be comprehended. An aesthetic ethics will often need to encompass disparate normative elements, some of which are clearly incommensurable on their own terms, but which contribute intensity and complexity as contrasting elements within the context of a larger whole.

An Epistemological Question

Throughout this book I have been pursuing a *religiously* and *intellectually* adequate theological ethics. In light of the modern commitment, I have argued, an intellectually adequate theological ethics must be naturalistic. That means,

---

[82] *Reenchantment without Supernaturalism*, 306.

among other things, that it must reject epistemic as well as ontological supernaturalism. But any theological ethics must also be theological. It must make some claims about God. Consequently, an *intellectually* adequate theological ethics demands some answer to the epistemological question of how God is to be known.

This epistemological question is highly problematic for both McFague and Gustafson. In the main, and despite her pragmatic wager that God is on the side of life and its flourishing, McFague does not have an answer to this question.[83] For religious reasons, there is much that she has to say about God, but intellectually speaking, her position is basically agnostic. Gustafson's approach is only slightly less precarious. He can say that he regards the patterns and processes of interdependence within nature and history as indicators or signs of the divine governance. But he admits that he can only say this "in piety." He offers no evidential warrant for his affirmation. Griffin, on the other hand, addresses the question of how God is to be known in terms of the human capacity for direct prehension or experience of God. It is a fundamental mistake, in the view of all process thinkers, to regard sensory experience as the only or even the primary form of human experience. Griffin's account of nonsensory experience, including the direct (prehensive) experience of God, constitutes a major contribution to an intellectually satisfactory theological ethics.

In light of Griffin's epistemology of prehension, is it possible that Gustafson has understated, or misconstrued, the role that piety plays in his theological affirmations? Amending Troeltsch, we have seen him declare that "the idea of God is admittedly not directly accessible in any other way than by religious piety."[84] In response to Midgley's question—does the ordering need an Orderer? —we have seen him say that he does not claim a logical need for an Orderer. However, in piety he can affirm an Orderer.[85] These statements are illustrative of a kind of double-mindedness that afflicts Gustafson's position. On the one hand, there is the world, which can be known through experience, science, and reason. On the other hand, there is God, whose existence is to be affirmed only in piety, as the object of the religious affections.

An implicit epistemology is at work here that seems to assume a fairly clear distinction between the cognitive and the affective. But Gustafson tells us in other contexts that he insists on holding the affective and the cognitive together *in theology and well as ethics*.[86] They are not to be sharply distin-

---

[83]Cf. 141–42 above.
[84]Cf. 57 above.
[85]Cf. 56–57 above.
[86]E.g., Beckley and Swezey, 212; my emphasis.

guished. He writes, for example, of an "interpenetration of affectivity, intellect, and will in making judgments and choices."[87] What about a similar interpenetration in apprehending God and the world? Must the one (God) be affirmed only as a matter of piety or affectivity, the other (the world) known only as a result of cognitive activity? I will not attempt any observations about the relations of the affective and the cognitive in human knowing in general. I only suggest that, on his own account, what Gustafson calls piety may rightly be described as a mode of cognition as well as a mode of affectivity.

If Griffin is right, then human beings do have direct experience of God. It is reasonable to claim that such experience may engender certain religious affections. It seems equally reasonable to claim that the conscious awareness of such experience would constitute a kind of knowledge. Religious piety should then be understood as arising from experience of the divine, and as possessing both affective and cognitive elements. Indeed, at one point Gustafson argues that the experience of awe, for example, derives from a perception that is "prior to explanations." In piety, it comes to be regarded as a religious experience, but it may also be construed and denominated in some other way, such as aesthetic.[88] I would argue that the experience of awe, though it be occasioned by some sensory experience, is in large measure a nonsensory experience, an apprehension of ultimacy, transcendence, mystery, or beauty marked by such feelings as wonder, dread, and reverence. Moreover, given Gustafson's view of piety, it seems just as true to say that such an experience engenders piety as it is to say, as he does, that in piety it is construed to be a religious experience. If so, then the piety that is engendered must derive from an experience or perception that is both cognitive and affective. There may be no logical necessity for Gustafson to affirm an Orderer, but there may very well be an experiential basis for this affirmation.

Furthermore, if it is correct to claim that what Gustafson calls piety denotes, at least in part, a way of perceiving or apprehending that is basically nonsensory, then other features of Gustafson's ethics become more comprehensible. Nonsensory experience may include the experience of value, as Griffin clearly maintains.[89] Even if such experience is not conscious, it must

---

[87] *Ethics I*, 191.
[88] Cf. *Ethics I*, 226–28.
[89] Griffin provides the following especially vivid statement of the capacity to experience value: "The reason why we are not generally conscious of the "physical world" (or "nature") as filled with intrinsic value is that it is only in nonsensory prehension that we experience other things *as value-laden*. For example, we directly prehend our prior occasions of experience, and "remember" them with their joys, sufferings, and desires. We also directly experience, if in more blurred fashion, our bodily members, feeling their excitement, their enjoyment, their suffering, their thirst and hunger. If we would generalize this knowledge of what the "physical

be in some sense felt. Every experience leaves its impression on the body of the experiencing subject. In this way it affects other perceptions. It must thereby affect our interpretation of conscious perceptions. Nonsensory perception also includes the experience of relationships. Our conscious sensory perception may be of discrete entities, whose relations to one another do not register on our sensory organs. This was the empiricist Hume's dilemma—we can see constant conjunction, but we cannot see cause and effect. Yet even Hume had to assume, for all practical purposes, that causal relations exist. In fact, as Griffin argues, we experience much more than the eye can see, or the ear can hear.

Acknowledgment of the reality of nonsensory experience of value and relationships makes the following account by Gustafson of the process of moral decision-making even more compelling:

> The final discernment is an informed intuition; it is not the conclusion of a formally logical argument, a strict deduction from a single moral principle, or an absolutely certain result from the exercises of human "reason" alone. There is a final moment of perception that sees the parts in relation to a whole, expresses sensibilities as well as reasoning, and is made in the conditions of human finitude. In complex circumstances it is not without risk.[90]

In other words, and first of all, moral discernment is a matter of practical reasoning. There is no single moral calculus or set of rules that can be employed to derive the "ought" in any but the most simplistically defined situations.[91] How then is the "ought" derived? It is derived in an act or process of intuition that is informed by a number of factors, says Gustafson, including an evaluative description of the circumstances, an analysis of the features that can be affected by the means available, the values and principles held by the individual engaged in discernment, his or her overall perspective and generalized beliefs about the world, and his or her affectivities and dispositions.[92] There are clearly critical, reflective, and analytical elements in this process of moral discernment. There are interpretive elements that derive

---

world' is like, we would not think of it as devoid of values, but as a throbbing multiplicity of energetic, passionate, appetitive events striving for, and realizing, values"; "Whitehead's Deeply Ecological Worldview," 199.

[90] *Ethics I*, 338.

[91] In passages leading up to this statement, Gustafson critiques other approaches to ethical decision-making, including those of the moral dogmatists, those who employ a checklist of "facts," a framework of analytical principles, and a few moral principles, and those who rely almost entirely on moral intuition; cf. 329ff.

[92] Ibid., 333ff.

from an individual's own particular perspective and beliefs. But there are also important affective and evaluative dimensions.

I would argue that the affective and evaluative dimensions of the process of moral discernment are not simply brought to the circumstances in question, but are in significant measure evoked by those circumstances as experienced by the individual. What Gustafson describes as a "final moment of perception," in which the "ought" is (however imperfectly) perceived, is not simply imposed upon the data of experience by the one who is engaged in moral discernment. This moment of perception is in fact—as Gustafson says—a discernment. It is a discernment not merely of what is or of what may be, of actuality and of possibility, but of what ought to be. We should not find this surprising, if we understand that value is intrinsic to all occasions of experience, that our nonsensory perceptions or prehensions include experiences of value and relationship, and that all our actions are influenced by the divine subjective aim. In short, the descriptive-empirical account of moral discernment given by Gustafson can be further elaborated in terms of Griffin's process conceptuality. In large part, Gustafson and Griffin are employing differing language, at different levels of conceptualization, under conditions of finitude, to describe very similar processes of moral discernment for an aesthetic ethics.

Conclusion

My intent throughout this book has been to identify the elements that are necessary for the articulation of a theological ethics that is both transparently naturalistic on the one hand, and robustly theological on the other. The approach as been to consider the thought of three major contemporary Protestant thinkers, James Gustafson, Sallie McFague, and David Griffin, whose writings differ significantly in style and methodology, yet exhibit substantial elements of congruence that I see as crucial to this task. In the first place, all three of these thinkers may be regarded as naturalists in the sense that they all share the modern commitment to reason and experience. Second, all three explicitly engage in a critique of anthropocentrism in theology and ethics, and—with significant qualification only in the case of McFague—may be said to hold a theocentric perspective. Third, all three understand themselves to be critical realists, though Gustafson often tends toward a naive rather than a critical realism, McFague lacks methodological coherence and abandons talk of realism soon after her *Models of God*, and critics of Griffin might charge that his abstract theorizing, including his Platonic conception of the primordial nature of God, exceed the bounds of what may reasonably be termed realism, whether critical or otherwise. Nonetheless, they are all ontological realists and epistemological fallibilists of one sort or another, differing chiefly regarding how much they think we can know either about God or the world.

I have identified other common themes and elements of congruence in the writings of these three thinkers that derive from their respective attempts to transcend metaphysical and ethical dualisms in a more processive, relational view of existence, one that stresses the interdependence of all things and expresses itself in an ecological outlook and special regard for the natural world. We have also noted that each of these three thinkers self-consciously regards his or her own work as a form of advocacy, an attempt to persuade, even to effect a conversion. In Gustafson's case, the conversion is from anthropocentrism to a radical theocentrism in which we are to comprehend ourselves and all things in our and their relation to God. For McFague, it is a conversion from androcentric and anthropocentric perspectives to love and care for the earth and all its inhabitants, in particular; a conversion to a feminist, ecological sensibility more generally; and a conversion to cosmocentrism or theocentrism at the conceptual or theological level. For Griffin, the conversion is largely a conceptual one, but with enormous moral and ethical implications, away from scientific materialism on the one hand and intellectually untenable supernaturalism on the other, to a panentheistic, panexperientialistic worldview in which all things are to be comprehended in terms of the general metaphysical principles of the universe, of which God is the chief exemplification. In my judgment, the conversion called for in each case is appropriate and necessary for an intellectually and religiously adequate theological ethics. My criticisms of these three approaches relate primarily if not exclusively to the adequacy with which each thinker has articulated a coherent and compelling case on behalf of the proposed conversion.

One of the more problematic features of the approaches examined, most evident in Gustafson and Griffin, is the attention to large temporal and spatial wholes as the contexts for ethical reflection. However, this regard for larger wholes also happens to be integral to their critique of anthropocentrism, and to their general ecological outlook. All three thinkers call for an enlargement of interests and sensibilities, as well as a holistic perspective, as an antidote to anthropocentrism. The attention to larger wholes is partly a theoretical problem, inasmuch as there does not appear to be any definitive way to specify the relevant whole or context for ethical reflection regarding any particular matter of moral significance. The focus on larger wholes poses an even greater practical problem, inasmuch as it greatly increases the amount of information and complexity of knowledge required for adequately informed moral decision-making. Indeed, for all practical purposes, it may be impossible to say when a moral decision is adequately informed, given this broad ecological outlook. The result, as I have tried to show, is an aesthetic ethics that calls for breadth and depth of knowledge, careful description, and practical reasoning, but also a kind of holistic sensibility and perceptive intuition in which decisions must be made and actions taken that are seldom if ever without risk. In light of Griffin's epistemology of prehension, however, the case can be made that the experiential basis for such decision-making and action is far more than meets the eye. Consequently, the decisions we make, and the actions we take, are often more sound than the reasoning we can give for them.

It should also be emphasized that Gustafson, McFague, and Griffin each understands him- or herself to stand within the Christian tradition. And each takes seriously the need to be accountable to that tradition. This is not always acknowledged or appreciated by critics, some of whom can hardly see beyond that fact that each of these thinkers departs from certain beliefs typically associated with Christian orthodoxy. Because each of them rejects supernaturalism, each of them rejects those formulations of traditional doctrines that necessarily entail supernaturalistic or scientifically refutable claims. They are all theists, however, and they all regard the person of Jesus Christ to be in some unique way integral to their own theological understanding and articulation of their faith. While they do not grant *a priori* authority to scripture or tradition, I think it can be said that they all see "sedimentations" of interpreted human experience of the divine in scripture and tradition.[93] It is unmistakably evident that they are all deeply indebted to the language and thought of the Christian tradition for the expression of their theological views, however much they may argue the need for transformation in our understanding or reformulation in our articulation of certain traditional Christian teachings.

One example of a traditional Christian teaching that Gustafson, McFague, and Griffin each find necessary to reformulate is the doctrine of sin. In the first place, each of them implicitly rejects any notion of a historical "Fall" from an Edenic state of perfection. Even a mythical interpretation of the doctrine of the "Fall" would seem incongruous with their thinking. In the second place, they do not attribute cosmic significance to human sin. The whole of creation is not implicated, and corrupted, on account of human perfidy.[94] Neither do they assign any role to biology in the transmission of sin. Gustafson explicitly repudiates the notion of utter depravity, the idea that human beings are so infected by sin that even their natural capacities for reasoning are severely impaired. McFague and Griffin would surely agree. In fact, all of these departures from traditional Christian views of sin are neces-

---

[93]Cf. Chapter 3, 99.
[94]McFague is especially insistent, however, that future life on our planet is in jeopardy due to human sin.

sitated by the modern commitment, with its acceptance of experience and reason as final arbiters of human knowledge.

However, in ways that are continuous with Christian tradition, all three thinkers continue to associate human sin with human finitude, and with the human propensity to self-centeredness. They also recognize the enormous capacities of human beings for evil and destruction. Their critique of anthropocentrism is simultaneously a critique of egocentrism. It is a call to recognize our place, to accept our finitude, to acknowledge our interdependence with all that exists. It is a call for wider sympathies, an enlargement of interest and compassion, in order to attain a greater realization of the possibilities for life inherent in the world of which we are a part.

As first noted in Chapter 1, there is a remarkable congruence or convergence among Gustafson, McFague, and Griffin on a number of issues critical to the articulation of a satisfactory theological ethics. It is this congruence that suggests the possibility of a creative synthesis of their approaches. When it comes to the actual elaboration of a serviceable theological ethics, it should be emphasized, I find Gustafson's work on the whole to be much more satisfactory than that of McFague or Griffin. McFague and Griffin, after all, are not primarily ethicists, whereas Gustafson is not only "the master teacher of [his] craft," but also one of its master practitioners.[95] Much of his work involves the appropriation of specific and extensive knowledge from the natural and social sciences in the tasks of empirical description, practical moral reasoning, and prescription.[96]

However, as we have seen, there are significant weaknesses in Gustafson's theocentric ethics that can hardly be satisfactorily addressed without the sorts of contributions McFague and Griffin have to make. A *religiously* adequate theological ethics needs religiously adequate language, including theological metaphors that are evocative of religious piety. These metaphors must be congruent with our conception of reality, and they must also be morally appropriate. While admitting the need for such metaphors in the worship life of the Christian churches, Gustafson has openly, and I believe mistakenly, resisted the incorporation of more robust metaphorical theological language in his theological work. Griffin has not taken up the task of formulating

---

[95]Cf. Chapter 2, 45, n. 2. It is not uncommon for other theological ethicists who are critical of facets of Gustafson's conceptualization of his theocentric ethics to hold his practical moral and ethical reasoning in high regard. I have previously footnoted Gordon D. Kaufman's and Robert Bellah's observations in this connection; Chapter 2, 81, n.172.
[96]Gustafson is sometimes criticized for the lack of a social or cultural critique, however; cf. Robert Bellah, Gustafson as Critic of Culture," Beckley and Swezey, 143–58. Both McFague and Griffin articulate more trenchant critiques, McFague with respect to our relations with the natural world, Griffin with respect to our political life.

religiously adequate theological language. McFague has elaborated a metaphorical theology that appropriately engages and critiques the Christian tradition, and has articulated promising alternative metaphors for God and the God–world relation. She has been a path-breaker, whose convincing case for metaphorical theology helps provide a basis for others like William Everett to continue the experiment of invoking and employing new religious language, including more appropriate metaphors for God. This is McFague's most significant contribution to theological ethics.

An *intellectually* adequate theological ethics needs a conceptually adequate construal of the God–world relation, including the nature of divine agency, in order to account for variable divine influence in the world. Gustafson's and McFague's variations on a theology of nature approach to the reconciliation of scientific and theological perspectives have much to commend them, but they both fall noticeably short on this score. An intellectually adequate theological ethics must also provide some non-supernatural account of how God is to be known. Gustafson's resort to piety, and McFague's retreat to epistemological agnosticism, annulled by her "wager" of belief, fail here as well. Griffin's process interpretation of reality, with its naturalistic panexperientialism and panentheism, meets the test of a conceptually adequate construal of the God–world relation. Griffin's doctrine of prehension specifically provides an account of how God is to be experientially known (and is suggestive of the possibility that Gustafson's "piety" may be another way of speaking about the experience of apprehending, perceiving, and knowing divine reality). These are Griffin's most important, though not his only, contributions to the kind of theological ethics that holds promise of meeting the intellectual challenges of today's world.

I began this book by noting Gustafson's insistence on the importance of theological construal for ethics. Yet it now seems that his construal of the world is just as significant for his construal of God as vice versa. The same holds true for McFague and Griffin, though in different ways. Integral to Gustafson's theocentric emphasis is a conviction that there are serious conceptual and ethical problems with an anthropocentric ethics. Clearly McFague's existential moral concerns, arising from gender discrimination, nuclear and ecological perils, and economic exploitation, help shape her conceptualization of God. Griffin's "hard-core common sense notions," set in the context of a naturalistic, scientific account of the world, clearly establish an agenda that he must address in the philosophical development of his conception of God. Perhaps this is only to say that just as our conceptualizations shape our interpretations of our experiences and their importance, so do reflections on our knowledge and experiences occasion the need for conceptualization.

There is no straight line that leads from theology to ethics, or the other way, for that matter.

In this light, I want to recall a conviction stated in the opening chapter: The articulation of a theological ethics is not a linear process, beginning with theology and ending with ethics, but a much more complex holistic undertaking. If such an undertaking sometimes begins with empirical observations or ethical concerns, with feelings of piety, apprehensions of mystery, or convictions of meaning, that does not speak against the integrity of the theological enterprise, nor does it measure the adequacy of the concomitant moral judgments. When making moral judgments, one must seek a coherence that encompasses what is known and what is believed, what is experienced and what is taken on authority, what is felt and what is reasoned, what is discerned to be and what is discerned to be required—or at least a gestalt of patterns and relationships that is sufficiently evident to warrant one's interpretation of the situation and sufficiently indicative to authorize one's discernment of what that situation calls oneself and others to be and do.

My claim is that the work of James Gustafson, Sallie McFague, and David Griffin can be creatively appropriated to provide the necessary elements for the articulation of an aesthetic theological ethics of just this sort, one that is naturalistic and theocentric in terms that are religiously and intellectually adequate for our times.

Bibliography

Barbour, Ian G. "Experiencing and Interpreting Nature in Science and Religion." *Zygon* 29 (1994) 457–87.
———. *Nature, Human Nature, and God*. Minneapolis: Fortress, 2002.
———. *Religion in an Age of Science*. New York: HarperCollins, 1990.
———. "Response to Critiques of *Religion in an Age of Science*." *Zygon* 31 (1996) 51–65.
———. *When Science Meets Religion: Enemies, Strangers, or Partners?* New York: HarperCollins, 2002.
Beckley, Harlan R. "A Raft That Floats: Experience, Tradition, and Sciences in Gustafson's Theocentric Ethics." *Zygon* 30 (1995) 201–9.
Beckley, Harlan R., and Charles M. Swezey, editors. *James M. Gustafson's Theocentric Ethics: Interpretations and Assessments*. Macon, Ga.: Mercer University, 1988.
Bromell, David J. "Sallie McFague's 'Metaphorical Theology.'" *Journal of the American Academy of Religion* 61 (1993) 485–502.
Cahill, Lisa Sowle. "Consent in Time of Affliction: The Ethics of a Circumspect Theist." *Journal of Religious Ethics* 13 (1985) 22–36.
Cahill, Lisa Sowle, and James F. Childress, editors. *Christian Ethics: Problems and Prospects*. Cleveland: Pilgrim, 1996.
Cobb, John B., Jr., and W. Widick Schroeder, editors. *Process Philosophy and Social Thought*. Chicago: Center for the Scientific Study of Religion, 1981.
Davaney, Sheila Greeve, and John B. Cobb Jr. [Review article] "*Models of God: Theology for an Ecological, Nuclear Age*." *Religious Studies Review* 16 (1990) 36–42.
Dean, William. [Review article] "*God and Religion in the Postmodern World: Essays in Postmodern Theology*." *Process Studies* 18 (1989) 208–12.
Everett, William Johnson. *The Politics of Worship: Reforming the Language and Symbols of Liturgy*. Cleveland: United Church Press, 1999.
Gamwell, Franklin. *The Divine Good: Modern Moral Theory and the Necessity of God*. New York: HarperCollins, 1990.
Gould, Stephen Jay. "Nonoverlapping Magisteria." *Natural History* 106 (1997) 19–20.
Griffin, David Ray. *A Process Christology*. Philadelphia: Westminster, 1973.
———. "Creation Out of Chaos and the Problem of Evil." In *Encountering Evil: Live Options in Theology*, edited by Stephan T. Davis, 101–19, 129–36. Atlanta: John Knox, 1981.
———, editor. *Deep Religious Pluralism*. Louisville: Westminster John Knox, 2005.

———. "The Divine, the Demonic, and the Parable of the Tribes." The 2003 Brennan Lectures, Lecture II. Delivered at Christ Church Cathedral, Louisville, Kentucky, June 2, 2003. A draft of the second chapter of a book with the proposed title, *Thy Kingdom Come*.

———. "Divine Goodness and Demonic Evil." In *Evil and the Response of World Religion*, edited by William Cenkner, 223–40. St. Paul, Minn.: Paragon, 1997.

———. "Empire Now and Then: Jesus, and the Reign of God." The 2003 Brennan Lectures, Lecture I. Delivered at Christ Church Cathedral, Louisville, Kentucky, June 1, 2003. A draft of the first chapter of a book with the proposed title, *Thy Kingdom Come*.

———. *Evil Revisited: Responses and Reconsiderations*. Albany, N.Y.: SUNY Press, 1991

———. *God and Religion in the Postmodern World: Essays in Postmodern Theology*. Albany, N.Y.: SUNY Press, 1989.

———. *God, Power, and Evil: A Process Theodicy*. Philadelphia: Westminster, 1976.

———. "The Holy, Necessary Goodness, and Morality." *Journal of Religious Ethics* 8 (1980) 330–49.

———. "Morality and Scientific Naturalism: Overcoming the Conflicts." In *Philosophy of Religion for a New Century: Essays in Honor of Eugene Thomas Long*, edited by Jeremiah Hackett and Jerald Wallulis, 81–104. Dordrecht: Kluwer Academic Publishers, 2004.

———. [Review article] "On Ian Barbour's *Issues in Science and Religion*." *Zygon* 23 (1988) 57–81.

———, and Richard Falk, editors. *Postmodern Politics for a Planet in Crisis: Policy, Process, and Presidential Vision*. Albany, N.Y.: SUNY Press, 1993.

———, and Huston Smith. *Primordial Truth and Postmodern Theology*. Albany, N.Y.: SUNY Press, 1989.

———, editor. *The Reenchantment of Science*. Albany, N.Y.: SUNY Press, 1988.

———. *Reenchantment without Supernaturalism: A Process Philosophy of Religion*. Ithaca, N.Y.: Cornell University Press, 2001.

———. *Religion and Scientific Naturalism: Overcoming the Conflicts*. Albany, N.Y.: SUNY Press, 2001.

———. "Religious Experience, Naturalism, and the Social Scientific Study of Religion" and "Rejoinder to Preus and Segal." *Journal of the American Academy of Religion* 68 (2000) 99–125, 143–49.

———, editor. *Sacred Interconnections: Postmodern Spirituality, Political Economy, and Art*. Albany, N.Y.: SUNY Press, 1990.

———, editor. *Spirituality and Society: Postmodern Visions*. Albany, N.Y.: SUNY Press. 1988.

———. *Two Great Truths: Christian Faith and Scientific Naturalism*. Louisville: Westminster John Knox, 2004.

———. *Unsnarling the World-Knot: Consciousness, Freedom, and the Mind-Body Problem*. Berkeley: University of California Press, 1988.

———. "Values, Evil, and Liberation Theology." In *Process Philosophy and Social Thought*, edited by John B.Cobb Jr. and W. Widick Schroeder, 183–96. Chicago: Center for the Scientific Study of Religion, 1981.

———, William A. Beardslee, and Joe Holland. *Varieties of Postmodern Theology*. Albany, N.Y.: SUNY Press, 1989.

———. "Whitehead's Deeply Ecological Worldview." In *Worldviews and Ecology: Religion, Philosophy, and the Environment*, edited by Mary Evelyn Tucker and John A. Grim, 190–206. Maryknoll, N. Y.: Orbis, 1994.

Gustafson, James M. "A Response to Critics." *Journal of Religious Ethics* 13 (1985) 185–209.

———. *Ethics from a Theocentric Perspective*, Vol. 1: *Theology and Ethics*. Chicago: University of Chicago Press, 1981.

———. *Ethics from a Theocentric Perspective*, Vol. 2: *Ethics and Theology*. Chicago: University of Chicago Press, 1984.

———. *An Examined Faith: The Grace of Self-Doubt*. Minneapolis: Fortress, 2003.

———. "The Idea of Christian Ethics." In *Companion Encyclopedia of Theology*, edited by Peter Byrne and Leslie Houlden, 691–715. London: Routledge, 1995.

———. *Intersections: Science, Theology, and Ethics*. Cleveland: Pilgrim, 1996.

———. "Just What Is 'Postliberal' Theology?" *Christian Century* 116 (1999) 353–55.

———. "Liberal Questions: A Response to William Placher." *Christian Century* 116 (1999) 422–425.

———. "The Place of Scripture in Christian Ethics: A Methodological Study." *Interpretation* 24 (1970) 430–55.

———. "Response to Rottschaefer, Beckley, and Konner." *Zygon* 30 (1995) 221–26.

———. *A Sense of the Divine: The Natural Environment from a Theocentric Perspective*. Cleveland: Pilgrim, 1994.

———. "A Theocentric Interpretation of Life." *Christian Century* 97 (1980) 754–60.

———. "Theological Anthropology and the Human Sciences." In *Theology at the End of Modernity*, edited by Sheila Greeve Davaney, 61–77. Philadelphia: Trinity, 1991.

———. "Tracing a Trajectory." *Zygon* 30 (1995) 177–90.

———. *Treasure in Earthen Vessels: The Church as a Human Community*. New York: Harper and Row, 1961.

Hartshorne, Charles. "Science, Insecurity, and the Abiding Treasure." *Journal of Religion* 39 (1958) 168–74.

———. *Omnipotence and Other Theological Mistakes*. Albany, N.Y.: SUNY Press, 1984.

Hauerwas, Stanley. "Time and History in Theological Ethics: The Work of James Gustafson." *Journal of Religious Ethics* 13 (1985) 3–21.

Haught, John F. *Science and Religion: From Conflict to Conversation*. New York: Paulist, 1995.

Keller, Catherine, and Anne Daniell, editors. *Process and Difference: Between Cosmological and Poststructuralist Postmodernisms*. Albany, N.Y.: SUNY Press, 2002.

Kaufman, Gordon D. "*Models of God*: Is Metaphor Enough?" *Religion and Intellectual Life* 5 (1988) 11–23.

Konner, Melvin. "Following a Trajectory: On 'Tracing a Trajectory' and 'Explaining and Valuing,' by James M. Gustafson." *Zygon* 30 (1995) 191–200.

Lindbeck, George A. *The Nature of Doctrine: Religion and Theology in a Postliberal Age*. Louisville: Westminster John Knox, 1984.

McCormick, Richard A. "Gustafson's God: Who? What? Where? (Etc.)." *Journal of Religious Ethics* 13 (1985) 53–70.

McFague, Sallie. "An Earthly Theological Agenda." *Christian Century* 108 (1991) 12–15.

———. *The Body of God: An Ecological Theology*. Minneapolis: Fortress, 1993.

———. "Cosmology and Christianity: Implications of the Common Creation Story for Theology." In *Theology at the End of Modernity*, edited by Sheila Greeve Davaney, 19–40. Philadelphia: Trinity, 1991.

———. "God as Mother." In *Weaving the Visions: New Patterns in Feminist Spirituality*, edited by Judith Plaskow and Carol P. Christ, 139–50. San Francisco: Harper and Row, 1989.

———. "Ian Barbour: Theologian's Friend, Scientist's Interpreter." *Zygon* 31 (1996) 21–28.

———. "Imaging a Theology of Nature: The World as God's Body." In *Liberating Life: Contemporary Approaches to Ecological Theology*, edited by Charles Birch, William Eakin, and Jay B. McDaniel, 201–27. Maryknoll, N.Y.: Orbis, 1990.

———. "Intimate Creation: God's Body, Our Home." *Christian Century* 119 (2002) 36–45.

———. *Life Abundant: Rethinking Theology and Economy for a Planet in Peril*. Minneapolis: Fortress, 2001.

———. "The Loving Eye vs. the Arrogant Eye: Christian Critique of the Western Gaze on Nature and the Third World." *The Ecumenical Review* 42 (1997) 185–93.
———. *Metaphorical Theology: Models of God in Religious Language*. Minneapolis: Fortress, 1982.
———. *Models of God: Theology for an Ecological, Nuclear Age*. Philadelphia: Fortress, 1987.
———. "Response." *Religion and Intellectual Life* 5 (1988) 38–44.
———. "Sallie McFague." In *Essentials of Christian Theology*, edited by William C. Placher, 101–16. Louisville: Westminster John Knox, 2003.
———. *Speaking in Parables: A Study in Metaphor and Theology*. Philadelphia: Fortress, 1975.
———. *Super, Natural Christians: How We Should Love Nature*. Minneapolis: Fortress, 1997.
———. "The World as God's Body." *Christian Century* 105 (1988) 671–73.
Meilander, Gilbert. [Review article] "*Ethics from a Theocentric Perspective*, V. 1: *Theology and Ethics*; V. 2: *Ethics and Theology*." *Religious Studies Review* 12 (1986) 11–16.
Meland, Bernard. *The Realities of Faith: The Revolution in Cultural Forms*. New York: Oxford University Press, 1962.
O'Connor, June. [Review article] "*Metaphorical Theology: Models of God in Religious Language*." *Religious Studies Review* 12 (1986) 204–5.
Peacocke, Arthur. *Theology for a Scientific Age: Being and Becoming—Natural, Divine, and Human*. Enlarged ed. Minneapolis: Fortress, 1993.
Placher, William. "Being Postliberal: A Response to James Gustafson." *Christian Century* 116 (1999) 390–92.
Preus, J. Samuel. "Response: Explaining Griffin." *Journal of the American Academy of Religion* 68 (2000) 127–32.
Proudfoot, Wayne. *Religious Experience*. Berkeley: University of California Press, 1985.
Ramsey, Paul. "A Letter to James Gustafson." *Journal of Religious Ethics* 13 (1985) 71–100.
Reynolds, Terrence. "Two McFagues: Meaning, Truth, and Justification in *Models of God*." *Modern Theology* 11 (1995) 289–313.
———. "Walking Apart, Together: Lindbeck and McFague on Theological Method." *Journal of Religion* 77 (1997) 44–67.
Rottschaefer, William A. "Gustafson's Theocentrism and Scientific Naturalistic Philosophy: A Marriage Made in Heaven?" *Zygon* 30 (1995) 211–20.
Schilbrack, Kevin. [Review article] "*Reenchantment without Supernaturalism: A Process Philosophy of Religion*." *Journal of the American Academy of Religion* 70 (2002) 639.
Segal, Robert A. "Response: In Defense of Social Scientific Naturalism: A Response to David Griffin." *Journal of the American Academy of Religion* 68 (2000) 133–41.
Sideris, Lisa H. *Environmental Ethics, Ecological Theology, and Natural Selection*. New York: Columbia University Press, 2003.
Stout, Jeffrey. *Ethics after Babel: The Languages of Morals and Their Discontents*. Boston: Beacon, 1988.
Swezey, Charles. "Bibliography of the Writings of James Gustafson, 1951–84." *Journal of Religious Ethics* 13 (1985) 101–12.
Tracy, David. "*Models of God*: Three Observations." *Religion and Intellectual Life* 5 (1988) 24–28.
Toulmin, Stephen. "Nature and Nature's God." *Journal of Religious Ethics* 13 (1985) 37–52.
Weaver, Mary Jo. "A Discussion of Sallie McFague's *Models of God: Theology for an Ecological, Nuclear Age*. Introduction." *Religion and Intellectual Life* 5 (1988) 9–10.
Whitehead, Alfred North. *Science and the Modern World*. New York: Free Press, 1925.

www.ingramcontent.com/pod-product-compliance
Lightning Source LLC
Chambersburg PA
CBHW051632230426
43669CB00013B/2275